FOSTER CHILDREN IN A LIFE COURSE PERSPECTIVE

DAVID FANSHEL is Professor, Columbia University School of Social Work, and is the director of the study.

STEPHEN J. FINCH is Associate Professor, Department of Applied Mathematics and Statistics at the State University of New York at Stony Brook.

JOHN F. GRUNDY is a senior research associate and computer analyst at the Columbia University School of Social Work.

FOSTER CHILDREN IN A LIFE COURSE PERSPECTIVE

DAVID FANSHEL, STEPHEN J. FINCH
JOHN F. GRUNDY

COLUMBIA UNIVERSITY PRESS
New York

Columbia University Press
New York   Oxford
Copyright © 1990 Columbia University Press
All rights reserved

Library of Congress Cataloging-in-Publication Data

Fanshel, David.
Foster children in a life course perspectives : the Casey Family
Program experience / David Fanshel, Stephen J. Finch,
John F. Grundy.
p. cm.
Includes bibliographical references.
ISBN 0-231-07180-9
1. Foster home care—United States—Case studies. 2. Foster
children—United States—Case studies. 3. Casey Family Program.
I. Finch, Stephen J. II. Grundy, John F. III. Title.
HV881.F364 1990
362.7'33'0973—dc20
90-35629
CIP

Printed in the United States of America

c 10 9 8 7 6 5 4 3 2 1

CONTENTS

FIGURES

PREFACE

The Casey Family Program is a privately funded agency that continues to grow in size and is now located in more than a dozen western states. The major emphasis of its service program involves the maintenance of children in long-term foster family homes. The research described in this volume was commissioned by the agency as part of a program of self-evaluation.

It is the hope of the authors that this book contribute to the cumulative scientific information about children in foster care. In addition to its many substantive findings, we are hopeful that the model of life course analysis that underlies our investigation will prove attractive to agencies and scholars concerned with child welfare services. It is also important that funding sources be willing to entertain supporting the "long distance runners" among researchers who are willing to tie up their scholarly careers to such extended investigations.

One of the authors, David Fanshel, was approached by The Casey Family Program at Columbia University in late 1983 with the proposal that he consider undertaking a study of outcomes of the service effort to date. A relatively new program on the child welfare scene, the first children had been accepted into care in 1966. With the 20th anniversary of the founding of the agency rapidly approaching, there was interest expressed by the board of trustees in an objective study of outcomes, with inadequacies, as well as achievements, to be revealed. The ultimate purpose of the research was to enhance the quality of service to the children. The study got fully under way in September 1984 and was funded for three continuous years.

Fanshel had been approached at the suggestion of Joseph H. Reid, former executive director of the Child Welfare League of America. He had been a key consultant when the program was originally conceived and founded. He was of the opinion that Fanshel's prior experience in conducting a well-known longitudinal study of foster children in New York City provided good background for a research initiative with The Casey Family Program.

The authors recognize that compromises in research design have been made in the effort to span the lifetimes of our subjects and that these may give some of our readers pause. The use of content analysis to recreate measures of the preplacement histories of the subjects and the course of their lives as seen at intake into the program, their experiences while in care and the circumstances of their exit from the program's care involved a major investment of project funds and probably represents as ambitious a use of this technique as has yet been reported in studies of social programs. In our view the method has paid off handsomely and allowed us to experience the equivalent of a longitudinal investigation without having to wait decades to accumulate the kind of life course data we have created through coding case record protocols. Nevertheless, we look forward to the development of longitudinal data bases for foster children in which the data collection takes place prospectively in a real-time mode.

The research was carried out collaboratively by the three authors. While each of us brought to the occasion specialized skills in subject matter expertise, statistical analysis, and computer programming, the analysis and interpretation of the data and the preparation of the volume in its final form represent a combined effort. Ordering of names is not intended to signify priority in authorship.

D.F.
S.J.F.
J.F.G.

ACKNOWLEDGMENTS

We wish to thank The Casey Family Program for making possible a rewarding research experience. The board of directors of the agency contracted for this research as part of a program of self-evaluation. They provided generous financial support and allowed the researchers complete freedom in the conduct of the study and in the interpretation of findings.

The Casey Family Program division directors were cooperative in arranging for the shipment of records and in answering all manner of inquiry from the research staff. The smooth exchange of materials owes much to their helpfulness. Arthur R. Dodson was helpful and supportive, especially in the defining stage of the study, in his role as executive director of the agency.

Appreciation is owed to the case readers who performed the arduous content analysis task requiring their reading of more than six hundred case records and filling out the long schedule required for each case. Henry Ilian, Jeanne Bertrand-Finch, Mary Fitzpatrick, and Margaret Schmidt showed a high degree of professionalism and concern for the children about whom they were reading.

Amelia Chu, research assistant throughout the project, performed demanding research tasks such as coding complex material, data entry, and computer programming work with skill and dedication. Angela Sinanian carried the main responsibility for computer entry of coded data and did this with efficiency and impressive accuracy.

Jaime Alvelo directed the field operations of the follow-up study in

Seattle and Yakima in Washington. He collaborated with Fanshel in the construction of the follow-up interviewing schedule and in its field testing. He hired and trained the four interviewers who conducted the interviews with the former wards of the program. In order to oversee the study, he established temporary residence in Seattle. The success of the follow-up study owes much to the skill and commitment he brought to the research enterprise. His performance was at the highest level.

The interviewers employed in the follow-up study were Sid Copeland, Patti Gorman, Joan K. Heinmiller, and Mary L. Kline. Making contact with the subjects and securing their participation was a crucial task and this was carried out in a resourceful manner. Our in-depth analysis of the data secured from the interviews shows a coherence of information that reinforces our sense of the professionalism that guided the interviewing process.

Jeanne Bertrand-Finch gave generously of her time in reading all drafts of the manuscript. She provided perspectives for improvement in writing based upon her rich practice experience in child welfare and we found her comments most useful. She is not, of course, responsible for our final formulations of the many issues explored with her.

Dr. Tenshang Joh studied the performance of factor analysis on data from linear recursive path models. His results provided important guidance on the interpretation of the factor analyses discussed in chapters 8 and 9. Dr. Qimei He wrote the program that calculated the intraclass correlation coefficient and estimated the correlation of the errors of measurement of our data. He also performed simulations and numerical calculations that examined the experience of using factor analysis as an index construction strategy. These calculations studied a much less complex strategy than the one described in chapter 2, but they also led to important insights and increased confidence in the results we report in this book.

The study was conducted at the Columbia University School of Social Work, which provided a full measure of support in a variety of services. Dean George Brager and his successor Dean Ronald Feldmen were most encouraging as were the faculty and doctoral students with whom the work was discussed at various times. The climate for productive work could not have been better.

We feel indebted to the two anonymous readers who read the earlier draft of the manuscript for Columbia University Press. They provided insightful suggestions and criticisms in their comments. These were helpful to us in our further writing.

A large measure of thanks is owed to the former wards of The Casey

Family Program who agreed to participate in research interviews in two cities in the state of Washington, Seattle and Yakima. They furnished us with critical data that proved invaluable in the overall study. Those who carry responsibility for the care of foster children are likely to find their insights deepened by the direct quotations from the subjects provided in chapter 10.

FOSTER CHILDREN IN A LIFE COURSE PERSPECTIVE

## CHAPTER ONE

Doing Good For Children:
A Man Named Jim Casey

One day in 1965, an immaculate but otherwise simple-looking man appeared at the offices of the Child Welfare League of America on Irving Place in New York City. Well beyond his seventieth year, he had an open, intelligent face that easily broke into a broad smile. He browsed through the pamphlets about child welfare on display in the main entrance room and proceeded to ask Regina Cavanagh, the receptionist, about the purposes of the League and the needs of the children it represented. The visitor was obviously someone who was self-assured and skilled in dealing with strangers.

Something about the manner in which he presented himself and the way he posed questions about failing children suggested that he was not engaged in idle pursuit. The receptionist sensed that the visitor was a man organizing himself to become engaged in a project. She passed along a suggestion to the secretary of Joseph H. Reid, the executive director of the League, that he might want to spend a few minutes with a man who had dropped in, named James Emmet Casey, who had many questions to ask and had hinted at having funds to invest in a child welfare program of some sort. Reid agreed to see the gentleman—who, he later learned, was always called Jim Casey by those who knew him—for a short encounter. Little did he know that this meeting would be the first of many between them and that they would be planning for a new foster care service that would come to have national significance.

Although younger by several decades, Joseph Reid was the kind of man who could appeal to Jim Casey because of his recognized leadership qualities in his chosen field, his ease in human relationships, and the absence of pretentiousness in his makeup. Both men were pleased to find they had common roots in Seattle, Washington, where Casey had started his business activity and where Reid had developed his career as a social worker in a children's residential treatment facility. Reid found the older man's questions about children in trouble interesting and his views intelligent. At some point Reid learned that the stranger who had dropped in was the president of United Parcel Service, and he became alert to the fact that Casey had resources to invest in an innovative new service program.

Jim Casey personified the American success story, a veritable Horatio Alger figure on the American business landscape. Born in Nevada in 1888, he was brought to Seattle by his family while still an infant. Because of the illness of his father, Jim Casey began to help support his family when he was only eleven years old. With his brothers, he had started a messenger service in Seattle in 1907 in very modest basement quarters. His company began by delivering packages on bicycles for local clothing stores and other merchants. After a brief sojourn away from Seattle prospecting, Casey returned to the arena of messenger work. By the time he was thirty years old, he had become the prime mover in the development of what was to become a vast company whose name and brown delivery vans—always neatly maintained in accordance with his precepts—were to become a well-established institution in the United States. In guiding the growth of the United Parcel Service, Casey developed a national reputation as an unusually skilled business manager, one who was able to infuse his organization with a high standard of performance. Among other innovations, he was one of the first to develop profit-sharing programs.

Casey and his two brothers and sister had long talked about establishing some kind of a child welfare service for deprived children as the type of memorial to their mother, Annie Casey, best suited to represent her personal attributes. They were united in the desire to honor her memory by funding a program that would secure the benefits of strong family life for problem-ridden children. At the time he visited the offices of the Child Welfare League of America, Jim Casey was in a position to influence the distribution of very substantial charitable funds accumulated in an endowment derived from earnings of the United Parcel Service.

CONCERN FOR CHILDREN WITH PROBLEMS

Jim Casey arrived with a plan in his mind and a detailed outline of that plan in his pocket, a plan to assist needy children in becoming useful United States citizens. His interests focused upon children moving into their adolescent years who were showing problems of delinquency or were otherwise on the road to becoming involved in deviant careers. Coming from a relatively deprived background himself, Casey felt a sense of sympathy as he came to understand that youthful antisocial behavior was rooted in poverty, family break-up, and the failure of society to welcome these youngsters into the mainstream of opportunity. He and his siblings particularly appreciated the strong family life they had been exposed to in their formative years even in times of financial adversity.

Joseph Reid knew the problems of children deprived of the care of functioning families as well as any person in the United States. He had used his influence to secure funding of a major national study by the League of the foster care system. Henry S. Maas, a professor at the School of Social Welfare at the University of California at Berkeley, directed a research team that studied the conditions of foster children in nine communities. The book reporting the results of the study, *Children in Need of Parents*, had an important impact when it was published and is still regarded as a landmark investigation in child welfare (Maas and Engler 1959). While the report of the research was quite balanced and careful in its assessment of the evidence, the findings tended to be discouraging in the description of many children captured for extended periods in a foster care system that was intended to provide temporary placements.

Maas and Engler found that a high proportion of the foster children had been abandoned by their parents, were unvisited and in a state of limbo. The children who remained in foster care placement for more extended periods showed significantly more behavioral problems than those who had been in care for shorter periods (Fanshel and Maas 1962). The overall view was that the welfare of deprived children was being undermined by a seemingly mindless and poorly managed system. The study findings put foster care services under a cloud of suspicion as not serving children well, and reactions to these findings helped launch the sustained movement for reform that took place in the years that followed.

Joseph Reid and Jim Casey came to a shared point of view about the new program that was to be brought into being. Jim Casey left Reid with the same plan in his mind and in his pocket. But he left with something additional, which was of great importance to Jim Casey—approval and encouragement from someone knowledgeable in the field of child welfare. He then telephoned to Seattle requesting that the next steps be completed to put The Casey Family Program in operation.

It made sense to both men that an agency be established in Seattle that would offer care in foster family homes to children deprived of their families. This effort would reflect Reid's conviction that, despite the negative findings of the Maas and Engler study, extended placement in foster care need not constitute an unsuitable environment for a child if return to the biological parents was not possible and adoption was ruled out as a likely alternative because of the child's age or other factors. This was in accord with Jim Casey's view that the provision by an agency of a service that offered strong family life could be a powerful force in the rescue of children who were on a downward spiral because they had the misfortune of having been born to families replete with serious problems.

In his summary recommendations written as a final chapter in the Maas and Engler book, Reid had set forth the perspective that long-term foster care was a necessary service for some children:

> It is not possible to overemphasize the importance of every child welfare agency's concentrating on the family as a whole and not the individual child in care. However, we must also face the fact that there are thousands of children in care for whom there is a family in name only and for whom the parents, because of their own irremediable inadequacies, will never be able to function fully. Therefore, for thousands of children foster care is preferable to their being in their own homes, for there simply is no own home and no possibility for one. Just as communities must make certain that there are adequate preventive services and services for work with parents, they must also make certain that they recognize the need for strong professional foster care services for those children unfortunate enough to be born to parents who can never fulfill their full parental responsibility (1959:338–389).

It was Reid's view that teenagers with unstable life histories who were showing problems in the community could be considered for placement with foster families if an agency had the assets to deliver good service. Recruitment of foster families who had the innate capacity to understand and tolerate the behavior of these children or who could be helped to achieve this was an essential ingredient of such a service program. Reid had made a special point of highlighting the role of foster parents in this context:

A concerted effort is also needed to discover—in part through more intensive and systematic study and in part through better use of existing knowledge—the kinds of foster parents who are able to provide a relatively enduring family life for children with emotional difficulties. Identifying the motivation that makes of parents good foster parents and then seeking out such families can do much to reduce the number of re-placements in foster care which emotionally disturbed children are subjected to and the extent of disturbance among such children which is reinforced by their repeated changes in homes. We need to determine what services foster parents require in order to be more accepting of these children, including such mundane things as regular baby-sitting services financed by the agency to enable foster parents to have sufficient freedom to maintain their own emotional health (1959:390).

Reid also pointed to the need for professional social work staff, with capacity to work therapeutically with the children and supportively with the foster families, as a vital aspect of such a service organization.

Reid found that Jim Casey had quite well formulated ideas about what would be required to make a new program successful. His thinking about service delivery issues in this area had the strength of solid experience in building a successful corporation in which considerable initiative was encouraged at the local level and where employees were offered stable employment and financial incentives for years of loyal service.

AN AGENCY COMES INTO BEING

The Casey Family Program was established in Seattle, Washington as a privately endowed social service agency. It accepted its first child into care in 1966. The aim of the program, as developed in the discussions between Jim Casey and Joseph Reid, was to provide "quality planned long-term foster care for children and youth when this is the best permanent plan." This aim has guided the agency since its inception. Thus, the agency has primarily placed children in foster boarding home care who have little prospect of being reunited with their natural families. It has sought to serve children who are victimized and troubled and so are likely to represent a challenge to caretakers.[1]

The agency was to be funded entirely from private sources, ruling out public subsidy as a basis for program support.[2] The plan was to secure the best trained social work staff available, to compensate them adequately, and to assign caseloads of reasonable size. Foster parents were to be recruited with an aim of obtaining strong families, already successful with their own children, to care for upset youngsters without families they could count on. The agency was to be accredited by the appropriate standard setting organizations to ensure the highest quality of service. The agency's substantial endowment was to be treated as an available resource for children when a child's identified needs required purchase of specialized services. Such needs might be in the areas of health, educational remediation, recreation, higher education, psychotherapeutic treatment, interim institutional care for children who were having a difficult experience in foster home placement, or in other areas.

Those well informed about child welfare services may question whether the service delivery model that guides The Casey Family Program is appreciably different from what is offered by other child welfare agencies providing foster family care as a basic service to children. Although in many ways what is being offered resembles foster family care placement services conventionally practiced throughout the United States, the kinds of children to be served are not "conventional" foster children. They represent a more challenging group of youngsters, most of whom have been in a large number of placements in the past and are, therefore, at fairly high risk in any subsequent care arrangement. Thus the program is special in the character of its caseload.

What Joseph Reid apparently had in mind was that foster family care could be expanded to a distressed population of children, in a form not radically different from the services being provided by other agencies but under better conditions made possible by the generous flow of charitable funds. This agency reflects a significant initiative from the private sector. Its staff tend to be paid at higher levels than those of other agencies offering similar services, and they have smaller case loads. As a consequence, there is less staff turnover, a widespread problem in the child welfare field. Another feature of the agency is that foster parents receive extra income in recognition of their special role.

Jim Casey approved of what he saw in the early beginnings of the Seattle program and after several years gave his support to the development of new divisions. From the time of the first children coming into care in 1966, the agency expanded at a steady rate. Table 1.1 shows the divisions of The Casey Family Program and the reported size of the caseload of each at the end of 1986, the time of the twentieth anniversary of the program.[3] Some of the divisions shown in the table were only recently established so they had few or no children in care. The table also contains the projected size of the caseload for each division. While the number of children in placement at any one time is relatively modest, the western program's current location in fifteen division sites situated in thirteen states gives it a significant national base.

The small size of each division's caseload reflects Jim Casey's desire that growth be limited at each site in the interest of the program's being able to deliver a more personalized service. According to the 1986 report, many of the divisions are not slated to go beyond 55 children as the normal caseload size, with only two (Seattle and South Dakota) serving as many as a hundred.[4] In the interviews with former wards of the agency in the follow-up study described in this book, they often said that the agency took on the aura of extended family and that this was particularly meaningful when a foster family placement was interrupted and a new foster home had to be found. Such comments would have gladdened Jim Casey's heart because they confirmed his sense of what these children needed.

THE NATIONAL POLICY CONTEXT FOR THE DEVELOPMENT OF A NEW SERVICE AGENCY

The Casey Family Program is an effort to utilize a well-known form of care, foster family home placement, in more creative ways for a challenging population of children. The emergence of such an agency also has special meaning now because residential institutional care for children showing behavioral difficulties is becoming prohibitively expensive and shrinking as a resource in many areas of the country. Indeed, some observers regard it as an "endangered species."[5] There is hope that difficult children, such as those placed with this agency, can be cared for in family situations with good results at less cost.

This agency's emphasis on serving children with foster families until they reach young adulthood has taken place in a period in which those concerned with child welfare throughout the nation have regarded foster care with considerable ambivalence. The Maas and Engler study was followed by further intense national scrutiny of the foster care system. Reports by the Children's Defense Fund (1978) and the National Commission for Children in Need of Parents (1979) were typical of a number of reviews of foster care as a service for children that condemned in scathing terms the inability of foster care agencies to meet the needs of children for some degree of permanence in their living arrangements. Such criticisms reached a crescendo in the late

TABLE 1.1   The Divisions of The Casey Family Program
in Order of Founding: Social Work Staff, Children in Care 1986,
and Projected Caseloads

Division	Social Workers	Children in Placement 12/31/86[a]	Children in Placement at Full Development
Seattle[b]	6	103	100
Yakima	3	52	55
Idaho	4	58	65
Montana	4	78	65
California	3	55	55
Oregon	4	54	65
South Dakota	6	52	100
North Dakota	5	42	80
Arizona	3	46	55
Hawaii	3	36	55
Austin	3	24	55
San Antonio	3	0	55
Louisiana	3	0	55
Wyoming	3	17	55
Oklahoma	3	0	55
	56	617	970

SOURCE: 1986 Annual Report (The Casey Family Program 20th Anniversary)
[a] Includes 41 youths emancipated from care in student aid program and 2 in subsidized adoption.
[b] The Seattle Division was called the Western Washington Division until 1985 when its name was changed.

1970's and helped to pass federal legislation bringing about a national policy change.

The Adoption Assistance and Child Welfare Act of 1980 (Public Law 96–272) has been described as one of the most important and far-reaching pieces of federal legislation in the area of child welfare to be enacted in recent history (Allen and Knitzer 1983). The legislation has established "permanency planning" as the major national orientation to children separated from their families. The Casey venture, whose foundation is the legitimacy of extended foster care for an especially vulnerable group of children, departs from this major orientation.

PROGRAM VARIATIONS IN TIME AND PLACE

The services offered the children by this program were not so rigidly standardized that all children were exposed to a fixed experience. With the passage of time, the points of view that guided the formation of the program changed as the board of trustees and staff became engaged with the realities of serving a group of challenging children. While the core formulations that Jim Casey enunciated were retained, these children were exposed to some variation in the service environment depending upon when and where they entered care. Some examples of changing perspectives and policies are the following:

1. There was less emphasis upon work with the children's families in the early years of the program since the plan was to accept children whose families were no longer a resource for them. With a growing awareness of the active involvement of a number of children with their families, the Western Washington Division (Seattle) had an advisory committee study the issue in 1977. Its report sought to correct what was regarded as an inadequate approach to work with families (The Casey Family Program 1977). A greater concern with the children's families seems to pervade the program now.

2. Although the term "delinquent children" (or those who were at risk of becoming delinquent) often appeared in the program's early descriptions of the types of children to be served, other types of children were admitted from the agency's start. For example, the agency accepted children with developmental disabilities in their backgrounds or those with a history of mental hospital care. Some of these admissions reflected dependency situations with special needs such as multiple sibling placements. The majority of children, however, coming into care were unsocialized youth who were in danger of becoming deviant as adults.

3. The agency has recently changed its policy toward subsidized adoption as a possibility for children who have become especially close to their foster families and now accepts it as a stated goal for some children in its care.

4. The divisions in which the children were placed varied from each other somewhat reflecting the local environments and the personal characteristics of the staff because a certain amount of local autonomy in shaping the service program was encouraged within the context of overall program policy. Jim Casey's experience in the United Parcel Service reinforced his view that some local initiative could bring out the best in a work force and thereby serve the organization's purposes. For example, there appears to have been variation among the divisions in the extent to which local mental health professionals were retained

to offer clinical treatment to children who required this as opposed to having agency social work staff carry major responsibility for this work. Depending upon the availability of regional institutional resources, there was also variation in the purchase of institutional and group care for children as interim placements for those who were not adapting well to foster family care, a strategy discussed in chapter 7.

5. The program modified its admission policies by choosing to accept children who were already successfully residing in a foster home placement not connected with the Casey Family Program and who were not problematic or delinquent. That is, the agency used its resources to make permanent a successful foster home placement. We call these arrangements "package placements" because the foster home came with the child. Of the 585 children, 23.1% (135) were in such placements These children were on average less hostile and adapted better to foster care and were more likely to remain in the foster home until emancipation at age 18.

CENTRAL HYPOTHESIS: A CHAIN OF CONTINUITY IN LIFE COURSE

Children enter foster care at varying ages. Some come as infants while others are placed as teenagers. A child who is older is more likely to have experienced significant events, often traumatic, that have affected the child negatively. A central hypothesis underlying this study was that these events and the child's adaptation to them were likely to influence the way new placement arrangements were experienced. An agency dedicated to the caring for adolescents, such as this one, would tend to have many youngsters who had experienced prior placements with other agencies. Some of these placements may have been in group settings, and others may have been in foster family living arrangements where tolerance for the behavior of the children evaporated. A child who had been expelled from prior foster family placements would be expected to challenge the Casey program's arrangements. Our statistical analysis documented and elaborated this central hypothesis of continuity of life course experience.

A feature of our research was that we made an effort to determine important aspects of the pre-Casey life experiences of these children and to trace the course of their adjustments while in Casey care and afterward. We focused not only on the placements of the children in foster care but also on changes in living arrangements taking place outside agency systems, such as a child leaving his parents to live with his grandparents or to live with a father who had been separated from the mother.

There is little precedent for this kind of "tracking" of the child's living experiences in the research literature about foster care. The placement histories of children are rarely taken into account in looking at outcomes of subsequent agency efforts. An example of a presentation of such information that is useful for clinical purposes is Figure 1.1, which displays this aspect of the life of one child in the study. It reveals the turbulence of her history and some of the damage inflicted upon her.

The Case of Mary: A Fragmented Childhood

At the age of two, Mary and her only sibling had been abandoned by their mother and been left for a short while in the care of their father. When he could not cope, the children were sent to their grandparents, where they lived for two years. When the grandfather died, the grandmother had a nervous breakdown, and the children were then placed in a foster home.

At the time Mary was referred to the program at the age of twelve, she had already been exposed to a dozen living arrangements including two failed public agency efforts to provide her with adoptive placements. She had had a fragmented childhood saturated with rejection and neglect. The case reader documented that she had been scarred by her experiences and, out of mistrust for adults, had developed defenses that served her poorly. Foster parents who extended themselves to her were fended off and subjected to hair-raising episodes of nonconformity.

By the time Mary left the program at age sixteen, she had experienced eighteen living arrangements since her birth and had run away from her last three foster homes. The agency had no further resource for her and reluctantly returned custody to the family court and public social service department. The agency learned that by the time Mary was 21 she had already given birth to two children who were in informal foster boarding home placements and was expecting the birth of twins. None of the putative fathers were involved in helping her cope with her current circumstances.

Closed Case Study

The population of children reported on in this book are the 585 children who entered the Casey program and whose cases were closed on or before December 31, 1984. Six divisions of the program were in existence long enough to warrant inclusion in this study. These divi-

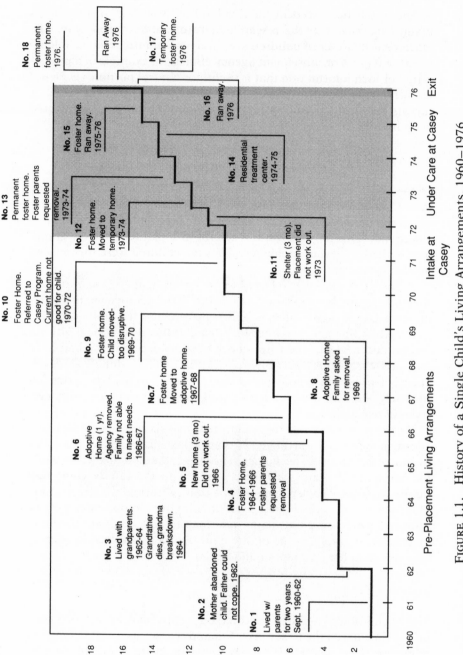

FIGURE 1.1.   History of a Single Child's Living Arrangements, 1960–1976

sions and the years children began to enter their care were: Western Washington (1966), Yakima (1972), Idaho (1972), Montana (1973), California (1974), and Oregon (1977).

The major advantage of studying the closed cases was that the work could cover the program's history to date from "day one" and the task of reading and extracting information from case records could be done in a relatively brief period of time, one year, with little disruption of agency routines. The alternative was to undertake a prospective longitudinal study that would require many years of effort before yielding results. Our findings from this effort are contained in chapters 3, 4, 5, 7, and 8.

We used a technique called "content analysis" to extract data systematically from written documents. Content analysis has been developed over several decades, and scholars continue to perfect it (Krippendorff 1980; Weber 1985). In chapter two, we describe our application of the procedures of content analysis so that our case readers could extract information objectively from the case records.

Follow-Up Study of Subjects:
Test of the Validity of the Content Analysis

Carrying out a content analysis of case records that were not prepared with any expectation that they would be input to a research study caused us to consider the implications of using these narrative records as if they were valid representations of the children's experiences in care. Fortunately, a substantive and objective test of the worth of the extracted data was made possible by the decision of the board of trustees to fund a follow-up investigation of a group of cases from the Seattle and Yakima Divisions. It included 106 subjects who were seen, on average, seven years after they had left the care of The Casey Family Program. The results of this effort are valuable in their own right and form an important part of our study. Coincidentally, the follow-up data permitted a test of the predictive validity of the measures derived from the content analysis of the case records. We were able to establish from the analyses of the follow-up data, discussed in chapter 6 and Chapter 9, that the data derived from the content analysis predicted variables observed at follow-up.

GENERALIZABILITY OF THE RESULTS OF THE STUDY

As our readers review our findings and seek to place them in the context of previous research results about children in foster care, they must remember that the extrapolation of findings about one popula-tion to a different one is always hazardous. Nevertheless, we feel that this agency's caseload is particularly worthy of research attention. The Casey program selected a majority of the children in this popula-tion because their families seemed unable or unwilling to provide adequate care and not likely to be a resource for their future care. These children and their families suffered more destructive experi-ences than one would typically find among the foster care children served by most public or private social agencies. Almost a quarter of this population were, however, package placements of relatively well-adjusted children.

The range of children, then, was approximately the same as the range in the typical foster care agency so that the applicability of the findings here is quite broad. Because the power of our statistical techniques is larger when the range of the population is larger, this population was in fact a very good choice for study. Our readers should still remember that we did not study a contrasting group of children placed in other settings so that our study does not have the advantage of comparisons with a control group. Nevertheless, we hypothesize that the general patterns of association that we have found would be replicated in studies of other agency populations serving a comparably large range of children. As in all empirical research, our study is a call to other researchers to confirm or chal-lenge the associations we found.

Interpretation of the Results Reported

Many forces act to shape the way a child adjusts over time, and each can contribute a piece of explanation significant at different stages in the child's life. We seek to determine quantitatively the importance of such forces as a child's history of being abused, age at first separation from parents, and the number of placements experienced. We can use these variables as predictors of how children adjust while in care, their mode of departure from care, their condition at the point of departure, and how their lives are played out as adults. Some predic-tors overlap with each other in their ability to account for what happens to children, and others contribute uniquely to the explained variance. Much is left unexplained because human beings defy classi-fication and follow idiosyncratic paths. Despite advances in the be-havioral and social sciences, our measurement procedures were far from perfect. Given these conditions and the additional bounds result-ing from the imperfections of our measurements, it is remarkable that some significant explained variance is accounted for by the independent variables we used.

In the course of grappling with the data and the statistical analyses, our experience has been that the p-value reported with each statistical measure has been invaluable in weaving the findings into a more understandable picture. At the risk of burdening the reader with research detail, we have reported the p-value of each of our findings. Our experience has been that an association significant at the .001 level was usually undeniable empirically and obvious to us when we read the data file to verify the finding. These associations showed up consistently when we ran further analyses with more variables or on subsets of children. An association significant at the .01 level was almost always a stable finding. Occasionally, however, the finding did not appear consistently in further statistical analyses because it was obscured by the many other relations simultaneously influencing the association. When we report a finding significant at the .05 level, the finding is suggestive and worth noting, but it is wise to view such findings with the proverbial grain of salt. Subsequent analyses with more variables or with a restricted set of cases may not confirm the association's significance, suggesting that a more complex explanation may be required.

Those readers who are practitioners, policy makers, or child welfare advocates and who are caught up in powerful substantive issues in a dynamic field where controversy abounds might easily lose patience with what seems to be elaborate technical findings. Those most strongly involved in the issues discussed here sometimes say, "Don't bother to give me all that analytic stuff, just give me your findings. I'll take your word that you did your research piece correctly." This is a short-sighted approach because much of the support for foster care programs rests upon an uncertain base of evidence in which small pieces of explained variance become the empirical foundations of programs. The complexity and fragility of the evidence are no less a challenge to these readers than their efforts to explain why Johnnie who has had 15 placements before coming into his current service program is at extreme risk of not being helped to become stabilized. We hope that our readers accept our reporting of significance levels as our means of expressing the strength of our findings.

Concluding Note

We will document that these children often reflect in their life histories and in the problems shown in foster care the adversity that has befallen their families. In chapter 10, we report their own statements about the care they received from The Casey Family Program and about their own present lives. Tracing the turbulent lives of the children as revealed in the case records and in the follow-up interviews with a subset of the subjects, we simultaneously felt empathy for the youngsters who suffered an intense sense of abandonment because their parents had totally disappeared from their lives and another kind of anguish for those who had not suffered parental loss but whose lives were intertwined with the most destructive kinds of parents. Finally, we present our conclusions in chapter 11.

CHAPTER TWO

Research Methods: An Overview

We discuss our methods in this chapter. Some sections are marked with an asterisk (*) to indicate that they are intended for readers with a methodologic interest and can be passed over by others.

This study is a retrospective longitudinal study. The longitudinal character of our research results from our decision to extract information reflecting stages in a child's life from archival data, the children's case records. Our study is not the prospective longitudinal study often reported in the child development literature with data gathered in real time.[1] The data extraction has taken place years after the events and phases in the child's life occurred.

Another caveat is that the data extracted from the closed case records are doubly derivative. Since the caseworker reported about the subject on many occasions in an unstructured manner, the worker's hindsight may have affected the contents of the record. Further, the case reader's knowledge of the progress of the whole case may have biased the evaluations of the condition of the child.

A second source of data is the subjects themselves in the follow-up study. We thus do not have repeated measures over time from the same source as one would collect in the classic longitudinal investigation. Needless to say, we would expect more accurate data in a study whose measures are taken prospectively and repeated in exactly the same way for each subject.

We do not refer to the limitations of our approach with a sense of apology. There are no reports of research on foster children now available that cover large time spans such as we do in this book. The shortcut we have taken, not waiting twenty years or more to gather data prospectively, allows us to become engaged quickly with longitudinal-type data that offer considerable promise in the yield of results that can be extracted. With computerized tracking systems likely to be introduced into child welfare soon, we hope that future studies will reinvestigate these issues with designs overcoming the limitations here.

CASE READING INSTRUMENT FOR CONTENT ANALYSIS

The search for past information no longer directly available to observers is the raison d'être for content analysis. The case records have not been developed with the specific aim of supporting scientific research, and we knew that the agency divisions included in the study approached case recording tasks in a somewhat idiosyncratic manner, particularly early in their histories. Obviously, we had to be realistic in approaching information extraction tasks. After we balanced the imperfections inherent in data collected by a content analysis with what could be gained in the way of solid knowledge, we decided to take the greatest advantage that we could of the opportunities that were available.

The data on which this study is based derive from a content analysis involving the reading of case records by highly trained social workers who filled out a 72-page schedule that had been prepared for this purpose. A copy of the final version of this schedule is appendix A. The content of this instrument was based upon Fanshel's past experience in the conduct of research about foster children, foster families, and adopted children and from his knowledge of other studies. Many domains reflecting the complex phenomenology of foster care were included as shown by the variables listed in table 2.1.

Many ratings took the form of summated scales of the Likert-type (Selltiz, Wrightsman and Cook 1976:418–421). In such a scale, the reader specified the degree to which a condition held for the child being considered. For example, we asked the reader to provide a rating for each of sixteen items descriptive of the child's adaptation to care (e.g., expressed resistance to being in foster care). We gave the reader a series of ordered choices: "very much," "moderately," "a little," or "not at all" to indicate the degree to which the condition appeared in the description of the child's behavior in the case record. There were other questions that represented nominal scales such as the identification of the referral source of the case (self-referral, voluntary agency, family court, or other source). These scales were a fixed set of categories from which the case reader chose the most appropriate. We relied heavily upon fixed choice responses to questions because we wanted to minimize coding operations and to have the data in a state ready for computer entry and analysis.

Although the schedule is imposing in its appearance, most of the information extracted from the records was in precoded form so that some pages required only a check or two in appropriate boxes. Further, some sections did not apply to all children and could be omitted. Nevertheless, the data collection from the case records required a considerable effort that was quite expensive. More than three thousand hours were spent in extracting information from the records, an average of 4.7 hours per case.

In developing "closed ended" questions for the case reading schedule, we had to anticipate the major, theoretically relevant responses. To allow for answers that were not given in the list, the reader could choose the response "other" and specify in narrative form the special circumstances. In a number of important areas of the schedule, this spillover into the category "other" involved a substantial number of cases. When time permitted, an enlarged coding scheme was created, and the "other" responses were recoded. Where this was not possible, the narratives were entered into the computer.

Opportunities for more qualitative descriptions of the children were included in the content analysis operations. "Open-ended" questions did not have fixed choice responses and permitted the readers to answer in their own words. All such texts were entered into the computer, and they were useful in providing a sense of key issues in the care of the children.

We took the following actions to reduce the "static and noise" inherent in our content analysis and to enhance the rigor of the data collection:

1. Wherever possible, we asked for factual items in the case-reading schedule when there was a high probability that the information would be found in the case record. Examples of such items are: date of a child's birth, date of entry into care, child's school grade level at entry and at exit from Casey care, dates of interruptions of foster home placements while the child was in Casey care, the descriptions of the manner of a child's exit from care, indication that a psychiatric evaluation had been made of the child, and descriptions of purchase of special services for the child such as tutoring, specialized health care, and treatment for behavioral problems.

2. In developing items for the case readers to rate the quality of children's

adaptation and behavior while in care, we attempted to use descriptors of the children that summarized overall qualities in a grosser form rather than resort to subtle, intrapsychic phenomena unavailable except through direct observation of a child. We asked the case reader to make summary ratings of the total "aura" or "gestalt" that permeated narrative descriptions in a case record (e.g., ratings of the child's overall adjustment, level of performance in school, and challenge to caretakers).

3. Our reliability check of the data took the form of an independent reading of 53 cases by second readers who also filled out schedules. We used the intraclass correlation coefficient (Fisher 1970) of the two ratings to report the repeatability of our measures. This statistic is an estimate of the fraction of variance that would be explained if the readers' ratings were regressed on the "true" value.

4. We examined the construct validity of our measures by the consistency of the observed relationships with theory. For example, we would expect that children who suffered physical abuse before coming into care or who experienced a great many failed living arrangements would show evidence of maladaptive behavior when described in their Casey intake studies and would likely suffer more interruptions in their placements with foster families than children who had fewer interruptions.

5. Training of the case readers and continuous quality control checking of the completed schedules standardized the research procedures and the performances of the case readers.

OPERATIONAL PROCEDURES

It was important that the case readers be professionally trained, seasoned in work related to families and children, and amenable to the requirements of the research assignment. We recruited four doctoral students with practice backgrounds in clinical work at the Columbia University School of Social Work. When one reader resigned, we hired a replacement who had substantial child welfare experience.[2]

The readers were oriented to the case-reading schedule in several training sessions. The schedule was tested in draft form by having the four readers independently read a single case and fill out the schedule. There was full discussion of ambiguities in defining terms. This review procedure was repeated on several cases with two or three readers carrying out the reading task and led to reframing of some items and clarification of the intent of the rating scales.

The reading of the 585 case records took place between August 1984 and June 1985. From 40 to 80 records were read each month during the heart of the study. When interpretation of items required further definition, these were discussed with either Fanshel or Grundy. One of the readers was given supervisory responsibilities and reviewed completed schedules with the other readers routinely. These reviews were more intensive in the early part of the study. In the course of preparing the data on the schedules for entry into a computer file, a research assistant and Grundy identified inconsistencies. These were discussed with the readers to ensure common understanding of procedures. Because we intended to have about fifty randomly selected cases reread to estimate reliability, we discouraged the discussion of specific cases. There was exchange about professional practice issues revealed in the case records, and the case readers shared their reactions with us. Although reading the records and filling out the schedules was a difficult assignment, the readers appeared highly motivated and expressed satisfaction in participating in an effort that might be helpful in serving deprived children.

MEASUREMENT IN THE CONTEXT OF CONTENT ANALYSIS

Our research experience with foster care phenomena has led us to distinguish between two types of variables: status variables and ratings. A status variable is a variable indicating whether a relatively objective condition holds or does not hold for a child. Examples are whether the child experienced a disrupted adoption in his past, whether the child ever served in an institution for youthful offenders, and whether a child was emancipated from Casey care, discharged to parents or returned to the court. Such information tends to be factual and less prone to the problems of subjectivity introduced by the source of the information or the data collection procedure. The most common measurement problem for a status variable is missing data.

Ratings carry a great deal of weight in our study because the case reader is asked to record summary impressions obtained from the social worker's case records about important domains in a standardized form. These impressions are the data that were the basis of the study and are summary clinical evaluations of issues such as the child's adaptation to being in care, the degree to which the child was described as resistant to being in foster care, and the degree of challenge posed by the child to those taking care of him.

Overall, our experience in the content analysis effort was that the preplacement histories of the children and how they appeared at the time of the Casey intake study were described in more condensed and abstract narrative fashion in the case records than was true for the period reflecting the child's experience while in care. The case readers thus had to rely upon less than complete descriptions for the preplacement and intake variables. Since the measures developed for the under care phase were based on more nearly full descriptions, they were uniformly stronger, and we could extract measures of more specific details of the children's lives then.

Factor Analysis as a Variable Extraction Strategy

The variables in the case-reading schedule and in the follow-up questionnaire were too numerous and diffuse to analyze efficiently. We reduced the number of variables by developing measures that were extracted from the data at hand using a variable reduction strategy developed over many studies such as this one. Grundy's experience was particularly useful here. As the reader will learn in subsequent chapters, we created a number of indexes guided by this strategy.

These indexes are a key feature of our research effort. Simply put, an index is a composite of items reflecting what is perceived as a common domain of information. Aside from the fact that multi-item indexes are usually stronger measures than their individual components, this extraction strategy allows us to provide our readers with a portraiture of the children that they can grasp more readily.

When one does not have a theory exactly specifying the variables to be used in a study and seeks to find coherence among them through exploratory techniques, factor analysis is an effective variable extraction strategy. Many of our variables are Likert scales, and so we start our work by reexpressing them so that each has the same range. That is, each transformed Likert scale variable has the same minimum value, m, and the same maximum value, M.[3]

Through simulation studies of factor analysis with data of this kind, we have found that the varimax rotation of the principal components produces satisfactory results, and our discussions use this rotation.[4] We regard a variable as belonging to a factor when the absolute value of the rotated coefficient of the variable in the factor, its loading, is greater than .35.[5] Our strategy has eight steps.

1. Inclusion of Relevant Variables: The first step is to run the largest possible factor analysis including as many variables as are germane to any one time frame. Variables that describe other time frames are not included in this factor analysis. For example, one factor analysis considered variables descriptive of a child's experiences prior to entry into the Casey program while another used variables descriptive of the child's experiences while in the program.
2. Number of Factors: For each factor analysis, it is necessary to deter-

mine the number of factors in the solution used. The initial number of factors used is the number of eigenvalues greater than 1. We compute the varimax rotation of the solution with this number of factors. If no more than two variables belong to the last factor, we reduce the number of factors in the solution by one and recompute. This procedure is continued until the largest integer emerges such that the last factor in the solution with one more factor has only one or two variables belonging to it.

3. Measuring Internal Consistency of Index: The principal objective is to derive sets of clusters of variables such that each cluster has high item-criterion correlations and is orthogonal to the other factors. Items that appear in two or more factors are generally ambiguous or broader in concept than a simple component of a variable. Cronbach's alpha (Cronbach 1951) is a useful measure of internal consistency, especially for indexes derived from factors with less than 10 or 12 items. An alpha of .60 appears to be a reasonable cutoff from our experience. We view with caution measures with 10 or fewer items that had a Cronbach's alpha less than .60. If such a factor makes "sense" and represents a potentially important substantive issue, we retain it because it might be significant in later statistical analyses even if its   Cronbach alpha is somewhat lower than desired.

For example, the Index of Mental Illness in Background, based on a child's experience before entering the Casey program, had a Cronbach alpha of .40; but the items had substantive importance. They are: (a) previously cared for in a mental hospital, (b) the agency referring the child to Casey had provided mental care, and (c) there was a prior attempt of the child to commit suicide. In the analyses, there were some significant associations of follow-up variables with this index.

4. Reversing Scale When Coefficient Negative. When a variable has a negative coefficient in an index, then the index uses the reexpressed variable X' equal to the sum of the maximum and minimum possible values minus the value of the variable; that is,

$$X' = m + M - X.$$

We then examine the pattern of variables belonging to a factor.

5. Single Variable Factors: A factor with just one variable belonging to it does not require an index. If this variable has substantive value, we exclude it from the index construction process and use it in our subsequent analyses directly without attempting further reduction of variables.

6. Inclusion of Items in an Index: We next consider each factor in turn. The simplest situation is a factor containing variables that belong only to this factor. The index uses only the variables belonging to the factor and is the mean of the values of these variables.

The next simplest situation is that there is a set of variables that belong only to factor A, another set that belong only to Factor B, and a third set that belongs to both factor A and factor B but to no other factors. Then, we create three indexes. The first uses only the variables that belong to factor A, the second only the variables that belong to factor B, and the third the variables common to factor A and factor B.

7. Dealing with Remaining Variables: If there are variables remaining that have not been included in an index, we run a factor analysis on the variables that have not been assigned to an index and repeat the analysis procedure described above. In general, few indexes result from this step. The variables that are not used in the initial step are often very skewed (for example, status variables for a rare condition) or are measured with a great deal of error. In this study, 15% of the variables were not assigned to an index.

8. Assessing the Reliability of an Index: At this point, we calculate four measures of reliability: Cronbach's alpha, item-criterion correlations (the correlation of the item with the index minus the item), the correlation of each item with indexes other than the one containing the item, and the intraclass correlation of the index.

The most important evaluative statistics are the item-criterion correlations. Each correlation should, at a minimum, be statistically significant. Ideally, they should all be high and essentially equal. In this study, the item-criterion correlations ranged from .4 to .7. We compare the lowest item-criterion correlation in an index to the item-criterion correlations for the other items. If they are low as well, then we keep the item in the index. If the other items have item-criterion correlations that are higher, then we examine the Cronbach alpha for the index with the item deleted. If the Cronbach alpha for an index with the item removed is lower than the Cronbach alpha for the index with the item, then we keep the item in the index.

If an item has a higher correlation with an index other than the one that contains it, we examine the content of the item and the two indexes to see whether it makes more sense to delete the item or to move it to the other index. On rare occasions, we keep the item in the original index

Finally, we address the issue of the inter-rater reliability of index scores mindful of the fact that a single reader was making ratings based on a sense of what the records were conveying about a child in the various domains of concern to us. When we calculate the intraclass correlation coefficient of an index, we routinely compare it with the intraclass correlations of the component items. In general, the intraclass correlation of the index is greater than the intraclass correlations of the component items. Recognizing the inherent vulnerability of measures developed from archival data, we consider as dubious an index whose intraclass correlation is less than .6. When the index is sufficiently important, however, we use it even though the intraclass correlation documents that there is substantial error of measurement. This is in the exploratory spirit of our investigation. Our expectation is that further work in defining the concepts and making them operational would likely improve the quality of some of these measures. The most important measure with low reliability is our measure of a child's exposure to a disturbing sexual event prior to entry into the Casey program.

Handling Missing Data

When a case has values missing for variables in an index, the value of the index is the mean of the values observed for the case for variables in the index. This procedure permits the calculation of each index for most subjects. In our regression and factor analyses, we deleted each case that was missing information on any variable used in an analysis.[6]

Considerations of Validity

A high intraclass correlation reflects agreement between two case readers and is a necessary but not sufficient condition for a scientifically useful variable. The validity of the index scores, whether we were indeed measuring what we had made operational on the basis of the factor analyses, is the sufficient condition. One standard treatment of validity (American Psychological Association 1966) considers three types of validity: content validity, criterion-related validity (concurrent or predictive), and construct validity.

The content validity of the items included in the case reading schedule was not assessed in the manner typically used in psychometric test construction, because our study did not use paper-and-pencil tests. Our items were culled from various investigations of foster children conducted by Fanshel and others, and their relevance was determined by past usage.

As an example of concurrent validity, we treated the child's pre-Casey life experiences in an integrated fashion so that we sought to determine whether the number and kind of living arrangements the child had experienced and other salient measures reflecting the quality of life would be associated with the way the child was perceived at intake as a candidate for foster family care in sensible and predictable ways. A second example is that a child who had required care in a youth services institution offering confined care should be seen as more oppositional in behavior than a child not exposed to such care.

There was ample opportunity to prove the predictive validity of our indexes from the data gathered in the follow-up. For example, we would predict that a child who had experienced a stay in a mental hospital before entering Casey care would show significantly more emotional disturbance as measured by an index based on self-report at follow-up than other subjects.

Construct validation of a measure requires us to document empirically that it performs in accordance with theoretical expectations. Are the associations produced by key measures similar to the associations one would expect from existing theory? Put another way, are the findings consistent with established knowledge as derived from child welfare practice theory or from empirical results reported in the research literature? Our factor analysis studies of life course phenomena in chapter 8 and chapter 9 give us an opportunity to examine whether phenomena cluster together in a manner to be expected on the theoretical assumption of stability of adaptation and behavioral patterns over time.

We are able to set forth a network of relationships to test the validity of measures. For example, we report a two-item index reflecting a child's mode of exit from care and adjustment at departure. In the later follow-up, we have information that permits the development of measures of well-being, adequacy of housing, adequacy of income, satisfaction with educational attainment and other measures of the quality of life of the subjects as adults. If we assume stability of life course patterns, we would expect children leaving Casey care in better shape to report better quality of life when seen as adults than those who were more troubled at departure. Similarly, theory would dictate that the children who were most delinquent while in the care of The Casey Family Program would report on average significantly more arrests and involvement in crime at follow-up than those who were less acting out while in care. Of course, the validity of the follow-up measure is implicated in its own right. Bostwick and Kyte have observed that in the effort to establish the construct validity of a measure, the investigator is simultaneously involved in the construct validity of the other theoretical concepts. (1988:117)

Statistical Analyses

In seeking to track children using time dependent data, we have used multiple regression and factor analysis as our basic statistical procedures. Each index score characterizing child description domains in successive stages (that is, the intake period prior to entering care with The Casey Family Program, the period while in the program's care, and the point of departure from the program's care) was the dependent variable in a multiple regression analysis. The independent variables included demographic variables descriptive of the children (e.g., age, gender, and ethnicity), and variables descriptive of preplacement living arrangements of the children, including counts of these arrangements, percentage of pre-Casey time since birth away from the natural parents, and percent of pre-Casey time that the child spent in foster care. The independent variables included status variables specifying whether the child had a history of physical abuse, exposure to a disturbing sexual event, adoption disruption, or placement in a group home or institution and whether the child was in a package placement. We also included some interaction variables: whether a boy was physically abused, whether a boy experienced a premature disturbing sexual event, and whether a boy experienced both. The physically abused boy was a variable found significant in earlier research (Galdston 1979). The other interactions were included to treat exposure to a disturbing sexual event in the same way as physical abuse. In addition, variables that were dependent variables in the analysis of the early stages of a child's life were used as independent variables in the analysis of later stages. For example, we used the index measuring the extent of the child's hostility and negativity at entry into the Casey program as an independent variable in the analysis of the child's adaptation to Casey care.

Regression analysis was also used to predict the index scores developed from the follow-up interview responses with the former wards of the Seattle and Yakima Divisions. The independent variables were the indexes based on descriptions of the children in the four phases (pre-Casey, at intake, under Casey care, and exit) and the demographic variables describing each subject. The regression analyses permitted us to make substantive statements, for example, about the effects of such independent variables as a history of abuse experienced by boys on the increased likelihood of involvement in criminal activities as adults. It also made it possible to link the condition at departure from care of subjects to a greater sense of well-being reported at the time of follow-up.

The logical culminations of the regression analyses seeking to relate early life history and later outcomes are the factor analysis of the life course data for the population of 585 children covering the time from their births to their exits from the Casey program and the factor analysis of the 106 subjects in the follow-up group extending the span of time to an average of seven years after leaving Casey care.

TABLE 2.1   Coverage of Case Reading Schedule

Intake, Pre-Casey Domains

Background

Child's Face Sheet: Includes such items as gender, race, birth date, division of agency, school grade, court of jurisdiction, court status, referral date, referral agency, worker, birthplace, and religion.

Child's Living Arrangement and Placement History: Includes location, identification of relation where living or agency facility, begin date, end date, and reason moved.

Family Directory: Name, sex, relation, address, birth date, birthplace, religion, marital status and occupation (provided for each significant relative, e.g., mother, father, siblings, and others).

Child's Family System: For parents, identity by name, relation, religion, birth date, ethnicity, location at child's entrance into care, and location at departure from care. For children, same items as for parents plus identification of father and father's relation to mother (location codes for adults and for children provided). Paternity status of father (code provided).

Referral Source: Name, category, length of time child/family known, nature of contact of referral source to family and/or child.

Reasons for Placement

Factors Related to the Child's Need for Care: Reasons for placement, reasons for approaching Casey program, and contributory conditions (15 categories, such as whether the child was ready to leave institutional care).[2]

Factors Related to Mother Creating the Need for Care: Reasons for placement, reasons for approaching Casey program, and contributory conditions (31 categories, such as mother deceased).

Factors Related to Father Creating the Need for Care: Reasons for placement, reasons for approaching Casey program, and contributory conditions (31 categories such as father's whereabouts unknown).

Intake: Referral accepted for study; if not, basis for prior rejection and later reversal.

Risk Factors and Preplacement Events

Risk Factors About Child Identified at Intake: Expelled from previous foster home, difficulty accepting separation from natural parents, inability to accept intimacy of family life, rebelliousness, history of delinquent or semidelinquent behavior, personality problems making child difficult to live with; psychiatric evaluation indicating serious emotional problems, difficulty adjusting to normal school situation, health problems, developmental disability (record shows: mention as risk factor/some mention/no mention).

Preplacement Events: Disturbing sexual event, physical abuse, runaway episodes, acts of juvenile delinquency, suicide attempt, cared for in mental hospital, other noteworthy events (open-ended response).

Parental Functioning

Mother's Maternal Career: Ways in which she fulfilled maternal responsibilities, ways she was impaired or otherwise limited (open-ended questions).

Father's Paternal Career: Ways in which he fulfilled paternal responsibilities, ways he was impaired or otherwise limited (open-ended questions).

Child's Experience in the Care of The Casey Family Program

Experience in Casey Foster Homes

Child's Placement History: Home No._____, date entered, facility (foster home, therapeutic foster home, support facility, residential setting). If foster home: name, address, number of own children, number of other Casey foster children, number of non-Casey foster children, past experience (open-ended question), date left foster home. (repeated for each foster home in which the child was placed).

Foster Home No._____: Attributes as motive for placing child with foster family: able to tolerate aggressive children, rural family, lots of space, much experience raising children, tolerance for emotionally disturbed children, family being religious, family having worked well with Casey program, other (check all that apply).

Reservations About Foster Family When Selected: no/yes (details).

Unusual Features of the Foster Home as Relates to the Child: (open-ended question).

Summary Rating of Child's Foster Home (rating for each year child in care) Rating Categories: (1) strongly positive, (2) positive, (3) mixed or neutral, (4) some reservations, (5) strong reservation, not ratable.[8]

Challenge to Caretakers

Challenge of the Child While in Care, Extent Difficult To Care For (rating for each year child in care) Rating Categories: (1) no difficulty, (2) slight difficulty, (3) moderate difficulty, (4) substantial difficulty, (5) other, (6) unable to determine from record.

Interruptions in Placements

Interrupted Foster Home Placement (Foster Home No. _____) Categories: child ran away, foster parents experienced illness or death, foster parents moved out of state, foster parents experienced family problems;, foster parents asked for removal because of child's behavior, agency removed child because needs not well met, other (describe).

Adjustment

Summary Rating of the Child's Adjustment While in Care (rating for each year child in care) Rating Categories: (1) excellent, (3) adequate, (5) mixed; (7) poor.

Adaptation to Care

Ratings Covering Child's Adaptation to Care (for first year in care, at midpoint while in Casey care, last year in care). Items: Status in Foster Care: (1) Expressed resistance to being in care; (2) was anxious to return to natural parent; (3) felt at home in setting; (4) showed positive attachment to own mother—desired to see her; (5) showed positive attachment to own father—desired to see him; (6) ties to foster family were very close. General Behavior in Care: was resistant to adult supervision; tended to be moody or depressed; tended to be secure, free of anxiety; tended to be hostile and belligerent; showed difficulty in controlling behavioral impulses; tended to be relaxed, at ease; was friendly and outgoing in social life; was able to make close, intimate friendship ties; showed low tolerance for frustration of desires; showed poor concentration, had short attention span; was easy for foster parents to discipline; was usually cheerful and happy; tended to be rowdy; experimented with drugs; tended to drink alcohol to excess. (Rating Categories: very much, moderately, a little, not at all, does not apply, and no basis for rating).

Social Conduct

Problems Exhibited During Placement Experience: Items: had run away, had stolen petty items, had stolen major items, had stayed away overnight without permission, engaged in destruction of property, had been involved in activities of a delinquent gang, had been defiant of caretaker in a major way, had engaged in behavior dangerous to own physical safety, had used hallucinogenic or other drugs, had gotten into difficulty because of sexual behavior, other. (Response Categories: never, one occasion, several occasions, frequently).

Symptomatic Behaviors[9]

Symptomatic Behaviors Reported: Items: disturbing dreams; telling lies; soiling self; wetting self — daytime; wetting self — night; sleep disorder; destructive; poor appetite; nail biting; nervous tics; stomach disorders; sucking thumb; afraid or shy; allergy or skin disorder; colds; moody or depressed; excluded by children; overweight or underweight; too sensitive; too serious; under strain; accident prone; bizarre behavior; other (open-ended response). (Response Categories: none recorded; single incident; occasional incident; frequent).

Hobbies and Interests

Child's Achievements/Assets/Interests: Items: music, sports, art, mechanical crafts, dance, debate, computers, science, creative writing, community participation, 4–H clubs/animal care dramatics, clothing design, sewing, other hobbies (specify). Response Categories: no mention, some interest, strong interest, some achievement, outstanding achievement.

School Performance

Child at Age-Appropriate Grade Level When Entering Care: Response Categories: yes, no (years behind).

Overall Performance in Academic Work While in Casey Care: Response Categories: (1) below average, (3) average, (5) above average.

Child's Grade Upon Leaving Casey Care

Child at Age-Appropriate Grade Level When Leaving Care: Response Categories: yes, no (years behind).

Factors Causing Child To Be Behind in School: Response Categories: limited mental ability (IQ _____), unable to apply self to school work, expelled or suspended because of behavior, truancy, physical illness causing absence, other (specify).

School Related Problems While in Casey Care: Response Categories: discipline problem, emotional problems (phobia, nervousness, etc.), poor academic performance, underachiever, other (describe).

Child Attended Special or Modified School Program: Response Categories: program for emotionally disturbed, socially maladjusted children; reading school; classes for emotionally disturbed in regular public school; classes for retarded children; classes for physically handicapped children; classes for "slow learners"; other (describe).

Health

Child's Health Before Placement and While in Care: Conditions: weight problem—overweight, weight problem—underweight, vision impairment, hearing deficit, skin disorders, musculo-skeletal disorder, respiratory problem, cardiovascular problem, nervous system disorder, stature (problems in normal growth), diabetes, anemia, tuberculosis, congenital anomalies, nutritional/metabolic disorder, other (specify). (Categories of Response: major problem, minor problem).

Ways in Which Health Impaired Functioning: Response Categories: no indication in the record, yes (describe).

Child's Proneness to Illness: Response Categories: yes, somewhat, no.

Necessity of Program to Mobilize Nonroutine Medical Care: Response Categories: no indication in record, yes (describe).

Medical Incidents While in Care: Response Categories: no indication in record, yes (describe).

General View of Child's Health Revealed by Record: Response Categories: good health, fairly good health, moderate health, poor health, other (describe).

Moderate or Major Dental Problems While in Care: Response Categories: no indication in record, yes (describe).

Evaluation and Treatment of Child

Date of Psychiatric Evaluation: Summary.

Treatment by Psychiatrist: Response Categories: no indication of this, yes (describe).

Date of Psychological Evaluation: Summary.

Treatment by Psychologist: Response Categories: no indication of this, yes (describe).

Treatment by Other Professional: Response Categories: no indication of this, yes (describe).

Treatment by Casey Staff: Response Categories: (1) reference to fairly continuous and intense work with the child, (2) reference to time limited or episodic work on a relatively intense basis; (3) reference to moderate work activity on a continuous basis; (4) reference to relatively episodic, occasional work on a moderate basis; (5) no reference to such work in the record; (6) other.

Background of Adoption

Child previously placed in Adoptive Home: Response Categories: no, yes.

Child previously surrendered for Adoption: Response Categories: no yes.

Foster Family Approached About Adoption: Response Categories: no, yes.

Incidents in Care

Events Disturbing the Placements: Items runaway; truancy; expulsion from school; failure to be promoted in school; act of delinquency, stealing; act of delinquency, substance abuse; act of delinquency, violence; act of delinquency, other; suicidal attempt; serious challenge to foster parents; school dropout; teenage pregnancy; other.

Agency Action: Items: psychiatric evaluation, staff conference, child removed from foster home and placed in another foster home, child removed from foster home and placed in another facility, other (specify).

Contacts with Parents, Siblings, and Others

Persons Seen While Child in Care: Categories: mother, father, stepmother, stepfather, sibling(s), maternal grandmother, maternal grandfather, paternal grandmother, paternal grandfather, other relative, other nonrelated person. (Response categories for each year in care: never, occasionally, sometimes, often).

Where Contacts Tended To Take Place Between Child and Parent: Items: child visited parent's home, parent visited child's home, parent visited agency office, parent took child elsewhere. (Response Categories: never, sometimes, often, always).

Characterization of Mother's and Father's Tendency To Visit Child: (for each year in care): Response Categories: (1) never visited, (2) rarely visited, (3) infrequently visited, (4) occasionally visited, (5) visited fairly regularly, (6) visited regularly, (7) other.

Other Forms of Contact with Mother and Father (for each year in care): Categories: telephone calls, letters, card, gifts, other (specify).

Program's Attempts To Increase Parental Visiting (for each year in care): Categories: not applicable, parent not permitted to visit, not applicable, parent visited frequently, advice to parents of child's need for visits, provision of funds for travel, provision of funds for baby sitter, other forms of encouragement.

Factors Operating To Explain Lack of Contact: Categories: identity of parent not known, paternity not acknowledged, had never lived with child, had surrendered child, had expressed intention of surrendering child, parent lived out of state, parent's whereabouts were unknown, parent was institutionalized, other (specify).

Restriction or Prohibition of Parental Visiting by Program (for mother and father): Response Categories: (1) never; (2) yes, for limited time; (3) yes, over full course of placement; (4) other (specify).

Program's Attempts To Get Parents To Visit (for each year, mother and father): Response Categories: (1) parent visited, no special effort required; (2) major effort to get parent to visit; (3) moderate effort to get parent to visit; (4) slight effort to get parent to visit; (5) no effort to get parent to visit; (6) other (specify).

Circumstances Preventing Visitation (for mother and father): (open-ended questions).

Siblings of Child in Care

Background: Name, birth date, sex, same mother, same father, years lived in same household, living arrangements of sibling.

Contact of Sibling with Casey Child: Response Categories: no contact, occasional, once in six months, once in three months, monthly, more than once a month, in same foster home, other (specify).

Work with Parents

Service Contact with Parents (for each year in care, for mother and father): (1) parent not available for service contact; (2) no contact, no indication of effort to involve parent; (3) effort to involve parent but without success; (4) sporadic contact; (5) contact on regular basis.

Image of Parent

Image of Parent's Role in Child's Life Contained in Record (for mother and father): (1) essentially out of picture, totally absent; (2) parent a peripheral figure, presence rarely mentioned; (3) parent in the picture, sometimes sporadically; (4) parent pretty much in the picture, somewhat significant presence; (5) parent very much in the picture, a significant presence.

Child's Exit from Casey Care

Basis for Child's Ceasing To Be Ward of Program: Response Categories: emancipated from care, adopted by foster parents, adopted by others, returned to natural mother and father, returned to natural mother, returned to natural father, went to live with other person, ran away and did not return, returned to court by program, hospitalized, placed with other agency, imprisoned, other (specify).

Circumstances Under Which Child Left Care: Response Categories: (1) normal aging out, emancipatory process generally devoid of any sense of conflict or crisis; (3) ending on a positive note but some elements of turbulence and associated problematic behavior; (5) a less than serene ending with considerable evidence of emotional crisis and problematic behavior—some positive features to the ending phase gives the exit from care a mixed quality; (7) an acute crisis in the child's foster care status (e.g., child is being thrust out of the home)—a sense of failure accompanies the ending of care; (8) other (e.g., adoption).

Child's Living Arrangements Upon Emancipation: Response Categories: set up own independent domicile, remained in home of foster parents, entered military service, entered college or other educational institution, other (details).

Overall Adjustment at Termination of Care: Response Categories: (1) child making an excellent adjustment in all spheres of life; (3) child was making an adequate adjustment—his/her strengths outweighed the weaknesses shown; (5) child was making a mixed adjustment— generally the problems he faced were serious; (7) child was making an extremely poor adjustment.

Purchased Services for Child

Payment for care in residential treatment program, payment for therapeutic or counseling treatment, payment for medical treatment, payment for medical services, other expenditures.

CHAPTER THREE

Characteristics of The Children and Their Experiences Before Entering Care

In this chapter, we focus on the living arrangements and other experiences of the subjects before being placed with the Casey program. We also describe the ways in which the children were portrayed in the case records at their entry, particularly with regard to risk factors that would identify placement as challenging. A basic hypothesis underlying the study was that the experience of the children while in Casey care would strongly reflect life events that had taken place before their entry. That is, some continuity of the life course could be expected so that children who experienced greater deprivation, physical abuse, neglect, and instability of living arrangements would present a greater challenge to their foster parents.

The common theme of our hypotheses on this life course development is that an experience embodying rejection or mistreatment of a child gets played out in the child's increased subsequent hostility, which can be identified at the time of a child's entry into care. Conversely, an experience reflecting acceptance of the child is associated with lessened hostility. Although this theme is obvious, the determination of which traumatic or rejection incidents experienced by children with unstable life histories are most associated with the child's hostility and the estimation of the importance of each type of incident are complex and unanswered questions in the child welfare literature. From a practical standpoint, an understanding of a child's preplacement history and current behavioral tendencies help to define the challenge faced by the receiving agency and the child's foster family.

The first specific hypothesis was that our data would confirm the association that physically abused boys tend to be more violent than other children. The phenomenon that physically abused boys are subsequently more violent and that girls have a different response to physical abuse has been observed in several populations described in the psychiatric literature. For example, Galdston says:

> Little boys who have been physically abused tend to develop a proclivity to violent behavior as their prime mode of relating to others. In a group setting they tend to violate the person and property of other children to a degree that far exceeds the norm for their age. It is not so much that they are more violent than other children but, rather, that violence remains their dominant mode of relating to others. . . . The little girl who has been physically abused tends to be inordinately dependent upon autoerotic activities as her source of comfort in the context of exposure to other children. She relies upon hair-twirling, thumb-sucking, and clinging behavior to a degree that exceeds the range for girls of her age. . . . These patterns of behavior may be viewed as active and passive identification with the experience of violence. . . (1979:588)

Rogeness et al. (1986) reported findings consistent with Galdston's report. Their analysis revealed that abused and neglected boys in a population of children admitted to a psychiatric hospital had an increased frequency of conduct disorder diagnoses. They found that abused boys were more likely to have homicidal ideation, to set fires, and to show cruelty to animals. They found abused girls to be like other girls on these measures. Sandberg (1989) assembled the views of strategically placed informants including a judge, victims of child abuse, lawyers, psychiatrists, and researchers to confirm the hypothesis that child abuse and delinquent behavior by victims were strongly associated. Some experts in this field, have, however, expressed the view that there is no one discernible profile of abused children, some being negativistic while others show withdrawal symptoms (Martin and Beezley 1976:195).

The second hypothesis was that a child who experienced a great deal of prior turbulence in living arrangements would be more hostile and negativistic at entry. We define a "living arrangement" as a situation in which a child was residing in a domicile or other setting intended to be stable. In developing a count of living arrangements, we did not include as separate "arrangements" temporary living experiences in summer camps or short-term stays in hospitals. Children in this study, such as Mary described in chapter 1, have moved from one domicile or setting to another and are a stark contrast to the normal situation.

Why undertake a count of preplacement living arrangements? The parent-child deprivation literature has emphasized the damaging effects upon children of separation from parents. Many studies have shown that separated children have been more prone to experience emotional problems and have tended to be emotionally labile and antisocial (Akins, Akins, and Mace 1981). The emphasis in the maternal deprivation literature has been upon infants and the consequences of breaking the initial bond between parent and newborn. There has been scant attention given to further successive ruptures of living arrangements to which some children have been exposed. Indeed, the evidence that many of the children in our study experienced a large number of dislocations in living arrangements makes them appear even more at risk than most of the children described in the parent-child deprivation literature. Such children not only have experienced separation from their natural parents but also have been exposed to the break-up of living arrangements with its associated trauma repeatedly.

Estimating the extent of damage associated with a larger number of living arrangements is a particularly important practice issue since many foster care programs are designed to have at least two placements for each child: a diagnostic center placement and a subsequent permanent placement. Since so little is known about matching foster children to placement, many additional placements can occur for a child as the worker tries to find a stable placement.

The third hypothesis was that a child who experienced a disrupted adoption would subsequently be more hostile and negativistic. Our hypothesized direction of association is the result of considering a disrupted adoption as a rejection of the child that thereby results in increased hostility in the child. The influence of a disrupted adoption on the future course of a child's personality development has received only modest attention. Festinger (1986) estimated a disruption rate of close to 13% in a study of adoptions in New York City. She reports that the child from a disrupted adoption was likely to have had more placements of all sorts than an otherwise similar child whose adoption was not disrupted, suggesting that a child from a disrupted adoption experienced more problems in the earlier history or developed them during the stay in care. Kadushin and Martin (1988:592) also report that some 13% of adoptive placements are disrupted. In this study, 13.7% of the children had experienced a disrupted adoption.

The fourth hypothesis was that a child in a package placement (that is, one who was successfully placed in a foster home by a previous agency and whose placement in that home was not interrupted upon entry into the Casey program) would be less hostile and negativistic than children required to take on yet one more relationship with new foster parents. Our test of this hypothesis compares the experiences of the 135 children (23.1%) in package placements with those of the other 450 children.

We hypothesized that there would be an "exposure" effect for some of these measures. Exposure effects are part of everyday life and are not substantively important. For example, the dirtiness of a child's clothing would be associated with the length of time since the child put on some clean clothes. In this chapter we will report associations like these and label them as "exposure effects." We include them at the end of our reports because they are not terribly interesting.

Demographic Characteristics of Children

Overall, 57.5% of the population was male, and 42.5% were female. As would be expected from the population characteristics of the states in which most of the divisions involved in the study are located, a large majority of the children were identified as white. Almost 72% of the population was white, and it is likely that the figure is close to 78% if the 36 cases where ethnicity was not identified can be assumed to be white children. About 22% of the children were members of racial or ethnic minorities. About 7% of the children were black, 4% were Native American, and 3% were Hispanic. About 8% were of mixed racial or mixed ethnic backgrounds.

Source of Referral

Public social service departments referred more than seven of ten children (72.7%). Voluntary agencies provided 11% of the referrals. The juvenile courts were the third largest source, accounting for 7.9% of all referrals.

A common reason why children came to this program was that they were in foster care settings or other forms of institutional or hospital care and these programs were looking for new living arrangements for their wards, usually because they were not doing well in their care. Sometimes referrals were made because The Casey Family Program was perceived as offering special advantages to children. Foster family care arrangements accounted for 64.1% of the services provided by the referral sources. Residential treatment accounted for 17.4% of the prior service being rendered. In almost a tenth of the cases (9.6%), the referral source was legal action leading to the termination of parental rights. Presumably these sources were the juvenile courts or public protective service agencies.

The Families of the Children

The agency was created with the expressed purpose of serving children whose families no longer appeared to be a viable resource for them. The content analysis of the closed case records strongly confirmed that this admission policy was operative. Table 3.1 shows the frequency with which various factors contributing to the child's need for care were identified in the case records as mother-related and as father-related.

Roughly 60% of the children were separated from their mothers permanently.[1] Quite striking is the fact that 20% of mothers were deceased. A surprisingly large group of children had mothers described as alcoholic (20.2%). A total of 75% of the children were separated from their fathers permanently.

Summary of Living Experiences

In table 3.2 we display means, standard deviations, and intraclass correlation coefficients of variables describing the living arrangements and pre-Casey experiences of these children. The intraclass correlations of these variables were very high.

Age

This agency accepted children who were somewhat older as compared with other programs in the country. The median age upon arrival was 13.5 years of age compared with the national median of 9.9 years in 1985 (Maximus 1988). This suggests that this group of children would be more problematic than the norm because older children have usually experienced a greater number of separations and are also likely to have a more expanded repertoire of "acting out" behaviors than younger children. Although a review of developmental studies of normal samples of children supports the view that behavioral problems decrease with age (Quevillon et al. 1986:268), with a group of children who are atypical in having suffered multiple placements and exposed to parental mishandling, the age variable could

TABLE 3.1   Parental Factors Related to the Child's Need for Care
(N = 585)

	Mother-Related		Father-Related	
	Number	Percent	Number	Percent
Deceased	119	20.1	81	13.7
Parents rights terminated	62	10.5	40	6.7
Surrendered child	76	12.8	40	6.7
Whereabouts unknown	59	9.9	178	30.0
Abandoned child	87	14.7	78	13.2
Mentally ill, hospitalized	41	6.9	15	2.5
Mentally ill, other	35	5.9	13	2.2
Mentally retarded	17	2.8	4	0.7
Arrested or in prison	24	4.1	47	7.9
Physical abuse by parent	84	14.2	107	18.0
Sexual abuse by parent	10	1.7	52	8.8
Neglectful parent	239	40.3	101	17.0
Unable to cope (incompetent)	205	34.6	61	10.3
Inadequate finances	60	10.1	33	5.6
Parent-child conflict	122	20.6	58	9.8
Drug abuse	16	2.7	14	2.4
Alcoholic	118	19.9	107	18.0
Prostitution	21	3.5	0	0.0
Marital difficulty	163	27.5	118	19.9

NOTE: Percentages do not add up to 100 percent because multiple factors can apply in a given case.

be expected to show a different relationship to problematic behavior in that older children would be likely to show a more expanded repertoire of "acting out" behavior than younger children. Further, a child who is older at the time of admission into the agency will have less time to stabilize his situation before "aging out" of foster care. Additionally, older children are more peer focused rather than family focused so that developmentally these older children are separating from their families rather than bonding to them.

The mean age the children first experienced total separation from their parents (i.e., simultaneously separated from both their mothers and fathers) was 6.8 years. Figure 3.1 shows the mean age of separation for white and minority children and also shows the gender differences within these groups. The white children averaged 7.4 years at the time of separation compared with a mean of 4.9 years for the

TABLE 3.2   Summary of the Living Arrangements Experienced by
the Subjects[a] (N = 585)

Item of Information	Mean	Standard Deviation	Intraclass[b] Correlation
1. Age first separated from both parents (years)	6.80	4.90	.88
2. Years in non-Casey living arrangements out of home	5.21	4.16	.76
3. Years in non-Casey foster care	2.79	3.31	.86
4. Age at first placement with Casey program (years)	12.84	2.99	.94
5. Living arrangement number of first Casey foster home	6.89	3.26	.85
6. Years in Casey program foster care	3.58	3.03	.90
7. Percent of pre-Casey time away from both parents	42.09	31.82	.78
8. Percent of pre-Casey out-of-home time in foster care	50.39	39.76	.84
9. Time in Casey care as percent of total out-of-home care	41.93	27.17	.85
10. Percent of time in all foster care (through exit from Casey program)	70.87	28.56	.77
11. Total number of living arrangements (through Casey)	10.21	4.38	.86

[a] Eight cases were deleted where the children were accepted into care but the placement was aborted within a few days after admission.
[b] This statistic is a measure of the interrater reliability.

minority children (p<.0001). Within both groups, boys had earlier loss of contact with their parents than girls did (p<.0001).

Pre-Placement Living Arrangements

A page of the case-reading schedule was designed to capture the child's placement history in as much detail as possible. Knowledge of the location of the child's residence from birth and afterward and the dates each living arrangement began and ended permitted development of a count of the number of living arrangements and the length of time spent in each arrangement. From this, we computed the amount of time the child had spent with each and both of the parents and the percentage of life span—from infancy to the time of entry—lived in various settings (e.g., in the care of own parents, in foster family care with other agencies, in institutions, and in other living arrangements). The reader was also asked to record the basis for the ending of each living arrangement, such as death of a parent, request for removal of the child by foster parents, a disrupted adoption, the child being ready to leave an institution, or the child having been abused.

This page of the case-reading schedule represented one of the most time-consuming tasks facing the case readers. Records were carefully combed to locate places, dates, and reasons for the ending of placements. Where gaps in information existed, estimations of these facts were made from the narrative details found in the record.[2] The fruit of this effort was a count that had a high intraclass correlation coefficient, .88.

Out-of-Home Experiences

Table 3.2 shows that the children experienced on the average more than 5 years in living arrangements outside of their homes before coming into Casey care and almost 3 years in non-Casey foster homes. The entrance into Casey care was, on average, the seventh living arrangement these children experienced. The average time spent in the Casey program was 3.5 years. The percent of time in all foster care at exit from this agency was 70.8% of the child's life on average. Finally, the total number of living arrangements experienced by the children at exit from Casey care averaged more than 10.

Preplacement Risk Factors

The case-reading schedule provided a list of risk factors that usually had to be considered when a decision was made to accept or reject the referral of the child. Our view of these risk factors is guarded because no risk factor had an intraclass correlation greater than .60.

Some of the risk factors applied to a high proportion of the children. For example, almost half of the children (49.9%) were rated as showing personality characteristics that made the child difficult to live with. More than a third of the children (34.9%) were seen as presenting risks for future foster family placement because they had previously been expelled from foster homes when in the care of other agencies. More than a third of the children (35.4%) showed difficulty

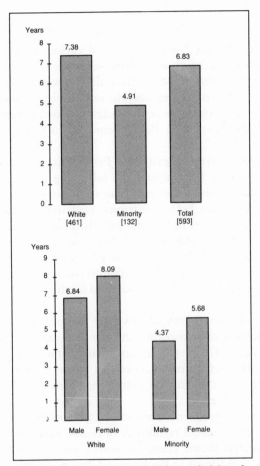

FIGURE 3.1   Mean Age When Child Left
Home, by Race/Ethnicity

in separating from their natural parents. The marginal nature of the adjustment of many of the children was revealed by the fact that more than a third (35.8%) were considered at risk because they had difficulty adjusting to a normal school situation. Almost a third of the children (31.0%) were behind their age-appropriate grade levels at the time they entered care. A fourth (25.5%) showed a history of delinquent or semidelinquent behavior. More than one fifth of the children (22.1%) had undergone a psychiatric evaluation. All of these factors stood out as potential threats to the viability of any placement.

Indexes Describing Children at Entry

As described in chapter 2, we constructed various indexes using composites of items on the case-reading schedule. Two of our indexes descriptive of the children at the time they entered the Casey Family Program had high intraclass correlations and Cronbach alphas as shown in table 3.3. These were the Index of Hostile-Negativistic Personality and the Index of a Background History of Juvenile Delinquency.

The Index of Hostile-Negativistic Personality is one of our most important measures. It combines the following items from the case-reading schedule: a preplacement history of personality problems; a psychiatric evaluation before entrance into the program that indicated serious emotional problems; expulsion from a previous foster home because of adjustment problems; and having as a reason for placement or a contributing factor for placement the child's showing evidence of a hostile-negativistic personality, being distrusting of adults, showing behavior difficulty at school, and having a severe personality problem.

The Index of the History of Juvenile Delinquency combines the following: showing of antisocial behavior as a reason or contributing factor for placement, a preplacement history of acts of juvenile delinquency, a history of runaway episodes prior to placement in the program, and a referral from a source that provided residential care to delinquent children.

Other indexes based on composites of items had low inter-rater reliability or low internal reliability of items, even though the factor analysis suggested them. These measures were as follows: Index of Child with Mental Illness in Background, Index of Child Embedded in Abusive Family Situation, Index of Child with Developmental Disability, and Index of Child in Conflicted Relationship with Parents.[3]

Findings Regarding Background of Disrupted Adoption

In this population, an adoption was usually disrupted because the adoptive parents requested that the child be taken back into foster care. Sometimes, an agency removed the child because of misgivings about the way the adoptive parents were responding to the child. Eighty children (13.7%) had a disrupted adoption before entry.[4] Of these, 9 children experienced two disruptions, and 6 experienced three or more.

The children with disrupted adoptions had been totally separated

TABLE 3.3   Indexes Descriptive of the Child at Entry

Measure	Mean	Standard Deviation	Intraclass Correlation	Cronbach Alpha
1. Index of Hostile-Negativistic Personality	5.74	1.31	.62	.72
2. Index of History of Juvenile Delinquency	6.07	1.30	.71	.71

from their parents at a mean age of 3.0 years compared with a mean age of separation at 7.4 years for other children (p<.001). They had also experienced a mean of 9.1 years in non-Casey living arrangements compared with a mean of 4.6 years for the other children (p<.0001). Their placement histories resemble the picture recently developed in a study of disrupted adoptions in New York City (Festinger 1986).

The children with disrupted adoptions were more hostile and negativistic at entry than other children (p<.001). On the basis of these results, therefore, there is some support for the third hypothesis associating disrupted adoption and subsequent hostility in the child.

Results Regarding Children in Package Placements

The children in package placements were somewhat older at the time of admission than the other children. Their mean age was 13.7 years compared with 12.6 years for others (p<.0001). They had also spent significantly more years in their pre-Casey living arrangements living away from both parents (p<.001). They were less hostile and negativistic (p<.0001) and had a less extensive history of juvenile delinquency in their backgrounds (p<.0001). They were also less involved in conflictual situations with their own parents (p<.001). They were likely to reflect cases where the parents were totally out of the picture, and the children were, therefore, more rooted in their foster homes. Our fourth hypothesis was strongly and consistently supported by these results.

Results Regarding a Background of Physical Abuse

Records of 235 children (40.2%) indicated that the child had experienced physical abuse prior to the Casey placement (Table 3.4). These children were more hostile and negativistic at entry (p<.0001) and tended to have had a more extensive prior history of mental illness (p<.10). We also compared the ratings assigned the children by the case readers on a four-point scale characterizing the challenge to foster parents presented by the child, ranging from no difficulty to substantial difficulty. The abused children presented greater challenges to their foster parents (p<.0001). They had, in the aggregate, a more extensive history of involvement in delinquent activities prior to coming into care than the other children (p<.0001) and were more likely to have come into this agency from a residential treatment center (p<.0001). Overall, we have a fairly strong picture of children with more severe problems of adjustment in the form of oppositional behavior.

The abused children had more extensive conflictual entanglements with their families (p<.01). This is also in accord with the clinical literature. Galdston observed: "The abused child develops an intense attachment to his parents and they to him. This often confuses the problem of diagnosis because the child and parents display an interest in each other which appears to belie the likelihood of parental abuse" (1979:589).

Results Regarding Exposure to a Disturbing Sexual Event

Records of 115 cases (19.7%) indicated that the child had been exposed to a disturbing sexual event within their families before entry. Although the case readers were specifically directed to extract information about "sexual molestation", a review of the cases involved suggested that the word "molestation" might be too dramatic for a number of the situations described even though it correctly described some of the experiences. Operationally, it is more appropriate to speak of "exposure to a disturbing sexual event."

The intraclass correlation coefficient for this indicator variable was .46, indicating a weak measure. Inspection of the case-reading schedules filled out by two readers in the 53 randomly selected cases used in the reliability study gave a sense of the codification problem. In some cases, one reader used case record narrative reporting a suspicion that the child had experienced an adverse experience in this area as an indication of molestation while the other reader did not. In other cases, one reader recorded the fact that the child had witnessed adult sexual activity or had seen a sibling or another foster child being molested as sexual molestation while the other reader chose not to describe these events as molestation. Sometimes the record indicated general sexual abuse of all children in the family without specifically identifying the subject as abused. Obviously, there is a classification problem that must be solved before preplacement history of sexual molestation can be used as data in longitudinally oriented studies of foster children.

There was a trend for children exposed to a disturbing sexual event to be more hostile and negativistic at entry (p<.10). Children exposed to a disturbing sexual event were more extensively embedded in an abusive family situation at entry (p<.0001), were older at entry (p<.01), and spent proportionately less pre-Casey time away from both parents (p<.05). We expected to find such differences.

Association of Physical Abuse, Exposure to a Disturbing Sexual Event, and Sex of Child

We used the techniques of loglinear analysis to evaluate the association between the sex of a child and these two abuse variables. The pattern of association for boys was different from the pattern for girls (p<.05). Table 3.4 presents the contingency table in percentage form

The nature of the association is rather complex. A much larger percentage of girls was exposed to a disturbing sexual event than boys: 34.8% of girls compared with 8.4% of boys (p<.0001). A somewhat larger percentage of boys was physically abused: 41.8% of boys compared with 38.0% of girls (p<.05). A child who was physically abused was more likely to have been exposed to a disturbing sexual event whether the child was a boy or a girl (p<.0001). Thus, 42.1% of the girls who were physically abused were exposed to a disturbing sexual event compared with 30.3% of the girls who were not physically abused but were exposed to a disturbing sexual event. Of the boys who were physically abused, 15.7% were exposed to a disturbing sexual event compared with 3.1% of the boys who were not abused but were exposed to a disturbing sexual event.

In practical terms, a girl who was physically abused had the greatest risk of exposure to a disturbing sexual event. A girl who was not abused had only a slightly lower risk. A boy who was not physically abused had a very low risk of exposure to a disturbing sexual event. A boy who was physically abused was very much more at risk of exposure to a disturbing sexual event than a boy who was not physically abused. Yet, a physically abused boy was still less at risk than a girl who was not physically abused.

TABLE 3.4   Children Exposed to Disturbing Sexual Event by
Indication of Physical Abuse and Sex of Child (N = 585)

	Boys Physically Abused			Girls Physically Abused		
	Yes	No	Total	Yes	No	Total
Disturbing Sexual Event						
Yes	15.7	3.1	8.4	42.1	30.3	34.8
	(22)	(6)	(28)	(40)	(47)	(87)
No	84.3	96.9	91.6	57.9	69.7	65.2
	(118)	(189)	(307)	(55)	(108)	(163)
Total	41.8	58.2	57.3	38.0	62.0	42.7
	(140)	(195)	(335)	(95)	(155)	(250)

Regression Results for the Hostile-Negativistic Index

Each hypothesis about associations with hostility at entry was confirmed in this analysis. The multiple regression explained .176 of the variance (p<.0001), compared with the intraclass correlation of .62. The most significant association was that a child who was physically abused was more hostile and negativistic at entry than an otherwise similar child who was not abused (p<.0001). The second most significant association was that a child who experienced more living arrangements before entry into this agency's care was more hostile and negativistic (p<.0001). Equally significant was that a child in a package placement was less hostile and negativistic than an otherwise similar child not in such a placement (p<.0001).

There were three weaker associations. A child with a disrupted adoption was more hostile and negativistic (p<.01). A nonwhite child was less hostile and negativistic at entry (p<.05). A child who had a group care placement prior to entry was more hostile and negativistic at entry (p<.05).

These regression results were very strongly supportive of the four hypotheses of this chapter. The coefficients of these variables calculated in the regression analysis allowed a comparison of the magnitude of the impacts of the traumatic events associated with the extent of hostility and negativism at entry. The increase in the extent of hostility associated with a physically abused child was equal to the increase in that associated with an additional 8 living arrangements experienced by the child prior to entry into this program. The increase in the extent of hostility associated with a disrupted adoption was equal to that associated with an additional 5 living arrangements. That is, the estimated magnitude of the impact of physical abuse on a child in this population was almost twice as large as the impact of a disrupted adoption. The converse of this finding is that the cumulative impact of turbulence in living arrangements was quite profound on these children. A succession of five temporary placements would be estimated to be as traumatic to a child as a disrupted adoption. This finding underscores the importance of finding a good match between foster parent and child. Reid's assessment of the importance of the foster parent as a major component of a successful foster program quoted in chapter 1 is thus dramatically supported. Regrettably, little more is known about these factors now than was known thirty years ago when Reid wrote his paper.

A related association was that a child who had a background of mental illness had a larger number of living arrangements before the first placement in Casey care ($p < .01$) and was older at first separation from both parents ($p < .01$).

Regression Results for the Index of History of Juvenile Delinquency

A major association here confirmed the hypothesis suggested by Galdston's summary that a boy who was physically abused had a more extensive history of delinquency before placement. The regression analysis explained .173 of the variance of the measure ($p < .0001$), compared with the intraclass correlation of .71. A boy who was suspected of being physically abused by his family had a more extensive history of juvenile delinquency at entry than an otherwise similar boy who was not abused or than a girl whether or not she was abused ($p < .0001$). A child in a package placement had a less extensive history of juvenile delinquency ($p < .0001$).

There were two additional associations that had little relation with substantive issues in foster care. A child who was older at entry had a more extensive history of juvenile delinquency prior to entry ($p < .0001$). This association is due to an exposure effect. A child who is older has had a longer period of time in which actions could be labeled as juvenile delinquency. A child who had been placed in a group home or other residential placement had a more extensive history of juvenile delinquency ($p < .0001$). This association between a pre-Casey group care placement and history of delinquent behavior is partially circular because the group or residential placement is one of the component variables of the index of history of delinquent behavior. Another association related to a residential placement being a component of the delinquency index was that a boy who was physically abused had a greater extent of residential placement before entry (p<.001).

DISCUSSION OF FINDINGS

Each of the four hypotheses was strongly confirmed. Our confirmation of Galdston's characterization of physically abused boys was a surprise to us. We had originally thought that the finding was a relic of a time when sexual stereotyping characterized boys as violent and girls as passive. That our analysis and other psychiatric studies have independently confirmed this description suggests that the association be more closely examined. The results from chapter 6 show that the pattern of physically abused boys being violent extends into adulthood. For practitioners, the findings in Rogeness et al. (1986) that abused boys more often engage in firesetting and homicidal ideation show the need to bring help quickly to this population. The foster care system includes many such youngsters in its ranks who would typically require group care settings. The festering damage to the child and the monetary cost to society constitute large penalties that might be reduced with early intervention.

The negative association with the number of living arrangements has important practice implications. First, the count of living arrangements has appeal as clinical tool because it provides an important measure of the degree of deprivation children have been exposed to. The data made amply clear that many of the children who had experienced turbulent living arrangements as shown by high counts showed telltale signs in the form of problematic behaviors that make them difficult to care for. Although counts of living arrangements have not been used previously in the published literature, they were such valuable predictors here that those serving children in foster care should consider routinely collecting these counts to determine the replicability of our findings. They are relatively easy to collect and aggregate, and they are a good measure of changes in the characteristics of children coming into care in a given service system over extended periods of time. It would also be possible to compare agencies with respect to the populations of children they are serving by use of the number of prior living arrangements as a measure of the difficulty of the caseloads.

Our finding of a positive association between physical abuse of a boy and exposure to a disturbing sexual event was not suggested by any of our hypotheses. We do not know of other studies of this issue. The practice implication is that a practitioner who is working with a physically abused boy consider the possibility of issues of sexual abuse as well. Since our findings were that physical abuse and exposure to a disturbing sexual event were not strongly associated for girls, a practitioner should not conclude that a girl who is not physically abused is less likely to be sexually abused.

CHAPTER FOUR

How the Children Fared in Casey Care

Our hypotheses concerning the progress of these children while they were in Casey care were the natural extensions of the hypotheses in chapter three consistent with our theme that rejections of the child generate increased subsequent hostility that continued while the child was in care. The increased hostility of a child would be subsequently associated with increased expressions of anger and destructiveness. There were two approaches to the quantitative modeling of our data that were consistent with our hypotheses.

The first was that these variables were associated in a causal chain. Simon (1954) and Lazarsfeld (1972) have discussed the properties of causal chain models. For example, in chapter 3 we showed that an increase in the number of living arrangements was associated with an increase in the extent of hostility and negativity when the child entered the Casey program. We would hypothesize that each of these variables was associated with the child's adaptation to care while in the program. If these variables were a causal chain with an increase in the number of living arrangements causing an increase in the extent of hostility and negativity at entry and in turn an increase in the extent of hostility and negativity causing a decreased adaptation to care, then the coefficient of the number of living arrangements would not be significantly different from zero in the regression of adaptation on extent of hostility and negativity at entry and number of living arrangements. As we show in this chapter, exactly this model described the association of these three variables.

54

A causal chain has an important statistical property called the Markov or "memoryless" property in the technical literature. The term "memoryless" is so prone to misinterpretation that we prefer to use the word "summarizable."[1] In this example, the extent of hostility summarized the impact of the number of living arrangements on the child's subsequent adaptation to care. The lack of significance of the number of living arrangements in the regression on adaptation must not be interpreted as meaning that the number of living arrangements and the adaptation of the child to care had no association with each other or that the number of living arrangements a child had experienced would show no influence on the pattern of a child's history, because the pattern has no "memory" of the earlier number of living arrangements experienced. Consequently, we prefer to say that the extent of the child's hostility summarizes the effect of the number of living arrangements experienced by the child because it is more likely to be understood correctly.

Operationally, the "plasticity" model of child development (or reversibility of trauma model, Kagan 1973) in which there is a fading out of the effects of earlier life experiences has properties that are very similar to the properties expected of variables in a causal chain model. In the plasticity model, the correlation of a variable describing the state of a child as a six year old would be modest with a variable describing the child as a twelve year old and would be very small with a variable describing the child at eighteen years of age. Langner (Langner and Michael 1963:378–379) observed exactly such a pattern in a study relating the life histories of individuals in a New York City study of their mental health status.

The second model is the traumatic event model. As an example of this model, an early rejection of the child would be so profound that there would be continuing associations between the variable measuring the rejection and later measures of the child even after measures of the child's condition during the intervening years are included. For example, if the early physical abuse of a boy were such a traumatic event, then the coefficient associated with the physical abuse of a boy in the multiple regression of the child's condition while in Casey care would be significantly different from zero even though we had included variables describing the child's condition at entry into the Casey program. In this and subsequent chapters, we find evidence supporting the traumatic nature of the early physical abuse of a boy and of an excessive number of early living arrangements, as well as lesser trauma from a disrupted adoption.

Although we began the analysis of this part of the study with very definite hypotheses about the nature of the associations of the variables, we did not have any preliminary hypotheses favoring either the plasticity or the traumatic event models. We have found evidence of both types of models in this study.

Methods

Sometimes a child appeared at ease and not particularly difficult to sustain in care. Yet, underneath the surface veneer the youngster might well have been in anguish owing to a deprived past. We used two approaches to measure how the subjects fared because the children were likely to show the quality of their adjusting in a variety of ways. The first was the use of ratings made by the case reader, and the second was the identification of conduct problems and psychological symptoms. We gave the case readers a list of symptoms derived from the Columbia University longitudinal study of foster children in New York City (Fanshel and Shinn 1978) and instructed them to indicate whether the case record reported the children as showing these symptoms. We extracted information on various domains of information from these data.

Adaptation to Care

This section of the form was filled out for three periods covering the child's time in care (first year, midpoint, and final year). It included such items as whether the child expressed resistance to being in care, was anxious to return to natural parents, felt at home in the placement, and showed close ties to the foster parents. It also included such behavioral descriptions as: whether the child was resistant to adult supervision, tended to be moody or depressed, was secure and free of anxiety, was hostile and belligerent, showed difficulty in controlling behavioral impulses, was friendly and outgoing in social life, was able to make close friends, showed tolerance for frustration of desires, and experimented with drugs. We constructed an index from these variables.

> The Index of Adaptation to Foster Care: It showed marked stability in the factor analyses with the 11 items always belonging to the first extracted factor for all solutions attempted. It provided a summary measure of the child's reactions to being in foster care and his overall adjustment. It included items describing whether the child: (a) felt at home in the setting, (b) showed close ties to the foster parents, (c) tended to be secure and free of anxiety, (d) tended to be

relaxed and at ease, (e) was friendly and outgoing in social life, (f) was able to make close intimate friends, (g) was usually cheerful and happy, (h) was resistant to adult supervision, (i) tended to be hostile and belligerent, (j) showed difficulty in controlling behavior, and (k) showed low tolerance for frustration.

Social Conduct

In this section, the reader indicated whether the child exhibited any of the following social conduct problems while in care (mentioned once in record, several occasions, or frequently): stole petty items, stole major items, stayed away overnight without permission, engaged in the destruction of property, was involved in activities of delinquent gang, was defiant of caretaker in a major way, engaged in behavior dangerous to own physical safety, used drugs, had gotten into difficulty because of sexual behavior, and had other social conduct problems.

We also used data on various incidents in care: runaway, truancy, expulsion from school, failure to be promoted, act of delinquency (stealing), act of delinquency (substance abuse), act of delinquency (violence), act of delinquency (other), suicide attempt, serious challenge to foster parents, school dropout, teenage pregnancy, and other incidents. These data were the basis of six indexes of social conduct.

The Index of Delinquent Behavior: It is composed of 12 items relating to the child's conduct while in the agency: (a) had engaged in the destruction of property, (b) had engaged in behavior dangerous to self, (c) had been defiant of caretaker (foster parent) in a major way, (d) had been involved in the activities of a delinquent gang, (e) had been suspended or expelled from school because of behavior, (f) had been truant from school, (g) had run away, (h) had stayed away overnight without permission, (i) had gotten into difficulty because of sexual behavior, (j) had stolen petty items, (k) had stolen major items or money, and (l) was reported to tell lies frequently.

We used five indexes based upon items from the overall delinquency measure and from the symptom list to reflect the various forms in which children acted out.

The Index of Destructive Delinquent Behavior: (a) had engaged in destruction of property, (b) had engaged in behavior dangerous to self, (c) described in symptom list as "destructive."

The Index of Sexual Acting Out Delinquent Behavior: (a) had stayed away overnight without permission, (b) had gotten into difficulty because of sexual behavior, and (c) had run away.

The Index of Sociopathic Delinquent Behavior: (a) telling lies, (b) stealing petty items, and (c) stealing major items.

The Index of School-Related Delinquency: (a) expelled or suspended from school because of behavior, (b) was truant, and (c) involved in activities of delinquent gang.

The Index of Drug Involvement: a) child described as having experimented with drugs, (b) child described as tending to drink alcohol to excess, and, (c) child described as having used drugs.

Symptomatic Behaviors

This section of the schedule called for an indication of whether any of the following behaviors was reported in the record (single incident, occasional, frequent): had disturbing dreams, told lies, soiled self, wet self—daytime, wet self—night, had sleep disorders, was destructive, had poor appetite, bit nails, had nervous tics, had stomach disorders, sucked thumb, was afraid or shy, had allergy or skin disorder, had colds, was excluded by children, was overweight or underweight, was too sensitive, was too serious, was under strain, was accident prone, showed bizarre behavior, and showed other symptomatic behaviors. We extracted two indexes from these variables:

The Index of Child Under Strain: (a) too sensitive, (b) too serious, (c) under strain, and (d) moody or depressed.[2]

The Index of Wetters and Soilers: (a) soiling self, (b) wetting self— daytime, and (c) wetting self—night.

School Performance

The following information was extracted in the case-reading schedule: whether child was at the appropriate grade level upon entering and leaving care; whether overall academic performance (rated below average, average, above average); whether there were factors causing the child to be behind such as limited mental abilities, inability to apply self to academic work, expulsion or suspension because of behavior, truancy, physical illness causing absence; whether the child showed evidence of the following school-related problems: discipline problems, emotional problems (phobias, nervousness), poor academic performance, underachievement, other problems. These variables were combined into an index:

The Index of School Performance: (a) child at age-appropriate grade level at entry into care, (b) child at age-appropriate grade level at exit from care, (c) child described as having limited mental abilities, (d) child's quality of academic performance, and (e) child cited for academic difficulties.

Other Summary Measures

Two summary ratings were required from the case reader covering each year the child was in care: (a) Summary Rating of the Child's Adjustment (a seven-point scale ranging from 1 = child making an excellent adjustment in all spheres of life to 7 = child making a poor adjustment). (b) Challenge to Caretakers: (a four-point scale ranging from 1 = no difficulty, presented almost no problems for caretakers in the living situation to 4 = substantial difficulty, presented serious and almost constant problems for caretakers).

We had two additional indexes.

The Index of Child Being Recipient of Psychiatric or Psychological Evaluation: (a) the variable indicating whether the child was the subject of psychiatric evaluation while in care and (b) whether the child was evaluated by a psychologist.

The Index of Attachment to Natural Family: (a) was anxious to return to natural parents, (b) showed positive attachment to own mother, and (c) showed positive attachment to own father.

Table 4.1 displays the correlations between index scores for boys and girls separately. In the main, the indexes have low correlation coefficients for both males and females. An exception is the correlation of .45 between the Ir 'ex of Adaptation and the Index of Delinquent Behavior for the females.

Behavior of the Children While in the Agency

The range of difficulties presented by children in the study population was shown by the distribution of the ratings of the case readers of the children according to their perceived challenge to the foster parents during the first year of care: no difficulty (5.7%), slight difficulty (27.8%), moderate difficulty (28.5%), substantial difficulty (34.9%), other and unable to determine (3%).[3]

TABLE 4.1   Correlations Between Index Scores for Boys and Girls,
Intraclass Correlations and Cronbach Alpha Coefficients

Index	1	2	3	4	5	6	7	Cronbach Alpha
1. Adaptation to care	(.63)	.29	.10	.00	−.15	.07	.13	.91
2. Delinquent behavior	.45	(.67)	.23	.03	.02	.25	.28	.79
3. Drug involvement	.27	.34	(.68)	−.08	.02	.07	.12	.71
4. Wetters and soilers	.04	.09	.13	(.88)	.03	.10	.08	.71
5. Family attachment	−.19	−.08	−.02	.10	(.43)	.02	.01	.68
6. School performance	.20	.36	−.01	.10	−.02	(.64)	.12	.68
7. Psychiatric/ psychological consultation	.21	.33	.15	.04	−.01	.20	(.75)	.52

NOTE: Correlations for males (N = 335) are above the diagonal; correlations for females (N = 250) are below the diagonal. Intraclass correlations for 53 cases are shown in parentheses on the diagonal; they are measures of interrater reliability based upon two independent readings of 53 randomly selected case records. The Cronbach alpha coefficients are calculated for the total population of 585 cases.

Although many children settled into care quite well, there was a substantial amount of "acting out" reported in the records. The most commonly occurring action was running away: two fifths (41.8%) of the children had run away at least once while in care. More than a third of the children (36.1%) had stolen petty items, and more than a quarter (26.0%) had gotten into difficulty because of sexual behavior. About a fifth (19.6%) had stolen major items, had engaged in the destruction of property (23.1%), or had been reported to use drugs (20.6%). Almost one child in ten (8.8%) had participated in the activities of a delinquent gang.

The symptom most frequently reported (65.6%) was that of moodiness or depression. Occurring less frequently were phenomena such as being excluded by children (25.6%), being accident prone (21.9%), being under strain (21.6%), being afraid or shy (21.1%), and having allergies or skin disorders (15.7%). The records of 76 children (12.8%) indicated that the child showed bizarre behavior. Some behaviors on the list rarely occurred. These included soiling (5.1%), wetting self in the daytime (5.4%), sleep disorders (5.4%) and poor appetite (4.0%).[4]

Figure 4.1 displays information about the percent of the children who showed conduct problems while in care separately for males and females. Males more often displayed conduct or behavior problems than females ($p < .0001$), were more extensively involved in destruction of property ($p < .001$), were more defiant of caretakers ($p < .0001$), more often stole and engaged in behavior dangerous to themselves ($p < .001$), and showed destructive behaviors more commonly ($p < .0001$), 30.5% of males showing destructive behavior compared with 11.1% of females. Males had bizarre behavioral symptoms more frequently than females did ($p < .0001$): 15.5% of the males compared with 9.1 of the females. Males were more often seen as being excluded by other children ($p < .001$): 30.2% of the males compared with 19.4% of the females. Previous research has consistently found disturbances of conduct more common in males than in females (Quevillon et al. 1986:269–270) There were only minor differences between males and females with regard to drug use and with respect to staying out overnight without permission.

Females were reported to show problems more frequently than the males with regard to sexual behavior ($p < .01$): 35.7% of the females compared with 18.8% of the males. This difference may reflect a greater sensitivity of the foster parents and agency staff to the possibility of the females becoming pregnant. Females were more likely to have weight problems; 23.0% of them were overweight or underweight compared with 10.9% of the males ($p < .001$).

Comparison of Indexes for Groups of Children.

In table 4.2 we compare the mean scores on the various indexes measuring the under care experiences of the subjects of the study for children who had experienced disrupted adoptions with the remaining children and for children in package placements with other children.

The 80 children (13.7%) with disrupted adoptions showed a greater extent of overall delinquent behavior ($p < .01$) and a greater extent of psychopathic behavior ($p < .001$). Again, these patterns seem to be a continuation of behaviors apparent at entry, when these children were rated as more hostile and negativistic.

The 135 children (23.1%) who were in package placements were rated as better adapted than others ($p < .001$) and displayed less overall delinquent behavior ($p < .001$), less destructive delinquent behavior

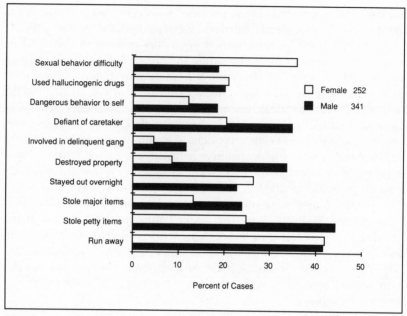

FIGURE 4.1   Percent of Boys and Girls Showing Conduct Problems
While in Care

(p<.001), and less psychopathic behavior (p<.001). These findings clearly support a theory of continuation of patterns that existed at entry, when these children were found to be less hostile and negativistic.

We performed the same analyses for children who were physically abused before entry compared with those who were not and for those who were exposed to a disturbing sexual event compared with those who were not. There was only one significant difference. Physically abused children had a greater extent of destructive delinquent behavior (p<.001), another finding consistent with Galdston's (1979) report.

MULTIPLE REGRESSION ANALYSIS FINDINGS

Adaptation to Foster Care in the Agency

Using as independent variables the demographic variables, the preplacement living arrangement information and the measures describing the children at entry, we found three significant associations that

TABLE 4.2 The Under Care Experience of Children in the Agency According to Two Background Status Factors: History of Disrupted Adoption and Package Placement

	History of Disrupted Adoption			Package Placement of Child		
	Mean Disrupted	Mean Other	Prob.	Mean Package	Mean Other	Prob.
Index of Adaptation to Foster Care	3.60	3.73	NS	4.35	3.52	.001
Index of Delinquent Behavior	5.62	5.99	.01	6.22	5.85	.001
Index of Destructive Delinquent Behavior	6.05	6.09	NS	6.51	5.96	.001
Index of School-Related Delinquent Behavior	6.15	6.45	.05	6.45	6.40	NS
Index of Sexual Acting Out	5.47	5.89	.05	5.99	5.78	NS
Index of Psychopathic, Lying and Stealing Behavior	4.82	5.51	.001	5.94	5.26	.001
Index of Drug Involvement	6.36	6.47	NS	6.42	6.46	NS
Index of Wetters and Soilers	6.73	6.62	NS	6.79	6.59	.10
Index of Child Moody or Depressed	5.58	5.56	NS	5.78	5.50	.05

together explained .21 of the variance (p<.0001), compared with the intraclass correlation of .63.

A child who was less hostile or negativistic at entry showed, on average, better adaptation to the foster care experience in the agency (p<.0001). The finding reflects a persistence in personality traits and behavior as the child proceeds on the life course in the foster care system. A child in a package placement showed better adaptation (p<.0001), confirming the one-way analysis. A child who was rated as having a history of juvenile delinquency prior to entry into the program on average showed a poorer adaptation to foster care while in the program's care (p<.0001).

A Causal Chain for Adaptation to Foster Care

One unique aspect of this study is our effort to describe the associations between the number of preplacement living arrangements and the child's subsequent history. We note that the correlation coefficient of the measure of the child's adaptation to care in the agency and the number of preplacement living arrangements was only −.14 and that this variable did not appear as significant in the multiple regression findings. Nevertheless, our data show a specific chain of findings from the previously reported correlation of −.29 between the number of preplacement living arrangements and the extent of hostile and negativistic personality traits shown by the child at entry into the agency and the correlation of .43 between the child's extent of hostile and negativistic personality at entry and the child's adaptation to care while in the program.

The correlation coefficients suggest a causal chain model in which there is an intervention of the measure of the child's hostile or negativistic personality between the child's number of preplacement living arrangements and the child's subsequent adaptation to foster care while in the agency.[5] The correlation of −.14 observed between the number of preplacement living arrangements and the child's subsequent adaptation to care is nearly equal to the product of the correlation between the number of preplacement living arrangements and the measure of the child's extent of hostile or negativistic personality and the correlation of the measure of the extent of the child's hostile or negativistic personality and the measure of the child's subsequent adaptation to foster care ($-.125 = -.29 * .43$). Simon specified this condition. Since the extent of the child's hostile or negativistic personality at entry occurred between the child's preplacement history and the child's adaptation to foster care, Simon's argument leads us to consider these variables as possibly linked in a causal chain.

The practical implication of this rather theoretical issue in statistical reasoning is that the strength of the evidence regarding the association between the number of preplacement living arrangements and the child's adaptation to care while in the agency is stronger than the rather modest correlation observed. The evidence includes the larger correlations between these two variables and the intervening variable, the measure of the extent of the child's hostile and negativistic personality at entry and the plausibility of the two associations combining to produce the chain. For this chain, the value of the child's hostile-negative index summarized the effect of the number of living arrangements the child had experienced in the sense that including the number of living arrangements in the prediction of the child's adaptation to foster care would not improve the prediction. Even though there is an overall association such that a child who has experienced more living arrangements would be less well adapted to foster care, the partial correlation between these two variables controlling for the child's index of hostile-negative behavior was essentially zero.

Similarly the physical abuse of a boy was not a significant variable in the multiple regression, but since it was associated with the extent of hostility at entry and a history of delinquent behavior at entry, these two variables summarized its effect.

Delinquent Behavior

The multiple regression analysis found four associations that explained .16 of the variance (p<.0001), compared with the intraclass correlation of .75. A child who had a more extensive history of juvenile delinquency at entry had more extensive delinquent behaviors while in Casey care (p<.0001). There is thus revealed consistency of behavior over time in this important domain. A child who was more hostile and negativistic at entry had more extensive delinquent behaviors while in Casey care (p<.0001). A child with a disrupted adoption was more delinquent in behavior while in this agency (p<.05). The last significant association is logically necessary and is simply an "exposure effect." A child who was older at entry into the agency had less extensive delinquent behavior while in Casey care than an otherwise similar child who entered at a younger age (p<.0001).

Destructive Delinquent Behavior

There were three highly significant associations found in the multiple regression analysis that together explained .14 of the variance (p<.0001) compared to the intraclass correlation of .54. A child who was less hostile and negativistic at entry showed less extensive destructive juvenile delinquent behavior while in Casey care (p<.0001). Girls on average showed less extensive destructive juvenile delinquent behavior than boys (p<.0001). A child who was older at entry into the program's care on average showed less extensive destructive juvenile delinquent behavior (p<.0001). The extent of hostility at entry here summarized the effects of variables operating earlier in the child's life. The age at entry association was another exposure effect.

Sexual Acting Out Delinquent Behavior

There were two very strong partial associations and two strong associations that together explained .08 of the variance (p<.0001) compared with the intraclass correlation of .57. A child who had a history of juvenile delinquency before entering the care of this agency on average showed more extensive acting-out, sexual behavior problems (p<.0001). The second very strong association was that boys on average showed less extensive acting out behavior than girls (p<.0001); we have noted earlier that this association may be a reporting effect. A child who had a hostile or negativistic personality before entry on average showed more extensive acting out behavior (p<.01). A child who was not in conflict with the parents on average showed more extensive acting-out behavior (p<.01). This finding is counterintuitive.

Sociopathic (Lying and Stealing) Behavior

The proportion of variance explained was .16 (p<.0001), compared with the intraclass correlation of .68. A child who had a history of juvenile delinquency prior to entry showed a greater extent of lying and stealing behavior while in the program's care (p<.0001). A child who had an adoption that was disrupted showed a greater extent of lying and stealing behavior (p<.01). A child who was more hostile and negativistic when the child entered care showed a greater extent of lying and stealing (p<.01). There was another length of exposure association: a child who was older at entry into the agency on average showed a lesser extent of lying and stealing behavior (p<.0001).

Drug Involvement in Casey Care

There were different associations for boys and girls. For girls, there was one association that explained .150 of the variance (p<.0001), compared with the intraclass correlation coefficient of .68. A girl who had a history of juvenile delinquency prior to entry had a much more extensive use of drugs while in Casey care. For boys, there was one association that explained .029 of the variance (p<.01). A boy who was older at entry was more extensively involved in drug usage while in Casey care.

Moodiness or Depression

The regression analysis found two associations that together explained .06 of the variance (p<.0001), compared with the intraclass correlation of .60. A child who was hostile or negativistic at entry was more moody or depressed while in care (p<.0001). A child who was exposed to a disturbing sexual event prior to entry was more depressed or moody while in care (p<.01).[6]

Psychiatric or Psychological Evaluation While in Care

The regression analysis explained .06 of the variance (p<.0001), compared to the intraclass correlation of .75. A child who showed a greater extent of hostile or negativistic personality at entry into the care of the program on average showed a greater extent of being the object of psychiatric or psychological evaluation while in care (p<.0001). Another length of exposure association is that a child who was older at entry into care on average showed a lesser extent of being the object of psychiatric or psychological evaluation while in care (p<.0001).

Attachment to the Child's Natural Family While in the Program's Care

The regression analysis accounted for .15 of the variance compared with an intraclass correlation of .43 (p<.0001). A child who spent a greater proportion of time before entry into the agency in foster care showed a less strong attachment to his natural family (p<.0001). A child who showed a greater extent of conflict with parents before entry on average showed a greater degree of attachment to the family while in care (p<.01). Although this finding may be somewhat counterintuitive at first reading, it is consistent with Galdston's summary, quoted in chapter 3 of a greater attachment of a child to an abusive family. That is, there must be a strong attachment before a great degree of conflict can arise. Since many of the children simply had no parents available to them in any form, "conflict" was not possible. A child who moved back and forth to parents on more occasions before placement in the program on average had a greater extent of attachment to his family while in care (p<.05). A boy who was exposed to a disturbing sexual event before entry showed a greater degree of attachment to his natural family (p<.05). A child who showed a greater extent of a hostile or negativistic personality at entry showed a greater extent of attachment to the natural family (p<.05). These associations were also supportive of Galdston's summary about the involvement of abused children with their families.

DISCUSSION

The most striking pattern in our results is the pervasiveness of the index of the foster child's hostile or negativistic personality and the index of the foster child's history of juvenile delinquency as significant predictors of the foster child's behavior while in care. The index of a child's hostile or negativistic personality was a very important predictor of the in-care indexes. The index of the child's history of juvenile delinquency was almost as pervasive. The causal chain relationship that we described for the measure of the child's adjustment while in foster care holds for the other variables as well. These findings were consistent with the plasticity model of development.

In combination with the findings reported in chapter 3, then, our results show that a child who has a hostile or negativistic personality at entry or who had a history of juvenile delinquency adapted less well to foster care, displayed more delinquent behavior later in foster care, and was under greater stress while in foster care. In chapter 3 we showed that the physical abuse of a child, a greater number of placements before arriving at the agency, and a disrupted adoption increased the extent of a child's hostile and negativistic personality. In particular, a boy who was physically abused had a more extreme history of juvenile delinquent behavior on average.

The next most striking pattern is that associations with variables describing possibly traumatic events in the child's preplacement history are relatively few, suggesting that the causal chain model summarized effectively the most important of the associations with traumatic events. The fact of a disrupted adoption had significant lingering effects over and above the increase in hostility at entry, confirming the traumatic nature of this preplacement event. These children were more delinquent in their behavior while in Casey care, showing particularly a greater extent of lying and stealing. The number of living arrangements at entry and physical abuse of a boy did not have any significant partial associations with in-care measures and were well summarized by the measure of hostility and negativity at entry.

Several of the measures in the form of indexes characterizing the child's experience in care showed relatively strong intraclass correlations and Cronbach alphas. The most useful overall measure, the Index of Adaptation, provided a summary description of how the child adjusted to the living situation in the foster home. This measure not only had strong measures of reliability and validity but also showed a strong association with measures describing the child at entry. A telling finding is that children who were more hostile and negativistic at entry adapted significantly less well to their foster families.

CHAPTER FIVE

Modes of Exit of the Children from Care and Their Adjustment at Departure

The manner of termination of a child's foster care placement is one of the most important "outcome" variables in any evaluation of a foster care program. Some children return home to their parents when their families have been reconstituted, presumably a positive ending to the placement. Others "age out" or become "emancipated" upon their 18th birthdays and go forth on their own to independent living. Some children end their status in care more precipitously by running away or by behaving in such a manner that their foster parents request their removal. When the agency finds the child's problems not resolvable within its resources, it then regretfully remands the child to the court of original jurisdiction.

Instability in foster care arrangements is frequently commented upon in the child welfare literature and is characteristic of the experience of many children in foster care. Stein (1981:105) reported that almost 50 percent of all youngsters are placed in more than one home, and more than 20 percent experience three or more moves (1981:105). Kadushin reviewed eleven studies covering almost 16,000 children and found that about one in five children had experienced three or more placements (1978:101).

There is a commonly held view that personality difficulties of children play a major role in the creation of interruptions in placements (Wiltse 1985:576). In a study at the Children's Aid Society in Toronto, Rosenblum (1977:87) found that about half of the disruptions of foster home placements were related to behavioral problems of the children.

70

The longitudinal study of foster care in New York City revealed that children whose behavior was characterized by their social workers as defiant and hostile tended to experience more replacement than other children (Fanshel and Shinn 1978:143).

In this chapter, we analyze the number of placements a child experienced while in the Casey program, the mode of exit from care, and the adjustment of the child at exit from the program.

Condition at Exit from Care

Two ratings were made by the case readers based upon a review of the circumstances surrounding the child's departure from care as described in the case record. The first was a response to the question: "Overall how would you characterize the circumstances under which the child left care?"[1] The second rating was the response to the question: "Considering the accumulated information available about this child, rate his/her overall adjustment at the time of leaving the agency."[2]

Hypotheses About Condition at Exit

We hypothesized that a greater number of placements while in the Casey program would be associated with poorer condition at exit. Since a package placement was a clearly successful one, we hypothesized that there would be fewer Casey placements for children in package placements and that these children would therefore be in better condition at exit than other children. We hypothesized a child who experienced a disrupted adoption would be expected to have more placements reflecting the hostility generated by the rejection implicit in the failed adoption. As a child who experienced a disrupted adoption became older, the trauma of a disrupted adoption would reduce to the trauma of one more placement among many placements. Therefore, while the child would be in worse condition, there would be no additional association between condition at exit and having a disrupted adoption once the number of placements was controlled for. A child who was physically abused was hypothesized to have experienced more Casey placements and to be in worse condition at exit. We had no a priori hypotheses about whether the causal chain model (the plasticity model) or the traumatic event model would be the better description of these children's development.

Modes of Exit

We defined five modes in which the children departed from the care of the program:

1. Emancipation at age 18: This was the most common single outcome, 37.4% of the children (n = 218) staying with the program until they reached age 18 and presumably were ready to commence independent living.[3] In this period of "permanency planning," a foster child's being emancipated on the threshold of adulthood is not usually considered a positive way of bringing an end to the placement experience. This is not, however, the case when one considers the mission of the agency and the average older age of children accepted into its care.[4]

2. Emancipation at age 17 or less: An additional 17.8% of the children (n = 101) left care to enter into independent living at less than 18 years of age. They did not stay with the program for the full time that had been contemplated when they were accepted into care. Some of these children became gainfully employed and set up their own living quarters, some joined the military service, some set up informal living arrangements with a person of the opposite sex, and others married. While the departure of these children would appear to represent a relatively benign ending to their careers in foster care, we hypothesized that leaving on an earlier basis than normally expected was associated with a higher proportion of problematic departures in this group than among those leaving after reaching their 18th birthdays.
   In sum, 55.2% of the children in the closed case study were emancipated.

3. Returned to parents: There were 20.2% of the children (n = 117) who were returned to one or both parents. This outcome contradicted the notion that the children accepted by the agency came from families that could no longer offer a viable living situation for the children.
   There was strong evidence in the records, however, of problematic relationships between the children and their families for the minority of cases where the parents were not totally out of the picture. Some sense of uncertainty thus surrounds this outcome regarding what the future might hold for the children.

4. Return to court and/or public social service agency: There were 20.7% (n = 121) who did so poorly in their placements that they had to be remanded to the court holding jurisdiction and/or to the public social service agency that formerly provided care. Most went on to more restrictive placements in institutional settings. These children did not succeed with this agency, and this category of exit has to be viewed as a failure in the sense that the plan at the time of admission for the child to be sustained in foster family care had to be abandoned.

5. Runaways: There were 3.9% (n = 22) who ran away from their foster homes and did not return to the program's care. These situations can

also be regarded as failures to achieve the agency plans when the child was admitted to care.

We hypothesized that the condition at exit of the children in these groups would be in the order above with those children emancipated at 18 in the best condition and the runaways in the worst condition.

Factors Associated with the Number of Casey Placements

The regression analysis found six associations that together explained .29 of the variance (p<.0001). There were two moderate associations with preplacement conditions. A child in a package placement experienced fewer total placements in the agency on average (p<.05). A child who experienced a failed adoption prior to first agency placement had more placements while in the agency (p<.05). The strongest associations were with "in agency care" variables. A child who was sexually delinquent had more placements while in the agency program (p<.0001). A child who was referred for psychiatric or psychological assessment was likely to be one who experienced a larger number of placements while in the agency (p<.0001). A child who engaged in destructive delinquent behavior experienced a greater number of placements while in the agency (p<.0001). A child whose school performance was good while in the agency experienced fewer placements while in the agency (p<.001).

These results suggested that the plasticity model was better for this variable in that there was only one relatively weak association with a traumatic event, that of a disrupted adoption. These results confirmed the theme of our hypotheses of continuity of development and rejecting situations generating anger that in turn led to less desirable outcomes. They also suggested that children with multiple Casey placements showed the extremely challenging behaviors of sexual delinquency, destructive behavior, and poor school performance. The program responded to these children with professional psychological services.

Children Emancipated at 18 Were in the Best Condition at Exit

In table 5.1, we show the mean scores of The Index of Adjustment at Departure from Care calculated for the children organized by mode of exit. From a one-way analysis of variance, the modes of exit had different average conditions at exit (p<.0001). Their ranking was the one hypothesized. That is, children who achieved emancipation at the

TABLE 5.1   Adjustment of Children at Departure from Care by Mode
of Exit (N = 579)

Group	Mode of Exit	Number	Mean Adjustment Score	Standard Deviation
1.	Emancipated at 18	(218)	5.35	3.44
2.	Emancipated Under 18	(101)	4.05	1.77
3.	Returned to Parents	(117)	3.97	1.51
4.	Discharged to Court	(121)	2.51	1.53
5.	Runaway	(22)	3.05	1.70
	Total	(579)	4.16	1.88

Analysis of
Variance

Source	D.F.	Sum of Squares	Mean Squares	F Rato	F Prob.
Between Groups	4	671.86	167.96	70.315	.0000
Within Groups	574	1371.14	2.39		
Total	578	2042.99			

Group Comparisons (least significant difference):

1,2,3 significantly better > 4
1,2,3 significantly better > 5
1 significantly better > 3
1 significantly better > 2

age of 18 left care under the most serene circumstances and on average showed the best adjustment. Their adjustment was significantly
better than the adjustment of any other group. The group showing the
next best condition upon departure included the children who had
been emancipated under the age of 18, followed by the children returned to their families. These two groups had essentially the same
means. The adjustment of these two groups was significantly better
than the adjustment of children who were remanded to court or who
ran away. The children who ran away and those returned to the court
or public social service agency showed the poorest average scores, the
latter group being in the poorest condition.

In order to show this important finding graphically, the children in
the population were rank ordered by their scores based upon the two
ratings cited. The quartile points were used to divide the group reflecting four classes of adjustment, which we have characterized as

good, adequate, marginal-guarded, and poor. Figure 5.1 displays the proportions of subjects falling within each quarter organized by modes of exit.

Relation between Condition at Exit and Number of Placements Controlling Mode of Exit

We tested the hypothesis that more Casey placements were associated with poorer condition at exit controlling for mode of exit with the multiple regression that used condition at exit as the dependent variable and number of Casey placements and mode of exit as independent variables. This regression explained .368 of the variance in condition at exit (p<.0001).

A child who had more Casey placements was in poorer condition at exit after we controlled for mode of exit (p<.0001). We show this graphically in figure 5.2. Children emancipated at age 18 were generally in better condition at exit than children in other groups, no matter how many placements they had experienced. The decline with the emancipated group was not large until the fifth Casey placement.

The figure has an obviously important story to tell. Foster care programs can draw encouragement from the fact that many children survived multiple placements to be in relatively good shape at exit. The findings suggest that a worker responsible for a child who has experienced foster home disruptions sustain efforts on behalf of keeping the child in a foster home program. Perhaps the experience in a disrupted placement allows the staff to gauge more accurately the qualities of a foster family that will better tolerate the child's acting out. That is, the social worker had more information to plan a better subsequent placement. It is also possible that some children drew strength from the consistent presence of the Casey worker and program and that this might have led to better adaptation in the subsequent placement.

The negative side is that a worker needs to be aware of the association between increased numbers of placements and poorer condition at exit. We can use the coefficients from the multiple regression to estimate the magnitude of the change in condition at exit associated with a large number of placements as we did in chapter 3. The deterioration in condition at exit associated with 7 additional Casey placements was roughly the same as the deterioration in condition at exit between those emancipated at 18 and those emancipated early. The deterioration associated with 9 additional placements was roughly equal to the deterioration in condition at exit between those emanci-

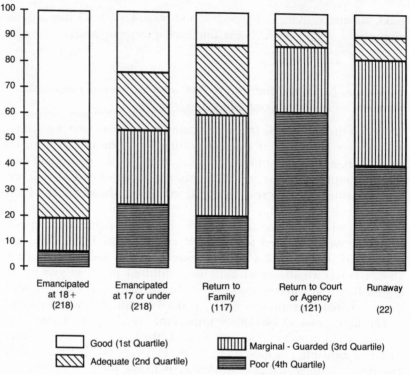

FIGURE 5.1   Adjustment of Children at Discharge from Care, by
Modes of Exit: Quartiles

pated at 18 and those who were returned to their families. This deterioration is the same in magnitude as the deterioration between those
emancipated early and those discharged to residential care. The deterioration associated with 16 additional placements would be roughly
equal to the difference in condition at exit between those emancipated
at 18 and those who were discharged to residential care.

The common theme of these results is that the deterioration associated with 9 additional placements may be great enough to destroy
the viability of foster care as a means of caring for the child. Inspection of figure 5.2 confirms the conclusions based on these calculations.

Disrupted Adoption Not Associated with Mode of Exit

In table 5.2, we show the mode of exit from care by whether a child
had experienced a disrupted adoption or not. The most obvious fact
of this table is that a lower proportion of children who experienced a

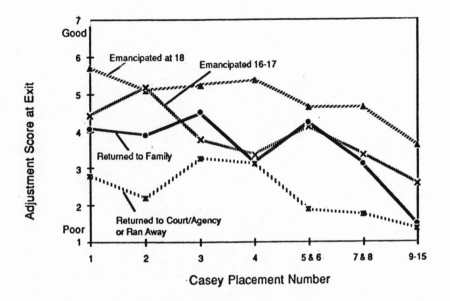

FIGURE 5.2   Adjustment of Subjects at End of Casey Care, by Mode of Exit and Placement Number

disrupted adoption were returned to their families compared with children without a disrupted adoption. Although we expected to find this association, we were surprised that 12.5% of the children with disrupted adoptions were ultimately returned to their families. When we exclude the 118 children who were returned to their families, we find that 74.3% of the children with disrupted adoptions were emancipated compared with 68.31% of children without disrupted adoptions. These percentages are quite similar. A much greater percentage of the children with disrupted adoptions were emancipated earlier than 18 compared with children without disrupted adoptions ($p < .0001$). This association is strong, and one of several possible explanations is that children who had experienced disrupted adoptions were more anxious to be on their own.

The average condition at exit of children with disrupted adoptions was essentially the same as the average condition of children without this experience. The trauma of the disrupted adoption evident at

TABLE 5.2 History of Adoption Disruption and Modes of Exit from Care

Disrupted Adoption?	Emancipated at Age 18		Emancipated Under 18		Returned to Family		Exit to Alternate Care		Runaway	
			(percentaged across)							
	No.	%	No.	%	No.	%	No.	%	No.	%
Yes (80)	27	33.7	25	31.2	10	12.5	17	21.3	1	1.3
No (505)	192	38.0	79	15.6	108	21.4	104	20.6	22	4.4
Total (585)	219	37.4	104	17.8	118	20.2	121	20.7	23	3.9

Chi-Square = 14.211   4 d.f.   p. = .007

entry and while in Casey care appears to have had a relatively small impact on the child's condition at exit and the child's mode of exit.

Children in Package Placements Were in Better Condition at Exit

We demonstrated in chapter 3 that children in package placements were less hostile and negativistic at entry and in chapter 4 that they were better adapted to subsequent foster care than other children. Table 5.3 shows the modes of exit by whether or not a child was in a package placement. Since a package placement was the continuation of a successful foster home placement, we expected a higher proportion of these children to have modes of exit reflecting a successful outcome. Indeed this was so: they showed a much higher proportion who stayed with the program until emancipation at age 18 (54.1%) as compared with other children (32.4%, p<.0001). Of the package placements, 72.6% were emancipated compared with 50.0% of other children (p<.0001). There were proportionately fewer failed placements. Children in package placements were in better condition on average at exit than other children (p<.001), a result consistent with their greater percentage of desirable outcomes.

Children with Difficult Problems at Entry
Were in Poorer Condition at Exit

We performed a multiple regression analysis with the combined measure (circumstances of departure and child's condition) as the dependent variable, and as the independent variables the following: those related to the prior living arrangements of the children, the measures of the child at entry, and measures of the child's experience in Casey care. These variables explained .44 of the variance in the child's condition at exit (p<.0001), compared with the intraclass correlation of .58. The degree of explanation was quite strong for data of this type.

There were three variables describing the child's condition prior to entry into the agency that were associated with the child's condition at exit. A child who had a greater extent of conflict with his natural parents prior to entry into the agency had a poorer condition at exit on average (p<.0001). A boy who was physically abused prior to his entry into the agency was in poorer condition at exit on average (p<.05). A child who experienced more living arrangements prior to the first separation from both natural parents was in poorer condition at exit (p<.05).

TABLE 5.3 Children in Package Placements[a] and Modes of Exit from Care

Package Placement	Emancipated at Age 18		Emancipated Under 18		Returned to Family		Exit to Alternate Care		Runaway	
	No.	%	No.	%	No.	%	No.	%	No.	%
					(percentaged across)					
Yes (135)	73	54.1	25	18.5	20	14.8	15	11.1	2	1.5
No (450)	146	32.4	79	17.5	98	21.8	106	23.6	21	4.7
Total (585)	219	37.4	104	17.8	118	20.2	121	20.7	23	3.9

[a] Child and foster family came under the supervision of The Casey Family Program as a "package" referral from the agency previously caring for the child.

Chi-square = 25.983 4df p=.0000

A child who was more hostile and negativistic at entry into the agency was in poorer condition at exit (p<.0001). There were no other associations significant at the .05 level with variables measuring the child's condition at entry.

Overall, there were four associations with variables measuring the child's condition while in care. A child who adapted to the agency's foster care better was, on average, in better condition at exit (p<.0001). A child who engaged in juvenile delinquent behavior to a greater extent while in the agency was, on average, in worse condition at exit (p<.0001). A child who was sexually acting out to a greater extent was, on average, in worse condition at exit (p<.01). A child who was more moody or depressed while in care was, on average, in better condition at exit (p<.05).[5]

Although the plasticity model had the most significant associations observed, the traumatic event model had substantial strength for this variable as shown by the findings that physical abuse of a boy and the number of living arrangements experienced before Casey placement had coefficients significantly different from zero.

The Context in Which the Findings Are To Be Evaluated

We must consider some cautions as we evaluate these findings. First, there are no absolute standards or conventional guidelines for defining a "good" outcome when the mission of the agency is to provide to children with unstable life histories living arrangements with foster families that can promote their well-being, growth, and development. There is no contrasting group with which to compare the children served by the agency, as would be the case if children were assigned to placements in the context of a randomized experiment or a matched pair study.

Even when a child cannot be kept in care until the age of 18, the time spent with the agency may still benefit the child. In a stormy life, several years of foster family living may offer some form of respite and some healing.[6] Even if this were not the case and no benefit could be demonstrated, the decision to take risks by accepting troubled children into care was an obligation the Casey program took upon itself as its sense of special mission among the spectrum of agencies serving children who could not live with their own families.

The large majority of the children who entered the care of the agency had experienced placement with a number of other agencies. More than a third were seen at entry as presenting risks because they had previously been expelled from foster homes when in the care of other agencies. About 45% of the children had previously experienced group care placements. At entry into Casey care, they were experiencing their seventh living arrangement, on average. The "outcome" studied here was the accumulated effect of a sequence of efforts by the child's family and the child welfare system, public and private. Their development was shaped by many types of programs and experiences.

The subjects studied represented the initial placements made by each of the agency's six divisions when they first opened their doors. The divisions had no experience in the selection of children at intake, in the recruitment of foster parents in the assignment of children to their homes, in their subsequent care, and in the development of case-specific treatment plans by social workers to address the needs of the children. As procedures were worked out in these areas, there may have been false starts and modifications in the way placements were arranged. After the start-up period of a social program, the outcomes of interventions should show more effectiveness in achieving service goals as the program gains experience.

In the study of closed cases, the population is biased toward inclusion of the most difficult cases. More of the children who did not succeed in the agency and were referred back to the courts were included in the population studied. The children who could be sustained within the program, most of them being better adjusted to the foster care arrangements, include those coming into care at the same time as many of the children in the closed case study but who were still in care. They reflect better outcomes, but they are not in the population studied, because their cases were still open on December 31, 1984, the defining date for inclusion in the study population. When complete cohorts of children entering care organized by year of entry are studied, the bias that tends to depress the proportion of successful outcomes indicated here is removed.

CONCLUSIONS

The placement experience was apparently beneficial, for the children left care in relatively good condition. Given the severe deprivation and instability suffered by the children before entering the program's care, the remaining in care of more than half the children through to emancipation is a noteworthy success. Although there were many successes, satisfaction with these results would have to be tempered by concern about the phenomenon of the 24.6% of the children who were returned to the courts or who ran away and whose placements apparently failed. Additionally, the relatively large number of placements that the children experienced in this agency has both positive and negative implications. The positive aspect is that the agency was able to provide some degree of stability for the children and that the agency had some success in providing foster homes for children who would typically be expected to be placed in group settings. The negative aspect is that increased numbers of placements were associated with undesirable outcomes for children. Prior to Casey placement, an increased number of living arrangements was associated with a more hostile and negativistic child at entry (chapter 3). In this chapter, we found that a greater number of Casey placements was associated with poorer condition at exit.

Among those children leaving care in poorer condition, our analysis has found significant associations that included variables reflecting the past deprivation of the child. These associations showed that greater conflict with the natural parent, a greater number of living arrangements prior to separation from both natural parents, and a boy's having been physically abused prior to his entry into care presaged poorer condition at exit. Further, our regression results found that a child with hostile and negativistic disposition was also in poorer condition. Thus, those children in poorer condition at exit tended to be those that presented the greatest challenges to care. These challenges were created before any involvement with the agency. These findings are supportive of the trauma model with events associated with greater conflict of child and parent as most destructive to the child.

The indications of our analysis are that this program had more than its share of success, suggesting that it has a strategy of care that allows children fated to reach adulthood without a return to their families to reside in a foster care setting even when they present the greatest of difficulties. This was exactly the aim of Jim Casey, the founder of this program. It remains a research task to isolate the elements of the strategy that are most effective and most easily transferred to other foster care programs serving children with unstable life histories.

## CHAPTER SIX

How They Fared After Foster Care

This chapter reports the results of the follow-up investigation of 106 former wards of The Casey Family Program who were part of the population of 585 children covered by the content analysis of closed case records. The adjustment of the subjects as adults in important areas of their lives and their reflections upon their foster care experiences with the Casey program are central features of the study.

Why Conduct a Follow-Up Study?

A follow-up study represents a genre of research in the behavioral and social sciences that carries with it a special sense of excitement. A major investment had been made in extracting information from case records to document the histories of the children. Four questions remained: (1) Do the case records contain a valid representation of the child's experience? (2) What does this massive information portend for the future course of the child's life? (3) What were the associations between the follow-up subjects' recollections of the foster home and the social worker with their condition at exit and the measures of their lives as adults? (4) What happened in the next phase of these children's lives?

The first question arises from the fact that the information has come from one source: the case records. While the reading of the case records by a second independent reader documents the reliability of the data from the case reading, reliability does not ensure the validity of the information. A follow-up study introduces a second perspective from a key participant in the drama: the child. Who is better equipped to tell what "really" happened? Thus the follow-up study provides the opportunity to confirm the impressions derived from the content analysis of the case records, and its results document the worth of the findings.

The second question deals with the value of the data about a youth for predicting what will happen to the subject in the adult years. For example, are those children who were returned to the courts because the agency could not find foster parents who could tolerate their behavior still exhibiting dysfunctional behaviors in their adult years? Have those who were in good shape when they left care been able to maintain a positive life course?

The third question, despite its obvious importance and the very explicit statement that Reid made of the research agenda (quoted in chapter 1), has not been systematically investigated. We had very limited resources in our investigation of this question. We had the status variables whether the subject reported receiving severe physical punishment in the last Casey foster home and whether the subject reported being exposed to an adverse sexual incident in that home. We had two indexes about the foster home: a measure of the subject's report of treatment there and of attachment to the foster home. Our two indexes about the social worker were a measure of the subject's report of the worker's responding to the subject's needs for relating to the family and a measure of the subject's report of the worker's extent of caring about the subject.

The fourth question has the widest human appeal. Are the scars experienced by abused, molested, and neglected children in their early years still strongly visible with the passage of time? How much of an emotional burden do they still carry? Conversely, can the worries of child welfare professionals and others concerned with these issues be relieved by accounts of former foster children who are succeeding in the adult world?

Hypotheses

Three themes in the hypotheses were at issue in this chapter. One theme was that there would be a continuation of the behaviors observed while the child was in care into the subject's behavior as an adult. A second theme was that the nature of the foster home and the conditions there would be significantly associated with the subject's condition at exit and his subsequent measures as an adult. A third theme was that the measures based on data extracted from the content analysis of the case record would have predictive validity for the measures based on the subject's responses at follow-up.

We included in our analyses variables that would show the impact of the number of placements experienced as a child both before and during Casey care, whether a child was physically abused or exposed to a disturbing sexual event before entry, and whether the subject's adoption had been disrupted. These three traumatic events had shown significant associations with earlier measures. We also included the indexes of the subject's condition at various times in development. The significance of these variables, especially ones descriptive of the subject when older, would support the plasticity model of development.

Methodology

The study was restricted to the two oldest divisions of the agency, the Western Washington (Seattle) Division, which opened in 1966, and the Yakima Division, which opened in 1972. The decision to limit the follow-up investigation to the two oldest divisions stemmed from a plan to keep this effort relatively modest in size. The Casey board of trustees decided that between 75 and 100 subjects were to be interviewed because they were unsure about what success could be achieved in locating the subjects and enlisting their cooperation. These two divisions were advantageous because they had the largest pool of cases to draw from and we could centralize the interviewing operations in one location (Seattle) and thereby contain costs.

A random sample of 100 cases selected from the Seattle Division's closed cases and 56 from the Yakima Division's was the initial group targeted for follow-up. We later added another 25 closed cases randomly selected from each of these two divisions. We then decided to focus on subjects who had received a substantial investment from the Casey program and considered only subjects who had been in the program more than one year. This excluded 26 cases; the majority of these cases had been in the program less than three months. There were thus 180 target cases in the initial sample.

Biases in the Follow-up Group

The study group is not a random sample of the children cared for in the Western Washington (Seattle) and Yakima Divisions. There were

106 subjects in the follow-up group and 74 in the non-response group (41% non-response).

The most common reason for non-response (39 subjects or 21.7% of the target sample) was that the study was finished before the subjects were located. Twenty-seven cases of the fifty selected in the supplemental sampling (15.0% of the target sample) were not found, because time ran out. Twelve subjects (6.6% of the target) in the initial sample could not be reached directly, although contact with their families or foster families indicated that they had been seen at some time during the past year or two. If the investigation could have remained in the field longer, we might have contacted these subjects directly.

The time and cost limitations of the study precluded our contacting 25 subjects (13.8% of the target). We had no trace of nineteen subjects (10.5% of the target). Our staff followed up some leads, but these efforts were not sufficient to locate them. We had the state of residence but no additional information for six subjects (3.3% of the target: they were living in Louisiana, Texas, Nevada, California, and the Philippines), and we made no further attempts to reach them.

The third most common reason for non-response (9 subjects) was the subject's refusal or inability to participate. Six subjects refused to participate after contact was made with them. Two of the six were in prison. A third subject refused to participate after seeing the questionnaire but agreed to write a statement in response to open-ended questions in the concluding section of the schedule. Three potential subjects were dead; a high count given the age group represented. One was killed in an accident; a second was murdered ("execution style"); and the third died of illness.[1]

The limited budget (in money terms and total study time) placed a constraint on the project. Those interviewed were subjects who were found most quickly and who consented to the study. Subjects who lived more than fifty miles from Seattle and Yakima were not interviewed in person. We found three of them and mailed them a copy of the interview schedule. They wrote in their answers on the schedule and mailed it back to us.

Those in the follow-up were systematically in better condition as foster children than those who were not: the follow-ups were less hostile and negativistic at Casey entry ($p<.01$), showed better adaptation to Casey foster care ($p<.001$), less destructive delinquent behavior while in Casey care ($p<.001$), less school related delinquency while in Casey care ($p<.01$), less sexual acting out while in Casey care ($p<.05$), less psychopathic behavior while in Casey care ($p<.01$), better school performance while in Casey care ($p<.01$), more extensive good behavior while in Casey care (p<.01), less psychiatric evaluation (p<.05), and better condition at exit from Casey care (p<.05). There was a trend (p<.10) for those interviewed to have been more likely to have been exposed to a disturbing sexual event before entry into Casey care. Those interviewed were like those not interviewed with regard to, all other measures. Most importantly, both groups had essentially the same level of physical abuse, history of juvenile delinquency, involvement in conflictual family situations, destructive delinquent behavior while in Casey care, drug involvement while in Casey care, and depression while in Casey care.

We conjecture that the associations we have found in these analyses are optimistic estimates of the entire set of relations. The prevalence of use of excessive physical punishment and of an adverse sexual experience in the foster home would be expected to understate the prevalences in the entire population. Those children who ran away from their foster homes may well have been fleeing abusive circumstances. Other subjects who did not agree to participate in the follow-up study may have done so because the conditions were oppressive and they chose not to reopen these issues.

The Interview

The interviews were carried out by four trained professionals, three of whom had masters degrees in social work and one a master's in nursing with additional training in psychotherapy.[2] All had very extensive experience in direct practice. The interviewers were encouraged to put the subjects at ease and to deal with any anxiety-related blocking shown in responding to sensitive questions. The narrative comments of the interviewees were additional sources of information in the effort to understand the meaning of the foster care experience to the subjects. Subjects were given a full explanation of the purpose of the study and care was taken to avoid pressuring them to participate. A payment of twenty-five dollars was offered to compensate them for the time given. Most were very pleased to be approached.

The interviewers asked a set group of questions with selective probing in each interview and recorded the subject's responses. Many of the questions were posed in a manner in which categories of response choice were made available to the subject. This facilitated the creation of computerized counts of item responses and index construction work designed to organize composites of items dealing with special themes into overall scores.

The interview was designed to cover important domains in the lives of the subjects.[3] Some groups of questions were taken from the published work of other investigators in related fields. Others derived from Fanshel's previous work. A substantial number of questions were created for the purposes of the follow-up study described here.

Demographics of Interviewed Subjects

The subjects were seen, on average, 7.1 years after leaving care with a minimum of one year and a maximum of 15 years. Thus some subjects were in their early twenties while others were in their midthirties. Sixty-one subjects (57.5%) were males, and 45 subjects (42.5%) were females. Almost four fifths were white and the remainder of minority status. Among the latter were 8 black, 5 Native American, 1 Filipino, 3 Mexican and 1 other Hispanic subjects. The subjects had been in the care of The Casey Family Program for a mean of 4.7 years (S.D. = 3.25) and had experienced an average of 2.5 placements while in the agency's care, much less than the average of 3.5 reported in chapter 3.

Indexes Measuring Important Domains

We created indexes following the procedures described in chapter two. We present the indexes in Tables 6.1 through 6.4. The indexes cover the major areas of the Casey experience (Table 6.1), personal equilibrium in the adult years (Table 6.2), getting on to the business of living (Table 6.3), and issues of crime and deviance (Table 6.4).

MULTIPLE REGRESSION ANALYSIS OF INDEX SCORES

We carried out a stepwise multiple regression analysis of each of the index scores. The independent variables included in the analysis reflected the various phases of the histories of the subjects: preplacement living arrangements and events, indexes reflecting the characteristics of the subjects at entry, and indexes measuring the under care experience of the subjects. We also used the demographic variables and the cross-product variables identifying a boy who was physically abused, a boy who was exposed to a disturbing sexual event, and a boy who was exposed to both. For the indexes that described the subjects as an adult (i.e., those in tables 6.2, 6.3 and 6.4), we also used measures reflecting the mode of exit of the subjects from care and their adjustment at the time of exit. In a second set of analyses, we sought to determine which of the adult measures were associated

TABLE 6.1   Indexes Developed from Follow-up Interviews:
The Casey Experience

Title of Index	Mean	Std Dev	Reliability (Alpha)	Sample Items
Attachment to Casey Foster Family (4 items)	3.61	1.29	.87	Did you feel secure in home? How close were you and they? Do you keep in touch?
Treatment by Casey Foster Family? (10 items)	4.40	0.83	.83	Were you treated kindly? Reasonable rules? Could you talk about self?
Role of Casey Social Worker (8 items)	2.80	0.97	.67	Explained placement reasons? Asked your opinion? Gave you information?
Casey Social Worker as Caring Person (4 items)	4.36	1.04	.73	Did worker care about you? Easy to talk with? Someone to depend on?

with our Casey experience variables. We added the six variables that we had from the subject's reports of treatment in the foster home and the report on relations with the worker.

THE CASEY EXPERIENCE

Adverse Sexual Experience

The interview contained a direct question about adverse sexual experiences in the Casey foster home in which the subject had the longest stay.[4] A female subject was more likely to report an adverse sexual experience in the Casey home than a male subject ($p<.05$): 24% ($n=11$) of female subjects were exposed to such incidents compared with 8% ($n=5$) of male subjects. No other associations were significant at the .05 level Specifically, there was no association whatsoever with a history of exposure to a disturbing sexual event.

TABLE 6.2 Indexes Developed from Follow-up Interviews:
Personal Equilibrium in the Adult Years

Title of Index	Mean	Std Dev	Reliability (Alpha)	Sample Items
General Well-Being (37 items)	3.59	1.00	.95	How have you been feeling? Bothered by nervousness? Waking up fresh and rested?
Emotional Disturbance (6 items)	4.41	0.73	.74	Ever had nervous breakdown? Patient in facility? Seen a psychiatrist?
Friendship (4 items)	3.36	0.98	.67	How many close friends? How often friends visit you? How often you visit?

Corporal Punishment

The interview also contained a direct question about whether the subject had experienced severe physical punishment in the Casey home of longest stay.[5] A quarter (25%, n = 26) reported that they were physically punished severely in the Casey home. A regression analysis with dependent variable whether the subject reported severe physical punishment found five associations that together explained .263 of the variance (p<.0001). A subject who was in a package placement was more likely to report receiving severe physical punishment (p<.01). A subject who was more extensively involved in delinquency while in Casey care was more likely to report receiving severe physical punishment (p<.05). The two subjects who as boys were both physically abused and exposed to a disturbing sexual event prior to entry were more likely to report receiving severe physical punishment (p<.01). A subject who spent a greater percentage of time in foster care before entry was less likely to report receiving severe physical punishment (p<.05). There was one association that was an exposure effect. A subject who was older at entry was less likely to report receiving

Table 6.3   Indexes Developed from Follow-up Interviews:
Getting on to the Business of Living

Title of Index	Mean	Std Dev	Reliability (Alpha)	Sample Items
Adequacy of Housing (3 items)	3.59	1.00	.47	How satisfied re: housing and neighborhood? Post-care housing problem? Feelings re: neighborhood?
Adequacy of Finances (9 items)	3.07	1.04	.86	Regard income as adequate? Ever run short of funds? What is annual income?
Educational Achievement & Satisfaction (8 items)	5.30	0.75	.72	Highest grade completed? Special problems doing best? Satisfied with education?
Employment satisfaction (3 items)	3.33	1.05	.43	Employed full or part-time? Happy with type of work? Do you have skills?
Family Building (3 items)	4.04	1.29	.74	Number depend on income? Number of children? Are you married?

severe physical punishment ($p < .001$). Since package placements lasted longer, that association may include an exposure effect as well.

Treatment by Foster Family

This index measured the manner in which the last foster family before exit from care had treated them. The ten items on which the index was based included the following questions: Were you treated kindly and accepted as part of the family? Did you have the right clothes? Did they have reasonable rules? Was recreation provided? Were you allowed friends? Was the home kept clean? Were you allowed to visit friends? Was there interest in your school work? Were you given an allowance? Could you talk to them about your concerns? The vast majority of subjects reported that they were treated kindly and accepted as family members in their Casey home of longest stay.

TABLE 6.4   Indexes Developed from Follow-up Interviews:
Issues of Crime and Deviance

Title of Index	Mean	Std Dev	Reliability (Alpha)	Sample Items
Involvement in Crime-Related Activities (10 items)	4.18	0.88	.80	Ever picked up or charged? Burglary? Disorderly conduct?
Armed Robbery (2 items)	4.80	0.77	.69	Charged weapons offense? Charged for robbery?
Substance abuse (9 items)	4.03	0.56	.70	Ever use nonprescribed drug? Use marijuana? Use cocaine?
Drinking (2 items)	3.97	1.07	.89	How often do you drink? How often do you feel high?

The multiple regression analysis found four significant associations that together explained .206 of the variance (p<.001). A subject who was more moody or depressed while in Casey care reported a poorer measure of treatment in the last Casey family (p<.01). A subject who had more living arrangements away from both parents reported a better measure of Casey foster home treatment (p<.01). A subject whose mother maintained a closer relationship with him during his Casey care reported a better measure of Casey foster home treatment (p<.05). A boy who had been both physically abused and exposed to a disturbing sexual event before entry into Casey care reported poorer Casey foster home treatment (p<.05).

The association between number of living arrangements and positive evaluation of the Casey foster family is an important judgment of the children about their Casey treatment. Since those subjects who had experienced a very wide range of treatments were more positive about their Casey foster family treatment than subjects who experienced fewer placements, we infer that the Casey treatment was comparatively better. There are two explanations of the association with the child's moodiness. One is that the child's moodiness caused the subject to perceive treatment more negatively. The other is that the poor treatment in the home caused the moodiness and depression. Our data are not detailed enough to permit us to distinguish these two explanations. The association with the extent of contact of the child with the natural mother parallels the association reported above. The two boys who were both physically abused and exposed to a disturbing sexual event had massive problems, especially as shown by the findings on involvement in serious crime. Determining whether these two children were beyond help or whether their treatment while in the Casey program contributed to their problems is beyond the scope of our data.

Foster Home Attachment

This measure is based on four questions about the last Casey foster family: Did you feel secure in this home? To what extent did they understand you? How close did you and the foster parents get? Do you keep in touch with the family?

A multiple regression analysis found three significant associations that together explained .161 of the variance (p<.001). A subject who received less extensive Casey psychiatric or psychological services reported a closer measure of attachment to the foster family (p<.01). A subject who had spent more time in Casey care reported a closer measure of attachment to the last Casey foster family (p<.05). A subject whose mother had a more extensive contact with her child while in Casey care reported a closer measure to the last Casey foster family (p<.05).

Simply put, those who had been less troubled while in care as shown by a lack of need for psychiatric or psychological services showed a more positive attitude in discussing the foster family. While somewhat counter- intuitive, the association with the extent of con-tact of the child with the mother while in Casey care suggests that a total loss of parents inhibits the ability of a child to trust and accept substitute caretakers. The finding supports the wisdom of working closely with the natural parents of a child in foster care. The association with the length of time in care is in the expected direction.

Social Worker's Relatedness to Subject's Needs

We measured the degree to which the subject regarded the Casey social worker as relating to the subject's needs. Our index used eight items: Did the social worker explain the reasons why the subject was in care? Did the social worker arrange for visits with the subject's parents? Did the social worker ask the subject's opinion about choosing a new place to live? Did the social worker visit the subject's school to see how the subject was doing? Did the social worker talk to subject about how long the subject would be in care? Did the social worker provide information about the child's biological parents? Did the social worker arrange for subject to see siblings? Did the social worker talk to subject about the "facts of life"?

The majority (70%) felt the social worker was someone who could be depended upon for help with personal problems. The most common criticism (57%) was that their social workers did not give them information about their biological families. Almost all of the subjects saw the social workers as caring about them (90%) and visiting regularly and keeping in touch (87%); 6% saw their social workers as not caring for them and 12% indicated that they did not visit regularly. There were content areas where the subjects reported the social workers as not getting involved in any discussion with them: e.g., how long they would remain in care (44%), information about the biological family (41%), and talks about the "facts of life" (68%).

The multiple regression analysis found two associations that together explained .161 of the variance (p<.001). A boy who had been exposed to a disturbing sexual event prior to entry reported a more positive measure of the relatedness of his social worker to his needs (p<.01). A subject who had a group care placement while in the Casey program reported a more positive measure of the social worker's relatedness to the subject's needs (p<.01). Both of these associations suggest a very positive and helpful response from the Casey worker to a child who had experienced a traumatic event and was in need of comfort and assistance and that came at a time the subject appreciated.

Social Worker's Caring About Subject

Our measure of the subject's evaluation of the social worker's personal concern for the subject while in Casey care used four questions: Did you feel your social worker cared about what happened to you? Did your social worker visit you regularly and keep in touch with you? Did you feel that your worker was easy to talk to? Did you find that you could depend on your worker to help you with problems? When asked, "Did the social worker make it easy to talk with her?", 83% of the subjects responded affirmatively and 15% negatively. When asked, "Was the social worker someone you could depend on for help with problems?," 70% were affirmative in their responses and 26% were negative.

The multiple regression analysis found three significant associations that together explained .180 of the variance (p<.001). A subject who had been away from Casey care more years had a less warm measure of the social worker's role (p<.001). A subject who was in better condition at exit reported a warmer measure of the social worker's role (p<.05). A subject who experienced a disrupted adoption had a more positive measure of the social worker's role (p<.05). This association is another instance of a positive evaluation of the Casey worker from a child who had suffered a traumatic event, here a disrupted adoption.

Condition at Exit

There were no associations significant at the .05 level or less between the variables descriptive of the foster home or Casey worker and the condition of the subject at exit from Casey care.[6]

PERSONAL EQUILIBRIUM IN THE ADULT YEARS

General Well-Being

This measure combines information gathered in the interview concerning how the subject has been feeling, whether the subject has been bothered by nerves, whether the subject has been in "firm control", whether the subject has felt sad, discouraged, or hopeless; whether the subject has been under a strain; how happy the subject has been; whether the subject has had a fear of losing his mind; whether the subject has been anxious; whether the subject has been waking up fresh; whether the subject has been bothered by illness; whether the subject's daily life has been interesting; whether the subject has felt downhearted, whether the subject has been feeling stable; and whether the subject has felt tired or worn out.[7]

Whereas three fifths of the subjects reported themselves in good spirits most of the time, a third reported themselves going up and down, under strain, and feeling dissatisfaction with life. More than a third suffered from problems of loneliness.

The regression analysis found one significant association that explained .095 of the variance (p<.01). A subject who was in better condition at exit from care, on average, reported a condition of better well-being (p<.01).[8] This association thus confirms the validity of the ratings of the condition of the child at exit made by the case readers. There were no associations significant at the .05 level with variables describing the foster home or the social worker interaction.

Emotional Disturbance

A subset of six questions taken from the Index of General Well-Being was used as a measure of emotional disturbance in the histories of the subjects. The index created for this purpose combined information on whether the subject had ever had a nervous breakdown, had ever been a mental patient in an institution, had seen a psychiatrist, had consulted a physician about emotional problems, had consulted with a psychiatrist or psychologist about emotional problems, or had consulted a social worker about personal problems.

The regression analysis model reported here explained .356 of the variance (p<.0001).[9] Subjects who had a greater number of group care placements while in Casey care had an index showing more emotional disturbance on average (p<.0001). A child who had a poorer condition of mental illness prior to entry (that is, whether the child attempted suicide, had severe depression, or had been in a mental hospital) reflected a greater extent of emotional disturbance as an adult (p<.01). A child who was exposed to a disturbing sexual event prior to entry into the Casey program had a greater extent of disturbance as an adult (p<.05). The two subjects who as boys were both physically abused and exposed to a disturbing sexual event prior to entry into the Casey Program had an even greater extent of emotional disturbance (p<.05). There were no significant associations with variables describing the foster home.[10]

Even though the mental illness measure had a low intraclass correlation, its predictive validation is clear. The association between the use of group care as a strategy for dealing with children and the subsequent measure of disturbance as an adult suggests that the Casey workers were effective at identifying disturbed children and bringing resources to bear on their treatment. Equally, the findings suggest that the treatments used were not completely effective. The findings strongly implicate the traumatic nature of exposure to a disturbing sexual event.

Friendship Patterns

We measured the capacity of these former foster children to become involved in intimate relationships after they left care, using the answers to four questions: How many close friends do you have? About how often have your friends visited you? How often have you visited your friends? How often has there been telephone contact?

A regression analysis revealed four significant indicators of adult friendship patterns that together explained .225 of the variance (p<.0001). Those subjects who had been involved with drugs while in the care of The Casey Family Program reported on average lesser involvement as an adult with friends (p<.001). Nelson et al. (1986:188) have identified solitary behavior as one of the signs associated with substance abuse by adolescents. A subject who reported an adverse sexual incident in the last Casey foster home reported less forming of friendships as an adult (p<.01). A white subject formed friendships more extensively as an adult than a nonwhite subject (p<.05). A subject who was returned to the parents more times before entry into Casey formed adult friendships less extensively (p<.05).

The finding on number of returns to parent before entry is another in a pattern linking excessive turbulence of living arrangements to undesirable outcomes. Finally, the association with the report of an adverse sexual experience in the Casey foster home of longest residence is part of a general pattern of abusiveness in care linked to undesirable outcomes.

GETTING ON TO THE BUSINESS OF LIVING

Adequacy of Housing and Neighborhood

This measure is based on the degree of the subject's satisfaction with housing circumstances, the housing problems encountered after leaving foster care, and feelings about the neighborhood in which the subject lived. During the five years preceding the interview the subjects had been quite mobile. Almost two fifths had moved five or more times.

The regression analysis found four significant associations in the backgrounds of the subjects that together explained .243 of the variance (p<.001). A child who experienced better adaptation to Casey foster care had a better level of housing adequacy (p<.01). A child who had more placements while in the Casey program had a poorer level of housing adequacy as an adult on average (p<.01). A subject who reported receiving severe corporal punishment in the Casey home of longest placement had poorer housing as an adult than a subject who did not report such treatment (p<.05). A white subject reported a better level of housing adequacy than a nonwhite subject (p<.05).

The adaptation to Casey care association and the association with the number of Casey placements are suggestive of the validity of the adaptation measure and the continuation of a difficulty of adjustment pattern shown in repeated placements. The association with the race of the subject is consistent with a pattern of national housing bias against minorities. The finding implicating use of excessive corporal punishment in the Casey home is consistent with the association of mistreatment in the Casey home and a variety of poorer outcomes as an adult.

Adequacy of Finances

We asked the subjects whether they regarded their income as adequate, whether their financial situation was getting better, how they regarded their income compared with others, whether they needed financial help to get along, whether they ever ran short of funds, whether they increasingly found themselves in debt, whatever was the amount of their income, and to what degree did they worry about money. Almost two thirds of the subjects were currently wage earners. About a tenth were receiving public assistance. Almost a third regarded their income as inadequate and found themselves often worrying about finances.

There were two clearly significant associations that explained .190 of the variance (p<.0001). A subject who was in better condition at exit from the Casey program reported more nearly adequate personal finances. A subject who reported receiving excessive physical punishment at the Casey home of longest residence reported a poorer financial condition as an adult (p<.05).[11]

Educational Achievement and Satisfaction

This measure summarized the subjects' views about educational achievement and combined their responses to questions about such areas as the highest grade level achieved, average grades, how they got along with teachers and with classmates, any special problems they had in doing their best, how well they felt they had been prepared for the work world, and how satisfied they were with their educational achievement. Whereas the majority of subjects characterized their school grades as at least adequate, three fifths identified special problems that had prevented them from doing their best and two thirds expressed regrets about school achievement.

The results of the multiple regression analysis found three significant associations with this measure of educational achievement that together explained .328 of the variance (p<.0001). Children who left Casey care in better condition had, on average, a higher measure of educational achievement (p<.0001). Subjects who were physically abused by their families before entering foster care showed, on average, a lower measure of educational achievement (p<.01). A male who reported an adverse sexual experience in his Casey home of longest residence had a poorer adult measure of education (p<.01). These findings confirm the extent of summarization in the condition at exit and the traumatic implications of early physical abuse of a child and of poor treatment in the foster home.[12]

Employment

The follow-up measure of adult employment is based on three items: (a) whether the subject is employed, (b) the subject's expressed happiness with the type of work, and (c) the subject's evaluation of extent to which work skills have been acquired. About half of the employed subjects were very satisfied with their current jobs and about a third were somewhat satisfied. About a third expressed much regret about opportunities wasted in preparing themselves for the world of work.

Since women in our society bear the greater share of the family burden and a somewhat lesser participation in the work force, we ran two regressions, one using only male subjects and the other using all subjects. For males, there were four associations that together explained .340 of the variance (p<.001). A male who had experienced a failed adoption reported a better level of adult employment (p<.01). A male who had a more extensive history of mental illness reported a better adult measure of employment (p<.01), a counterintuitive finding. A subject who engaged in juvenile delinquent behavior more extensively while in Casey care had a poorer measure of adult employment (p<.05). A subject who was in better condition at exit reported a better measure of adult employment (p<.05).

Among all subjects, there were eight associations that together explained .414 of the variance. A subject who was in better condition at exit again had a better measure of adult employment (p<.05). There were three relatively uninteresting associations. A male subject reported better adult employment than a female subject (p<.0001), reflecting a general societal pattern. A white subject reported better adult employment than a nonwhite subject (p<.01), another general societal pattern. A subject who engaged in more extensive wetting behavior reported a poorer measure of adult employment (p<.001). A subject who had more returns to his parents before entry into Casey care reported a poorer measure of adult employment (p<.01).[13] A subject who was older when first separated from both parents reported a poorer measure of adult employment (p<.05). A boy who was both physically abused and exposed to a disturbing sexual event before entry had a poorer measure of adult employment (p<.01). A subject who reported a greater attachment to his foster home reported a better level of adult employment (p<.01).

The substantive associations were provocative in their implications. The predictive validity of the condition of the child at exit was confirmed for a very important measure. There was a negative association between one measure of excessive turbulence in living arrangements in childhood, the number of returns of the child to the child's natural family, and the measure of the child's subsequent employment as an adult. The association with a disrupted adoption was positive, suggesting that the negative associations fade away with as the time from the disruption increases. The findings suggest that the positive treatment in the foster home can have a positive impact.

Job Stability and Satisfaction

This follow-up measure focused on the subject's current job and combined the answers to: years employed in the current job, whether subject had ever been promoted, degree of satisfaction with salary, stability of residence as related to employment.

For the male subjects, the regression analysis found three associations that together explained .266 of the variance (p<.001). A subject who was returned more times to his natural family before entry into Casey care had a poorer measure of adult job stability (p<.01). A subject who had a greater attachment to his foster home had a better measure of adult job stability (p<.05). A subject who had more extensive contact with his natural father while in Casey care had more stable adult employment (p<.05).

For all subjects, the regression analysis found three associations that explained .181 of the variance (p<.001). A subject who was returned to the parents more times before entry into Casey care had a lower measure of current job stability and satisfaction. This association is parallel to the results for the measure of adult employment (p<.01). A subject who spent more years out of the home had a better measure of adult job stability (p<.01). A subject who had more extensive contact with the natural father had a better measure of adult job stability (p<.05).

Number of Dependents

Three questions in the follow-up interview focused on the household and familial context in which the subjects were living. These were the subject's marital status, the number of adults in the subject's household, and the number of children in the subject's household. The measure that we used in the regression was equal to the sum of the number of adults in the subject's household, the number of children in the household, and one if the subject was married.

Almost two thirds of the subjects were married or living with someone in a paired relationship. Less than half the subjects were single (46.7%) About three tenths (29.9%) were married and 11.2% were living with someone. Another 11.2% were divorced or separated and one subject was widowed. About 12% were divorced, separated, or widowed. Most of the subjects (59.8%) reported a single adult, themselves, depending on this income, 35.% reported two adults, and 4.7% indicated that three family members depended on this income. A majority of the subjects (58.9%) reported themselves as childless, whereas 15.9% were parents of a single child, 17.8% had two children and 7.5% had three or more children.

The multiple regression analysis found one association that explained .153 of the variance of the family size measure (p<.0001). A subject who was in better condition at exit had a smaller family size measure on average (p<.0001).[14] There were no associations with foster home treatment or social worker measures.

ISSUES OF CRIME AND DEVIANCE

Involvement in Crime-Related Activities

An index based on 10 questions measured the involvement of the subjects in crime-related activities. Subjects were asked whether they had ever been picked up by the police or otherwise charged with a crime. They were also asked specifically whether they had ever been charged with the following violations of law: shoplifting, assault, parole violation, drugs, disorderly conduct, burglary, driving while intoxicated, or driving violation. They were also asked for a count of the number of times they had been charged with violations of law.

Difficulty with the police and other legal authorities before and after the placement of the subjects with the program varied with respect to the seriousness of infractions. Forty-four percent had been picked up by the police on charges at one time or another. Charges included shoplifting (n = 26), assault (18), drug-related infraction (13), disorderly conduct (12), driving while intoxicated (12), parole violation (7), forgery (6), and armed robbery (6). Thirty-two percent of the subjects had been convicted of the crimes with which they had been charged.

The regression analysis found six significant associations that together explained .534 of the variance ($p < .0001$). A male who was physically abused before entry into the Casey program had a much more extensive measure of adult criminality ($p < .0001$). A subject who engaged in more destructive delinquent behavior while in Casey care had a greater extent of adult criminality ($p < .001$). A male subject who reported an adverse sexual experience in the Casey foster home of longest residence had more extensive adult criminality ($p < .01$). Male subjects had a greater extent of adult criminality than females ($p < .05$). A subject who engaged more extensively in juvenile delinquent behaviors while in Casey care was more extensively involved in adult criminality ($p < .05$). This association was particularly strong for a boy who was physically abused ($p < .01$).[15]

The physical abuse of a male was obviously and firmly linked to this measure of self-reported criminality. The Pearson product-moment correlation was .55 ($p < .0001$). We see here an extremely strong confirmation of associations found in the previous chapters relating the physical abuse of a boy with violent and destructive behavior throughout the subject's life. In particular, a boy who has been physically abused and who has begun early delinquent behavior is extremely likely to be on a course leading to adult criminality. The association between destructive delinquent behavior while in the Casey program as measured in our content analysis of the narratives and the measure of adult criminality as reported by the subject directly is a major documentation of the predictive validity of our measure of destructive behavior and shows the continuity of the life course with regard to violent and criminal behavior. The abuse of a child, here the report of an adverse sexual experience in the Casey foster home by a boy, was consistently and broadly related to undesirable adult outcomes. That males are more extensively involved in adult criminality has been found consistently and is not related to foster care issues.

Involvement in Serious Crime

In order to measure more serious crime, we created a two-item index based on information on whether the subject had been charged with an offense involving the possession or use of an illegal weapon and whether the subject had been charged with burglary.

The regression analysis found four significant associations with involvement in more serious crime that together explained .284 of the variance (p<.0001). A subject who had been returned to the family or to court after discharge from the Casey program was more extensively involved in serious criminal activity as an adult (p<.0001). A male subject who reported both an adverse sexual experience and receiving severe physical punishment in his last Casey foster home (4 of 61 males) was more extensively involved in serious crime (p<.01). A subject who was less attached to his family while in Casey care was more extensively involved in serious crime at follow-up (p<.05). A boy who was physically abused before entry was more extensively involved in serious crime in adulthood (p<.05).[16]

These findings strongly support the hypothesis that an abused boy is at much greater risk of beginning a violent course of life that extends into his adulthood. A return of the boy to his abusing family may be counterindicated as shown by the association of return to family and increased involvement in serious crime. Conversely, a child who had a strong attachment to his family during Casey care was less extensively involved in serious crime during adulthood. This reinforces the hypothesis that positive family contact has a beneficial effect on the child that reduces the risk of subsequent adult involvement in serious crime. Similarly, the attachment of a male to his last Casey foster home was negatively associated with extensive involvement in serious adult criminality.

Drug Abuse Patterns

The measure concerning possible drug-related problems of the follow-up interviewees is an index based on nine items. If the subject responded "yes" to the question whether the subject had ever used a nonprescribed drug "like pot, cocaine...," then the interviewer asked about the following drugs: marijuana (pot, grass) or hashish, amphetamines, cocaine, barbiturates, heroin, LSD, angel dust, quads (Quaalude), Valium and Librium, etc. The subjects were also asked whether current use of drugs was greater than in the past.

About one in eight (13%) reported extreme difficulty with drug use. About a third of the subjects indicated that the use of drugs had been a source of problems in their lives at some time, and a third had used cocaine. A third of the subjects reported having used marijuana at least once or twice a week during the past year, and 18% used it every day. About a fifth of the subjects had used amphetamines during the past year,

The multiple regression analysis using all subjects found three significant associations that together explained .327 of the variance (p<.0001). A subject who adapted better to Casey care was less extensively involved with drug usage as an adult (p<.0001). Conversely, a subject who did not adapt as well to Casey care had a more extensive involvement with drugs as an adult. A male subject who reported receiving excessive physical punishment in his Casey home of longest residence was more extensively involved in adult drug usage (p<.0001). A subject who had a more extensive involvement in drugs while in Casey care had a more extensive involvement with drug usage as an adult (p<.01).

The regression analysis using just male subjects had three associations that explained .335 of the variance (p<.0001). Again, a male subject who adapted well did not use drugs as extensively as an adult (p<.01), and a male who reported receiving excessive physical punishment in the last Casey foster home used drugs more as an adult (p<.001). A male who felt that his Casey worker cared more for him used drugs less extensively as an adult (p<.05).

The measure of drug usage while in Casey care has an obviously strong predictive validity. The association between adaptation and subsequent adult drug usage validates the merits of the adaptation measure extracted from the content analysis. The physical abuse of a boy, this time with excessive corporal punishment in the Casey foster home of longest residence, was associated with a poor adult measure. There was a positive association upon the adult man of a boy's perception that his social worker cared for him.

Drinking Behavior

A two item index measured the subject's use of alcohol: how often the subject had consumed beer, wine or other alcoholic drinks during the past month and the frequency with which the subject had consumed alcoholic drinks during the past month to the point of feeling "high."

Thirteen percent of the subjects identified drinking as having been a major problem at some time in their lives, and 25% reported this as having been somewhat of a problem. The multiple regression analysis found two significant associations that together explained .152 of the variance (p<.001). A subject who experienced more living arrangements before the first separation from both parents abused alcohol more extensively as an adult (p<.01). A male subject abused alcohol more extensively as an adult than an otherwise similar female (p<.01).

These results confirm the theme that the exposure of a child to excessive turbulence of living arrangements, this time measured by the number of living arrangements before the child's first separation from both parents, is associated with an undesirable outcome in the child, this time alcohol abuse as an adult. A greater extent of alcohol abuse among males is a well known phenomenon.[17]

CONCLUSIONS

Viewed as a group, these findings suggest a continuity of life course. As an adult, a subject who was in better condition at exit from Casey care reported having better well-being, having more satisfactory adult employment, having gained a better education, having better finances, having a smaller size family, and having a warmer regard for the social worker. A subject who adapted better to Casey care had a better measure of housing as an adult and less drug usage. In general, these associations had very small p-values suggesting that these are clear findings.

A child who was placed in more group care placements while at Casey (usually because of the child's adjustment problems) was more emotionally disturbed as an adult. A child who used drugs while in foster care developed into an adult with lesser involvement with friends.

There were associations that were not continuations of life course but rather suggest the intrusion of traumatic events. The physical abuse of a boy by his family and excessive turbulence in childhood living arrangements had significant associations with adult characteristics. There were no major associations with a child's having an adoption disrupted.

A subject who was physically abused by the natural family before entry did not do as well in ultimate adult educational achievements. A subject who as a boy was physically abused was more extensively involved in adult criminality, specifically committing serious crimes such as burglary and armed robbery more extensively. The two young men who as boys were both physically abused and exposed to a disturbing sexual event were more mentally disturbed as adults and were even more extensively involved in serious crime.

In addition, there was a chain of behaviors from the physical abuse of a boy to adult drug usage and criminality. From chapter 3, a boy who was physically abused was more extensively involved in delinquent behavior before entry into Casey care. From chapter 4, a child who had been more extensively involved in delinquent behavior prior to entry was more extensively involved in delinquent behavior while in Casey care. From this chapter, a subject who was more extensively involved in delinquency while in Casey care was more extensively involved in criminal behavior as an adult.

There were important associations between the use of corporal punishment of the foster child while in the care of the foster home of longest residence and negative outcomes as an adult. A subject who reported an adverse sexual experience in the foster home was less able to make friends as an adult. A male who reported an adverse sexual experience in the Casey foster home was less well educated as an adult and more extensively involved in adult criminality. If in addition, he reported harsh physical punishment in the foster home, he was more extensively involved in serious crime as an adult. A subject who reported receiving excessive physical punishment in the Casey home of longest residence was less well off financially and lived in poorer housing as an adult. A male who reported receiving excessive physical punishment in a Casey foster home was more extensively involved in drug abuse as an adult and had poorer health.

On the positive side, there was an association between the subject's report of better treatment in the Casey home of longest residence and less depression while in Casey care. A subject who was more attached to the last Casey foster home had better adult employment. A male subject who was more attached to his last Casey foster home was less extensively involved in serious crime as an adult and had greater adult job stability and satisfaction. A male subject who regarded his social worker as showing greater concern for him was less extensively involved in substance abuse as an adult.

Jim Casey set out to care for youths who were on an inevitable downward spiral. The Casey Family Program found some of them. These results suggest that a boy who has been physically abused by his family and who has responded with delinquency is at a very great risk of embarking on a life course that is a litany of horrors: poor school performance and poor training for adult life, with continued violence and delinquency as a teenager. As an adult, he extends his delinquency to serious crime

Turbulence in living arrangements was directly and strongly related to hostility and negativity at entry. This was the start of a chain that continued to the child's condition at exit and subsequent adult performance. In addition, there were shadows of lingering effects that were not summarized in the measures we developed. A subject who had a turbulent living arrangement sequence as a child had poorer adult housing (with more Casey placements), poorer adult employment and job stability (with more returns to parent prior to entering Casey care), and more extensive alcohol abuse (more living arrangements prior to first separation from both parents).

A third theme emerges that the subjects remembered their workers favorably after experiencing traumatic events. There was a warmer evaluation of the social worker's relatedness by subjects who as boys were exposed to a disturbing sexual event prior to entry and by subjects who were put in a group placement while in the Casey program. Subjects who had experienced a disrupted adoption had a warmer regard for the worker's contact with the subject. A subject who experienced more living arrangements away from both parents had a more positive view of treatment in the last Casey foster home.

A fourth theme that the foster child's attachment to family and contact with natural parents has positive associations with the child's development at adulthood emerges somewhat dimly. A subject who had more extensive contact with the mother while in Casey care reported feeling closer to the foster family and receiving better treatment there. A subject who was more attached to the family while in Casey care was less extensively involved in serious crime.

A fifth theme is the importance of the interaction of the child in the foster home. A reported abusive relation was associated with negative adult outcomes. A positive relationship had positive outcomes. These findings were quite strong despite the bias that might cause us not to see the most abusive and worst of situations. Even though this was a first and very primitive effort to understand the impact of the care the child receives in an individual foster home on adult outcomes, we found very strong associations. These associations confirm the validity of Reid's position quoted in chapter 1. We want to stress the importance of understanding the "black box" that is the relationship of foster child and foster family. We are especially concerned, given the relatively high percentages of reported incidents involving attempts to take sexual advantage of the subjects and reported excessive use of corporal punishment, that many of the runaways might have been fleeing the most desperate of conditions. We regard it as a systematic weakness of foster care systems that they pay little attention to the runaway child.

The follow-up effort reported here has provided many results that can be useful in planning services for children who have had turbulent histories before coming into care. The overall results are sufficiently encouraging to warrant placing a high premium on the conduct of follow-up studies to illuminate the foster care experience of children. The subjects tended to be highly cooperative, indeed willing to share their views about their current and past situations. The interviewing schedule created for the investigation appears to have achieved its purposes quite well. Many useful domains of information have been illuminated and the majority of multiple-item indexes have come through as quite strong, reflected in high internal reliability measures and associations with earlier measures of the child.

The follow-up data support the validity of information extracted by the project's case readers from the agency records. The views of the former wards of the agency are firmly consistent in many areas with the pictures drawn from the records.

## CHAPTER SEVEN

Group Care and Replacement as a Tactic in Maintaining Foster Care

The present national and bipartisan philosophy of child foster care is that there is a hierarchy of placements. When the biological family cannot care for their child, the most desirable placement is that a child should be in foster boarding home care with reunification as a long-term goal. Otherwise, adoption or some long-term stable placement is the next most desirable outcome. The least desirable outcome is a group care placement, the placement of last resort and essentially a failure of the system. The rationale is that the biological family is best and that failing that, the biological family should be approximated as closely as possible.[1]

Foster family care and institutional or group care are two components in the repertoire of resources for children requiring out-of-home care, each appropriate according to the phase of the child's placement history. Janchill (1983) has documented the professional practice decisions when a group care placement is "appropriate." Zietz (1969) has observed that the institution and foster home need not be seen as competing services and has described the advantages of group care placements for certain kinds of children in terms that are consonant with the views of most other writers:

> The institutional community provides the child with opportunities to work through many problems and manifest various kinds of behavior that would not be permissible in most foster homes. Since these are children who have been damaged by emotional depriva-

tion and rejection, they have need for warm but casual relationships with a variety of adults in whom they can find continuous acceptance. The hostile, lonely child may have need to punish the adults about him by being aggressive, destructive, or cruel. This kind of behavior can be more readily absorbed, evaluated, and treated by the institution's professional staff than by foster parents. The institution also offers the child the opportunity of working his problems through at his own pace and spares him the pain and responsibility of having to form substitute parental relationships for which he may have neither the need, the desire, nor the capacity. . . . The institution also offers the child a variety of activities that will help him to grow and to become mature and independent (71–72).

In this chapter, we consider the role of group care placement as part of a strategy to prepare a child for foster home living in the Casey program. We are interested in the mix of foster family home and group care placements, the various times at which children were exposed to group care placements, the relation between a group care placement and a child's development, and the characteristics of the children who left foster family care and were then served in group care.

We were struck by the readiness of this agency to use foster boarding home placements for children who could not be sustained in such placements when in the care of other agencies and who had a repetition of such failures after coming to this agency. Specifically, we seek to document the frequency with which group care was used, the circumstances surrounding the decision to use this type of care, and the results of such efforts. Was the child returned to foster family care after group care placement? Was the child subsequently sustained in care until becoming emancipated at the age of 18? What was the child's condition at the point of departure?

Definition of Group Care Variables

We define a group care placement as the settings described in the records as "group home," "institution," "residential treatment institution," "group shelter," and "correctional institution" (Whittaker 1985). The study first focused on the group care experiences of the subjects while they were in the Casey program. After we observed that these children had group care placements before their Casey placements and that some were discharged to a group care placement, we included the status variables whether a child had a pre-Casey group placement and whether a child was discharged from the

Casey program to a group care placement. We were thus able to look at the patterns of group care that had taken place over each subject's life, ranging from no group care placements to having experienced group care on at least three occasions: pre-Casey, within Casey, and post-Casey. Our objective is to document the associations with group care placements and a sequence of multiple foster care placements.

Hypotheses

Since this study is pioneering in its concentration on sequences of placement arrangements, there are few data on the effects of sequences of group care placements on children in foster care. Although we can list many a priori associations that we expect to hold, there is not a body of organized empirical data supporting even the most basic of relations. For example, we would expect that the use of group care placements, as measured by the rate of group care placement, would increase as a child experienced an ever larger number of placements and became ever more rebellious and negative to family-type living arrangements. We would also expect that the rate of placing a child successfully in a foster home would decrease with the number of placements because we expect that such a child would present more specialized and challenging problems and demands on a foster home. Rather than list our a priori expectations explicitly, we have approached these data in a strictly empirical manner. In this chapter, we have tried to determine the characteristics of the Casey program's use of placement strategies because the results offer strong suggestions that this program has a strategy that is in fact effective.

We hypothesized that a group care placement while in Casey care would be associated with some positive therapeutic outcomes. That is, that a group care placement may be a positive strategy in caring for a foster child. We expected these associations to be smaller than the associations with whether a child had a group care placement prior to Casey care.

One area where there are clearly stated professional practice expectations is that of the characteristics of children in foster care that are appropriate for a group care placement. Our major formal hypothesis was that the placement of a child in group care while in the Casey program would be associated with factors that were appropriate and indicated this placement on accepted professional practice issues.

Summary of Findings

The Casey Family Program used group care placements at least once in 21.1% of the cases reviewed. These children were those who were likely to have been delinquent while in care, acting out sexually, or referred to a psychiatrist or psychologist because of staff concern about the child's adjustment. As the "more difficult of the difficult" (Kadushin 1967), these children who had a group care placement while in the Casey program were in a more distressed state at final exit from care than children who did not have a group care placement. Nevertheless, there was a significant association between improved condition at exit and Casey group care placement for those children who had very poor adaptation to Casey care. A child whose adaptation to Casey care was poor and who was placed in a Casey group placement had a condition at exit that was the same as a child whose adaptation was average and who did not have a group care placement.

Several other findings support the hypothesis that the Casey workers have an effective strategy for using group care placement in conjunction with foster home placement. An examination of the placement sequence of the children in the study revealed that a Casey group care placement was followed by an immediate termination of care in less than 10% of the group care placements. Once a child was placed in a Casey group care placement, roughly 25% of subsequent Casey placements were group care placements, and roughly 60% were foster home placements. That is, there was a "cooling off" of a majority of the children to the extent that they could accept a foster home placement afterward. Part of the strategy appears to reflect perseverance on the part of the agency in keeping children in its fold even when there were rather extended sequences of interrupted foster placements. There are no major trends downward or upward in the rates of subsequent Casey foster home placements as the number of Casey placements increases.

There was a provocative set of associations suggesting that the use of Casey group placement might affect the pattern of some adult outcomes. We were able to examine associations between the children's experiences in group care placements with their subsequent adult experiences. Since these findings are based on a rather small number of cases and on wide and undocumented variations in the nature of the group care placements, the reader should be duly cautious. No associations were found between group care placements and such important measures as the child's subsequent job experiences as an adult, employment status, health status, drinking and drug abuse as an adult, and well-being as an adult.

Since other researchers (in particular Galdston 1979) had previously found that boys had a different pattern of response to physical abuse than girls, we investigated whether boys and girls in the Casey program had the same patterns or not. Our results also showed this difference in patterns previously reported, and we indicate such a different pattern by specifically referring to boys. Boys who had Casey group care placements and group care placements either before or after their Casey placements (i.e., two types of group care placements in their life experiences) had deficits in significant areas of their adult lives. Boys who had a Casey group care placement and who were discharged from Casey to another group care experience were less well off financially and were more extensively involved in criminal behavior other than armed crimes. Boys who had both a Casey group care placement and a group care placement before entry into the Casey program were not as well educated as other Casey children as adults and were more extensively involved in armed robbery.

The Decision To Place a Child in Group Care

The data showed that 78.9% of the 585 subjects in the study were placed only in foster home settings while in the Casey program and were never placed in group care.

What factors were associated with a decision to place a Casey foster child in a group care program? There were four significant associations that together predicted .213 of the variance (p<.0001). A child who was delinquent while in Casey care was more likely to have had a group care placement while in Casey care (p<.0001). A child who was sexually acting out was more likely to have had a group care placement while in Casey care (p<.0001). A child who caused sufficient concern to require a psychiatric or psychological evaluation was more likely to have had a group care placement while in Casey care (p<.01). A child who was more moody or depressed while in Casey care was more likely to have had a group placement while in Casey care (p<.05).

The variables that were predictive of whether the child was placed in group care are those that were descriptive of the child's conduct while in the Casey program care and associated emotional states, measured by multi-item indexes in each domain cited, and are indicative of an unquestionably "appropriate" group care placement (Janchill 1983). A child who was delinquent or whose conduct necessitated a mental examination would necessarily be difficult to care for in a family setting. The association with the child's sexually acting out was regrettably all too expected and familiar. The finding suggests that training the foster family to anticipate the growing sexual independence of their charge and to learn appropriate responses could reduce the friction between family and foster child.

We were surprised that there was no association between whether a child was in a package placement and whether a child had a group care placement while in Casey care after controlling for these variables. The application of the logic that generated our hypotheses led to the conjecture that a child in a package placement would have been less likely to have had a group care placement while in Casey care.

Description of the Casey Strategy of Using Group Care Placements

The rate at which children were remanded to court or ran away, controlling for the number of Casey placements, was uniformly about 10%. Figure 7.1 shows the percentage of children who were remanded to court or who ran away from the Casey program by the number of Casey program placements that the child experienced. Since the graph is roughly flat at 10%, the program was as likely to continue with a child with eight previous placements as with a child with only one. Further, the program was almost as likely to place a child in a foster home after eight or so previous placements as after one.

This finding suggests a reevaluation of the sometimes held practice assumption that a child who has failed one foster home placement should ipso facto be regarded as not suitable for foster home placement.

Once a child had additional placements, the use of group care placement was rather high. Figure 7.2 plots the rate of group care placement by the number of previous Casey placements. Roughly 40% of subsequent placements were group care regardless of the number of previous Casey placements compared with an overall group placement rate of 21%.

The program did not use group care placement as a means of easing a child out of the program. Figure 7.3 plots the termination rate and the retention rate of children who were put into a group care placement in the sequence of Casey placements. Roughly 10% of the children who were put in a group care placement were terminated from the group care placement, and there was little if any trend in the rate with the number of placements. Roughly 80% of the children in

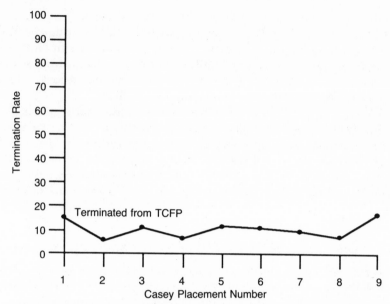

FIGURE 7.1 Termination Rate of Children, by Number of Casey
Placements Completed

group care placement were kept in the Casey program for at least one
more Casey placement, and this percentage too showed little if any
trend over the number of placements. The remaining 10% of the
children who were in group care placements but not terminated or
moved to another placement were emancipated or reunited with their
families from the Casey group care placement.

Figure 7.4 plots the rate of putting a child in a foster family home
placement subsequent to a group care placement and the rate of
putting a child in a second group care placement after a group care
placement. Roughly 60% of the children who were in a group care
placement were subsequently placed in foster family care. There appeared to be a slight trend downward with the number of Casey
placements. Roughly 25% of the children in a group care placement
were subsequently placed again in another group care arrangement.
There appeared to be a trend upward in figure 7.4 for this percentage.

Emancipation Status

A child who had a group placement while in Casey care was more
likely to be returned to court or to be a runaway and less likely to be
emancipated from care or to be returned to the biological family than

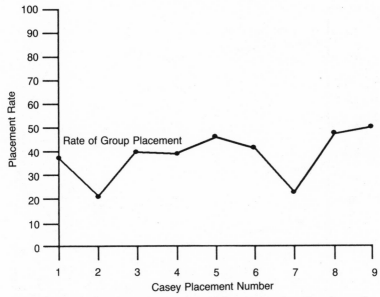

FIGURE 7.2   Rate of Group Care Placement, by Number of
Casey Placements Completed

a child who did not (p<.01). When we excluded the 118 children who were returned to their families from the total sample, we found the expected result that a child who had a group placement while in Casey care was less likely to be emancipated and more likely to run away or be remanded to the court (p<.05).

Condition of Subjects upon Departure from Casey Care as Related to Group Care

In chapter 5, we reported on the factors associated with the condition of the child at exit from the Casey program. We revised this analysis so that we could determine the associations with whether a child had a Casey group care placement. We found associations that suggest that group care placement while in Casey care had a positive effect on the child. These suggestions were very subtle, and, quite frankly, there are other reasonable interpretations that explain the associations reported without concluding improvement associated with group care placement.

The regression analysis using only associations significant at the .01 level or less explained .483 of the variance of the child's condition at exit, compared with the intraclass correlation of .58. As in chapter

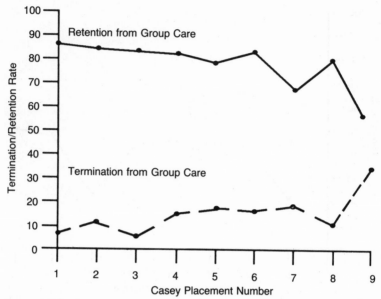

FIGURE 7.3   Retention and Termination Rates from Group Care

5, the associations with better condition at exit were better adaptation to Casey care (p<.0001), less destructive delinquency while in Casey care (p<.0001), less hostility and negativity at entry (p<.0001), less involvement in conflictual relations with parent (p<.0001), and less sexual acting out while in Casey care (p<.001). The associations with group care placements were that a child who had a group care placement prior to entry into Casey care but was not discharged to a group care placement was in better condition at exit (p<.01). A child who was placed in group care before entry and who was discharged to a group care placement was in worse condition at exit (p<.0001)

The associations with discharge to group care are somewhat circular because this was effectively an admission of failure in the child's case. The association with group care placement prior to entry into Casey care is positive but not conclusive. Although these children were in group care before Casey and were in better condition at exit, they may well have been placed in the Casey program precisely because they were in relatively good condition. In that event, the Casey program was bringing to fruition the effective treatment in the group care placement; alternatively, the selection process could be viewed as skimming off of the cases in best condition in the group placement program.

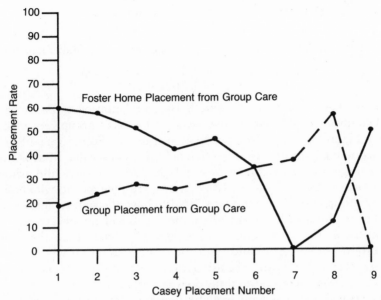

FIGURE 7.4   Rate of Placement from Group Care, by Number of
Casey Placements Completed

A multiple regression using an additional three variables explains
.496 of the variance and has additional positive, albeit weak, associations with group care placement variables. A boy who was in
group care placements both before and during Casey care was in
better condition at exit (p<.01). Additionally, a child who had adapted
poorly to Casey care and had been put in a group placement while
in Casey care was in relatively better condition at exit than another child whose adaptation to Casey care was equally poor
but who did not have a group placement while in Casey care
(p<.05).[2]

The regression with yet one more association was even more complex but positive and explained .504 of the variance. There was a
strong unequivocal association that a child who had a group placement while in Casey care was in better condition at exit (p<.01). This
association with group care placement was especially strong for children who adapted poorly while in Casey care (p<.001). Since the
association is complex and the issue so important, we will describe
the association in much more detail than has been our practice. The
model fitted for children who did not have a Casey group placement was

Fitted condition at exit for no Casey group care
= f(other variables) + .37 * Adaptation;

and the model fitted for children with Casey group placement was

Fitted condition at exit for Casey group care
= f(other variables) + 1.19.

That is, there was no association between adaptation to Casey care and condition at exit for children who had a Casey group care placement. Figure 7.5 graphs the two fits. The function f(other variables) is the same for both fits. The two fits yield the same value (that is, the lines intersect) for a child whose adaptation is 3.2. A child whose adaptation was less than 3.2 (that is, adapted poorly) and who had a Casey group care placement was fitted to have the same condition at exit as a child with typical adaptation who did not receive Casey group care. This fitted condition at exit was better than the fitted condition at exit for a child with the same adaptation who did not receive Casey group care. The fitted improvement was especially large for those children whose adaptation was very poor.

We can think of several explanations for this pattern of associations. The first is that this finding reflects measurement difficulties with the variables characterizing the adjustment of the children to Casey foster care. This variable was not perfectly measured in our study, as shown by the intraclass correlation of .63 for adaptation, the measure of the agreement between pairs of case readers. A child who had a group placement while in Casey care was, ipso facto, poorly adjusted. The finding above then might simply be that the group placement variable is a surrogate variable (instrument variable) for adaptation to foster care for children with group placement while in Casey care. In other words, the same mechanism holds for both groups of children, with the group placement variable operating as a more accurate reflection of adjustment than the raters' evaluations for children in the group care placements. The implication of this explanation is that the association is an artifact of imperfect measurement and is of no substantive importance.

The second explanation is that this finding was caused by the regression effect. Under this explanation, only the children with the most extreme problems were placed. The regression effect explanation argues that these children then regress toward the mean so that there would be much less of an association present. In addition to the regression effect, there is also a lowering of the correlation because of the restriction of the range due to selection of the most extreme cases for a group placement while in Casey care.

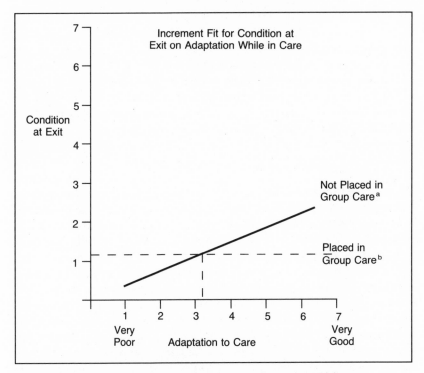

Notes: a. Fit for children not placed in group care is f(others) + .37 Adapt.
      b. Fit for children placed in group care us f(others) + 1.19.

FIGURE 7.5   Incremental Fit for Condition at Exit on
Adaptation While in Care

The first two explanations are not mutually exclusive and may well be operating jointly to produce the pattern observed. Our prevailing optimism led us to consider a third explanation. If, in fact, the group care placement had the effect of "cooling out" the child and helping the child overcome the problems that led to the placement, then the placement would have the effect of reducing or destroying the association between the child's adjustment and subsequent condition at exit.

Associations with Any Group Care

Many of the children in this agency experienced institutional or other forms of group care before entry into the Casey program, and a few had group care after exit from the Casey program. The next set of analyses summarized data considering these additional experiences with group care. Each child was classified as to whether the child had experienced a group care placement before the first Casey placement (noted as Pre = + if yes, and 0 if not), whether the child had experienced any group care placement while in the Casey program (noted as Within = + if yes and 0 if not); and whether the child had been discharged to an institution or other group care facility from the Casey program (noted as Post = + if yes, and 0 if not).

Follow-Up Measures by Pattern of Placement

We analyzed the experiences of the 106 former foster children seen at follow-up by the pattern of their placements in group care programs. There were very small numbers involved, and so the results have to be interpreted cautiously. For example, only 30 of the follow-up subjects had no group care placements (0-0-0), ten had group care while in the Casey program and were not discharged to a group care placement (0-+-0 and +-+-0), 48 had a group care placement before they entered the Casey program and no subsequent group care placements (+-0-0), 11 had no group care placements while in the Casey program but experienced subsequent discharge to a group care placement (0-0-+ and +-0-+), and six children had group care placements in all three phases (+-+-+).

There were no associations between group care placement experiences significant at the .05 level or lower for the subsequent job experience as an adult, extent of relating to other adults, employment status, health as an adult, well-being as an adult, extent of friends as an adult, drinking as an adult, substance abuse as an adult, recalled attachment to Casey foster parents, or treatment in the Casey foster home recalled in adulthood. We have already reported in chapter 6 that a subject who was in a group care placement while in Casey care had a warmer view of the worker.

There were some associations suggesting that children in group care placements were less well off as adults, especially boys who had group care placements over two or more periods in their lives. Group care placement before entry into Casey care and a group placement while in Casey care were associated with subsequent mental disturbance as an adult ($p<.0001$). That is, a child who had group care placement before Casey care and while in Casey care had a measure of mental stability indicating more unstable conditions such as having a nervous breakdown, having been a patient in a mental facility, or having seen a psychiatrist for emotional problems. A boy who was placed in group care both prior to entry and while in Casey care was more involved in criminality as an adult (p<.01). A boy who was placed in group care while in the Casey program and who was discharged from Casey care into a group care placement tended to be less well off financially (p<.05), but he was less extensively involved in serious crime such as armed robbery (p<.001). A boy who was placed in group care before Casey care and who was discharged from Casey care into group care had a larger family (p<.01), felt his social worker related less well to him (p<.01), had a less extensive amount of education as an adult (p<.01), and was more extensively involved in serious crime (p<.0001). Finally, a child who was in a group placement while in Casey care had poorer housing subsequently as an adult (p<.001).

Association of the Group Care Variables with Measures of Child Before and During Casey Care

Usually, the dependent variable in a regression analysis describes the subject at a time after the time of the independent variables so that an observed association has the possibility of a causal interpretation. We reversed this convention in the following analyses and offer these findings as descriptive and warn the reader not to attach a causal interpretation. For example, consider a boy who has turned out to have a decidedly bad outcome when studied as an adult: he has been involved in serious crime and is strongly addicted to drugs. Having life course data, we can seek to understand what went on in the child's past as prelude to the disasters in his life. We can look at the role of preplacement events in the child's life at three points in time: his characteristics at entry, his experiences in care, and his condition at exit. In studying the role of group care placements, we used regression analysis to look back at the precursors of the group care experience. The reader should not be confused that we are reversing causal direction, since it would be absurd to think that group placement while in Casey care caused the physical abuse of the child prior to entry into the Casey program.

Table 7.1 presents the averages for each of the eight possible combinations of status on these three variables for some key measures. Examination of table 7.1 shows that the means generally go down as one goes down the table. That is, those children who had no group care placements are in the best shape with respect to any of the measures presented, and those children with group care placements before, during, and after their Casey placement are in the poorest

TABLE 7.1 Mean Subject Index Scores on Entry, Under-Care and Exit Measures: by Patterns of Group Care Experiences Over Life Course

| | Entry | | | | Under-Care | | | | Exit | |
| | Hostile-Negative Personality | | History of Juvenile Delinquency | | Adaptation to Care | | Acting Out/JD | | Condition & Adjustment at Departure | |
Patterns of Group Care[a]	Mean	SD	Mean	SD	Mean	SD	Mean	SD	Mean	SD
No pre, no within, no post	6.32	0.93	6.58	0.89	4.21	1.24	6.40	0.73	4.97	1.59
(n)	(165)		(165)		(167)		(167)		(165)	
Pre, no within, no post	5.68	1.26	5.92	1.33	4.02	1.24	6.16	0.91	4.84	1.60
(n)	(195)		(195)		(195)		(195)		(191)	
No pre, within, no post	6.07	0.96	6.42	1.11	3.47	1.25	5.60	1.12	4.17	1.60
(n)	(26)		(26)		(26)		(26)		(26)	
Pre, within, no post	5.61	1.21	5.86	1.44	3.24	1.25	5.11	1.18	3.76	1.58
(n)	(36)		(36)		(36)		(36)		(36)	

No pre, no within, post	5.49	1.48	6.33	0.99	3.19	1.30	5.54	1.08	3.28	2.01
(n)	(39)		(39)		(39)		(39)		(39)	
Pre, no within, post	5.39	1.49	5.46	1.55	2.88	1.37	5.77	1.08	2.53	1.51
(n)	(71)		(71)		(72)		(72)		(72)	
No pre, within, post	5.07	1.65	5.53	1.27	2.67	1.12	4.76	1.36	2.30	1.09
(n)	(18)		(18)		(18)		(18)		(18)	
Pre, within, post	4.58	1.24	5.76	1.33	2.88	0.92	4.93	1.30	2.43	1.38
(n)	(23)		(23)		(23)		(23)		(23)	
Total mean, SD	5.77	1.29	6.08	1.28	3.72	1.35	5.95	1.08	4.20	1.87
(N)	(573)		(573)		(575)		(576)		(569)	
F Ratio	10.4395		8.3217		15.1730		19.6763		31.0203	
F Probability	.000		.000		.000		.000		.000	

Pre = group or institutional care prior to placement in Casey Family Program. Within = group or institutional care while client of Casey Family Program. Post = group or institutional care upon exit from Casey Family Program.

condition. Children who had a group care placement before their entry into the Casey program were very much like children who did not have a pre-Casey group care placement but who were otherwise similar (that is, each pair of groupings above were rather like each other). There were greater differences for children who had a Casey group care placement. By far the greatest differences occurred for children who were discharged from the Casey program to a group care placement.

There were some small associations between the sequence of the child's experiences in group care placements and the child's experiences before entry into the Casey program. For example, with regard to the extent of hostile and negativistic personality identified at the time of the entry, our model using group care experience explained .118 of the variance. Children who had no group care experience were the least hostile and negativistic on average. On the average, children who had a group care placement before entry into the Casey program were more hostile and negativistic at entry ($p<.0001$). Children who left the Casey program for a group care placement were more hostile and negativistic at entry ($p<.001$). Children who had group care experiences during their Casey placement and who left Casey for a group care placement also were more hostile and negativistic at entry ($p<.01$).

Overall, this model explained .096 of the variance in the extent of history of juvenile delinquency in children before entry ($p<.0001$). Children who had no history of group care experience had the least previous history of juvenile delinquency. Children who had a group care placement before their first Casey placement had a more extensive history of juvenile delinquency ($p<.0001$). Boys who were placed in a group care setting before Casey care and who left the Casey program to go to a group care setting had an additional greater extent of history of juvenile delinquent behavior before Casey care ($p<.0001$). This relation may well reflect the fact that these boys also had a greater proportion who were physically abused ($p<.01$). Children who had a group care placement before Casey care and who left the Casey program for a group care placement had, as well, a greater degree of mental illness before entry into the Casey Program.

The history of group care placements model used here explained .154 of the variance. Children who had no group care placements had the best scores on average on the Index of Adaptation to Foster Care. A child who left the Casey program to go into a group care placement had previously been much less well adapted on average ($p<.0001$). A child who was placed in group care while in the Casey program was much less well adapted while in care on average (p<.0001). A child who was placed in group care before, during, and after Casey care had been relatively better adapted while in the agency's care p<.01). Children who were placed in group care programs before their entry into the Casey program but not during their Casey placement or afterward adapted to foster care as well as children who had no group care experience.

 Overall, the history of group care placement explained .231 of the variance in the extent of delinquent behavior while in Casey care (p<.0001). Children who had no history of group care placement had the least extent of delinquent behavior on average. A child who had a group care placement while in the Casey program had a much greater extent of delinquent behavior (p<.0001). A child who was discharged from the Casey program to a group care placement also had a greater degree of delinquent behavior (p<.0001). There was an indication that a child who had a group care placement before entry into the Casey program also had an associated decrease in the index score indicating a greater extent of delinquent behavior (p<.05). The implication then is that group care placements were a continuing response to such behaviors. As expected, boys had on average more extensive delinquent behavior than otherwise similar girls (p<.01).

A similar set of associations held for destructive juvenile delinquent behavior while in Casey care. The percentage of variance explained was .172. A child who had a group care placement while in Casey care had more extensive destructive behavior (p<.0001). A child who was discharged from Casey care into a group care placement had a greater extent of destructive delinquent behavior (p<.0001). A child who was placed in group care before entry into the Casey program had more extensive destructive delinquent behavior (p<.05). A boy also had more extensive destructive juvenile delinquent behavior on average than an otherwise similar girl (p<.0001).

The placement of a child in group care while in the Casey program was associated with a greater extent of drug involvement while in Casey care (p<.0001). No other group placement pattern was associated with drug involvement. A child who was placed in group care while in the Casey program had a greater extent of sociopathic lying (p<.0001), and a child who was discharged from the Casey program into a group care placement also had a greater extent of sociopathic lying (p<.0001).

A child who had a group care placement while in the Casey program tended to be expelled from school for juvenile delinquent behavior (p<.05), to do more poorly in school (p<.0001), to be seen more often by a psychologist or psychiatrist because concern had risen about his or her problems ($p<.0001$), and to show acting-out behavior ($p<.0001$).

DISCUSSIONS AND CONCLUSIONS

One of our regression analyses suggests that a child who was adapting poorly to Casey care and who was subsequently put in a Casey group care placement was in much better condition than a child whose adaptation was equally poor but who was not put into a group care placement.

Our analyses of who was put into Casey group care placements found associations with variables that reflected appropriate placements. We did find an association with the extent to which a child was sexually acting out, suggesting that some training of foster parents and anticipation of problems might succeed in helping to maintain a placement.

Since the number of subjects followed up was relatively small and since there was such a high proportion of nonresponse, the ability of our analyses to find subtle associations is very limited. Nevertheless, there were a few findings with respect to measures of the follow-up as an adult.

There was a small association between an increased number of placements while in Casey care and condition at exit controlling for mode of exit. These findings, especially in combination with our earlier association of increased extent of hostility with a greater number of living arrangements, suggest that excessive numbers of placements are not beneficial to the child.

The suggestion of the regression analyses, these tables, and the cross-tabulations of institutional placements and mode of exit and condition at exit is that children who were placed in group care were in worse condition when they were placed than children who were not, and that as adults these children were subsequently not quite as well off in certain limited areas. In the course of time, however, these children appear to have made up most of the deficit in their backgrounds at the time of their Casey group care placement. Overall, the larger picture is that these children as adults were essentially as well adjusted and capable as the children who did not have a group care placement.

The Casey program was relatively successful at using an institutional placement to help a child adapt to foster care and to prepare for a subsequent foster home placement in the sense that a high percentage of these children had one or more subsequent foster home placements. We have no direct information about the specific strategies that are used to accomplish these tasks. Further analyses that can contribute to practice knowledge would be to consider the condition of the child with respect to behavioral tendencies before placement in an institutional setting and after such a placement, to see whether on average the placement serves to improve the child's reported adaptation and particularly whether conduct problems are reduced.

Our findings support the recommendations of the California Association of Services for Children following a recent study of ten thousand children in care:

- That data be collected and presented that more accurately reflect the changing nature and characteristics of the children in care;
- That such a study research new issues, such as why children "blow out" of their placements, or why children with similar presenting problems have varying dispositions in our current service system;
- That research be conducted to determine which intervention methods work—or work reasonably well—with which types of children (Fitzharris 1985).

CHAPTER EIGHT

From Birth to Exit:
Seeking Life Course Patterns in the
Experiences of Foster Children

In this and the next chapters, we report the results of our factor analyses, which further probed our data sets to cover the full expanse of the experience of the subjects from a life course perspective. In this chapter, we focus on the integration of information about the children from birth to the time of exit from The Casey Family Program. In the next chapter we extend our interest to the time of the follow-up interviews.

The integration of all findings into a consistent whole is an essential step in developing a modern theory of development. Insights can be expanded by linking earlier and later experiences in the lives of individuals—from birth to early adulthood. We have been interested, for example, in determining whether early trauma continues to show an impact on a child's life over the adolescent years and into adulthood. Specifically, does physical abuse by parents continue to have a demonstrable adverse effect on the child while in care and after leaving care? In a different domain, is a subject who was engaged in delinquent behavior before entering care and who was placed in a group setting for delinquent children likely to continue to show delinquent behavior while in Casey care and to report involvement in criminal activity when interviewed as an adult? In the mode of longitudinal investigation, we seek a more integrative approach to our data employing an analytic procedure that has promise of revealing continuity of experience in the lives of the subjects in important domains.

Do we have a right to expect continuity of experience? The hazardous part of the analytic journey, i.e., the possible failure to find continuity in the life course of the subjects, derives from the fact that the long spans of time involved and the many influences that may be at play helping to shape personality and behavior as a child grows up can cause associations to evaporate. Later experiences mitigate earlier experience involving deprivation or abuse. The child might have been antisocial and acting out at entrance into Casey care, have worn out a welcome in several foster homes, but finally was able to settle in with a foster family having the attributes sufficient to overcome the child's deficits. The very kind of program success one hopes for, even in the most obdurate of situations, can diminish the strength of associations with variables describing the child earlier and thus reduce predictive capability. There is always the possibility of chance factors to turn the tide in favor of the child who is likely to end up in failure: a teacher who takes a sympathetic interest, a neighbor's child who becomes a good friend, or a romantic interest that has a positive impact. And, of course, a negative chance experience can also be encountered that will throw a child off balance who was seemingly in good shape and lead to negative outcomes.

In chapters 3 through 7, multiple regression analysis was our principal tool. These calculations were the basis of our decisions to report an association or not. There were many possible choices, namely, 2^P, where P is the number of predictors. In addition, unusual patterns in the residual plots of these results led us to add interaction variables in our analyses. For example, in chapter 7, we used the interaction variable representing adaptation to foster care of children placed in Casey group care and found that it was significantly associated with condition at exit.

The richness of choice can lead analysts to overemphasize the importance of an association because they lose track of the number of possible associations they are prepared to report on. Statisticians (Mosteller and Tukey 1977) call this the problem of "multiplicity." Since the results of the varimax rotation of the principal components were so useful in constructing our indexes, we continued to use factor analysis. The results were so compelling that we report them here Since the techniques of factor analysis cannot be written in closed mathematical form, one of our students (Joh 1989) used numerical and simulation techniques to study the properties of factor analysis as we used it here. Joh showed that the varimax rotation of the principal components is extremely effective at correctly defining subproblems for later regression analysis and causal modeling. His study used fewer variables, and he did not examine the consequences of errors of measurement. Based on Joh's results, a major issue that we are concerned with in chapters 8 and 9 is that associations reported in the previous chapter appear in the same factor in these analyses.

We have chosen to use factor analysis as the analytic method to verify the life course patterns that have been reported.[1] An advantage of factor analysis is that it permits every variable in the data set—whether previously treated as an independent variable or as a dependent variable in the regression analyses—to show its association in the form of factor loadings with phenomena of interest. In the multiple regression analysis, predictor variables having stronger associations overshadow those that may be significantly correlated with the criterion variable but to a lesser degree.

The reader needs to be aware that there is little experience in longitudinal investigations of foster children using factor analysis in this manner, and the effort here represents an early exploratory effort. The focus is mainly on the child and does not include measures of the quality of the foster families serving the children nor does it take account of the effectiveness of the social worker's interventions or other important influences such as the schools the subjects attended, the churches that may have been part of their lives, and informal group memberships to which they were exposed.

Number of Factor Solutions and Evidence of Continuity of Life Course

Using factor analysis as an analytic tool for exploratory data analysis presents the investigator with the problem of making choices from the many available solutions. Using SPSS-X, our statistical computing program, we ran a series of factor analyses with the number of factor solutions to be extracted constrained to two as a start and working up to as many as twenty-four. With hundreds of pages of output resulting from these computer runs, the task was to determine the consistency of important themes characterizing the life course of the subjects over many factor solutions.

With a minimum number of factors in a solution, say two, the analyst has enforced a compacting together of many variables that have some affinity for each other, i.e., some minimum level of association. As the analyst moves to solutions with larger numbers of factors, more themes will emerge. Larger themes will be broken into several branches, each a subtheme in the larger. The variable loadings for these factors will reveal small clumps of content characteristic of limited subgroups of subjects sharing common features.

FROM BIRTH TO EXIT FROM CASEY CARE: RESULTS OF FACTOR ANALYSIS

On a technical note, we observe that the eigenvalues of the principal components of a correlation matrix provide an indication of the number of relations present in a data set. The analysis of the 576 children with complete data files found six eigenvalues greater than 2 (suggesting this many clear relations), an additional nine eigenvalues between 1 and 2 (suggesting this many possible relations), and two between .9 and 1.0 (indicating potential relations). On the basis of these values, most practitioners of factor analysis would choose a solution with between six and nine factors. We have taken our results more literally than most analysts. The consistency of the results both internally within each factor and across solutions was our guiding criterion.

Independent of this analysis, we ran simulation studies of the performance of factor analysis handling data with properties similar to what we found in these data. The results of these simulations suggested that factors with eigenvalues somewhat less than 1 occasionally correctly reflected the situation being simulated. Consequently, our ad hoc procedure has been to examine the interpretability of the findings of the factors with the smallest eigenvalues and to consider them when they contained plausible relations. In the description that follows, we start with the 17–factor solution.

Of course, there were many subjective decisions that we made in the course of digesting our results. The reader should refer to our presentation of the loadings themselves to review our decisions. We have found that the value of the factor analysis is the perspective that emerges from a detailed consideration of the output. We have found by experience and confirmed both by simulation and numerical calculation that the varimax rotation of the principal component solution produces statistics that can be quickly and accurately interpreted. Roughly speaking, a rotated loading that is less than .25 in absolute value often reflects noise. We report the loadings that are greater than .25 and interpret them in terms of their associations with the other variables with larger loadings in the factor. We use the product of the loadings to assess the direction and magnitude of the association.

The variables in one factor are associated with each other with magnitude of correlation roughly equal to the product of the loadings.

In our report of associations, we report those that are either theoretically interesting or were reported in earlier chapters. The reader should remember that there is an implicit set of associations with any variable in a factor with the other variables in the factor and that in the interests of brevity we cannot report all associations implicit in this analysis.

In addition, we have reported the results of many factors whose associations are essentially tautological from the definition of the variables. The first example is in factor 2 where we report the association between the percentage of time that a child spent away from both parents prior to entry into the Casey program and the years the child spent in non-Casey living arrangements. We ask our readers' forbearance and hope that they will understand that the fact that the analysis has shown an obvious association subsequent to other not so obvious associations means that the earlier findings are more conspicuous empirically than these associations that were logically necessary. For example, empirically, the most obvious finding from the analysis is the chain of associations showing the continuity of the pattern of delinquency while in Casey care, and this pattern is even more obvious than the logically necessary relations of factor 2.

The results of this analysis suggest a set of models for the development of children in foster care. The central issue is the correctness of the model as a tool in understanding children in general and children in foster care in particular. We now proceed to our discussion of the patterns suggested by the factor analysis of the 576 children whose records were complete on the variables we used here. For identification purposes, we label each factor by the variable with the largest loading in absolute value and follow that label with a short description of the major pattern of the variables with the largest loadings. For the reader wishing to examine some of the factor solutions described below, we provide in table 8.1 the list of variables included in the analysis and in table 8.2 the varimax factor rotation results for the seventeen-factor solution.

REVIEWING SEVENTEEN- TO TWO-FACTOR SOLUTIONS

Factor 1: Acting-Out Behavior While in Casey Care Delinquency as a Common Thread Through a Foster Child's Life

The most obvious pattern in the data was the continuity of delinquency throughout a child's life for that portion of the study population afflicted with such problems and, conversely, the consistent ab-

sence of delinquency in children not afflicted. The largest eigenvalue
is 6.6, a value indicating an obvious pattern. The child's extent of
acting-out or delinquent behavior while in the care of the program
had the largest loading, .86.[2] This was followed by the extent of
delinquent behavior while in school (with loading .74) and extent of
psychopathic behavior (.68). This factor is particularly striking when
we list the variables in their time sequence: a child's history of juvenile delinquent behavior before entry (.30) is associated with a child's
pattern of delinquency while in Casey care (.86), delinquent behavior
in school (.74), a child's psychopathic behavior (.68), the extent of
acting-out behavior (.63), drug involvement (.46), destructive delinquency (.39), and school performance (.35). Of course, the delinquent
behaviors while in care form a strongly correlated constellation of
behaviors. Finally, the chain of delinquent behavior is associated with
a child's poorer condition at exit from care (.34). In parallel fashion,
one can describe the subgroup of the study population relatively free
of such conditions.

This factor is very appropriately identified with acting-out behavior while in Casey care. The index appears in only one other factor
with a quite small loading, and the variable descriptive of delinquency while in school in Casey care appears only in this factor.

These associations are very stable across solutions and are the core
of the most important factors down to and including solutions with
only two factors. When the number of factors was reduced to 10, a
secondary set of associations was merged with the larger theme. The
secondary set of associations related depression and other psychological measures with juvenile delinquent behavior while in Casey care
and also associated greater numbers of placements with more delinquent behavior while in care.

The analysis thus found that a child who received Casey group care
(.42) was associated with more acting out, a child who had more
group care placements while in Casey care (.57) was associated with
having more delinquent behavior in care, a child who had a greater
number of Casey placements (.69) was more involved in delinquent
activities, a child who had a greater number of placements in Casey
before emancipation (.37) was involved in delinquent activity to a
greater extent while in Casey care, and a child who had a greater
number of living arrangements away from both parents (.43) was
involved in a greater extent of delinquent behavior.

Further associations suggested were that a child who was more
poorly adapted to foster care (.31) was more involved with acting out,
a child who was more depressed (.41) was more involved in delin-

Table 8.1   Variables Included in the Factor Analysis of
Birth-to-Casey Exit

Pre-Casey Variables:

1. Age of child at first Casey placement
2. Age first separated from parents
3. Years in non-Casey living arrangements
4. Percent of pre-Casey time away from both parents
5. Percent of pre-Casey out-of-home time spent in foster care
6. Placement number when first separated from both parents
7. Number of pre-Casey returns to parents after first separation
8. Total pre-Casey living arrangements away from both parents
9. Adoption disruptions before Casey
10. Child placed in group home, residential center, or institution pre-Casey
11. Child placed in institution for delinquent children pre-Casey
12. Prior foster home came to Casey with child (package placement)
13. Ethnicity (1 = white; 0 = minority)
14. Sex (1 = male; 0 = female)
15. Interaction of sex of child and indication of pre-Casey exposure to a disturbing sexual event
16. Interaction of sex of child and pre-Casey indication of physical abuse
17. Interaction of sex of child, indication of pre-Casey exposure to a disturbing sexual event and physical abuse
18. Interaction of indication of pre-Casey exposure to a disturbing sexual event and pre-Casey physical abuse
19. Indication of pre-Casey exposure to a disturbing sexual event
20. Indication of pre-Casey physical abuse

Variables 21–25: Index scores for children as seen at intake to Casey

21. I: Hostile-Negativistic Personality (7 items)
22. II: History of Juvenile Delinquency (6 items)
23. III: History of Mental Illness in Background (3 items)
24. IV: Child with Developmental Disability (3 items)
25. V: Child in Conflictual Situation with Parents (2 items)

Casey Variables:

26. Placement number of first Casey placement
27. Non-Casey care purchased by Casey
28. Number of non-Casey group/institutional placements between Casey placements

Variables 29–40: Index scores for children reflecting Casey care experience

29. I: Adaptation to Foster Care (11 items)
30. II: Acting Out, Delinquents (12 items)
31. III: Juvenile Delinquent—Destructive (3 items)
32. IV: Juvenile Delinquent—Expelled from School (3 items)
33. V: Juvenile Delinquent—Acting Out (3 items)
34. VI: Juvenile Delinquent, Psychopathic—Lying and Stealing (3 items)
35. VII: Drug Involvement (3 items)
36. VIII: Wetters and Soilers (3 items)
37. IX: Moody or Depressed (2 items)
38. X: Family Attachment (3 items)
39. XI: School Performance (5 items)
40. Psychiatric or Psychological Evaluation (2 items)
41. Mother's role in child's life while child in Casey care
42. Father's role in child's life while child in Casey care

Exit Variables:

43. Total number of placements of child while in Casey care
44. Casey placement number at exit from Casey care
45. Total living arrangements away from both parents at exit from Casey care
46. Years in Casey placements
47. Total years out of home at exit from Casey care
48. Index of Adjustment at Departure from Casey Care (2 items)
49. Emancipation status at exit from Casey care (1 = emancipated at 18, 2 = emancipated at less than 18, 3 = returned to family, 4 = remanded to court or public agency)
50. Exit from Casey destination: residential care

quent behavior, and a child who had undergone psychiatric or psychological evaluation (.44) was weakly associated with more involvement in delinquent activities. The measures of the child's prior involvement in delinquent behavior and involvement in psychopathic behavior while in Casey care shifted to a slightly different factor centered on the prior involvement of the child in delinquent activity and the child's placement in a group care facility before Casey entry.

This larger factor remains essentially unchanged until the number of factors is reduced to two. At this point, variables related to turbulence in living arrangements and the physical abuse of the child

TABLE 8.2 Varimax Factor Rotations Descriptive of Subjects From Birth to Exit: Seventeen Factor Solution (N = 576)

					Factors				
	1	2	3	4	5	6	7	8	9
Factor 1 Variables:									
22. Index: History of Juvenile Delinquency	0.30					-0.22			
30. Index: Acting Out, Delinquent in Casey Care	0.86								
31. Index: J.D.-Destructive Behavior in Casey Care	0.39					0.22	0.27		
32. Index: J.D.-School Expulsion Etc. in Casey Care	0.74								
33. Index: J.D.-Acting Out Behavior in Casey Care	0.64						-0.23		
34. Index: J.D.-Sociopathic, Lying & Stealing in Casey	0.68								
35. Index: Drug Involvement in Casey Care	0.46					0.23			
39. Index: School Performance in Casey Care	0.35					-0.25			-0.28
48. Index: Condition & Adjustment of Child at Exit	0.34				-0.61				
Factor 2 Variables:									
2. Age 1st separated from parents		-0.82	-0.22			0.33			
3. Years in non-Casey living arrangements		0.91				0.23			
4. % of pre-Casey time away from both parents		0.93							
6. First separation from both parents		-0.44							
8. Total living arrngmts away from parents pre-Casey		0.31	0.88						
9. Number of adoption failures before Casey		0.50							
38. Index: Family Attachment While in Casey Care		-0.26						-0.74	-0.48
47. Total years out of home at exit from Casey care		0.86			-0.26	-0.22			
Factor 3 Variables:									
7. Number returns to parents pre-Casey			0.52					-0.21	0.26
8. Total living arrngmts away from parents pre-Casey			0.88						
10. Child placed in gp ho/rtc/inst care before Casey		0.31	0.33						
21. Index: Hostile-Negativ., Maladjusted Personality			-0.28		-0.28				
26. Living arrangement # of first Casey placement			0.95						

Factor loading table (continued). Values shown in square brackets are enclosed in boxes in the original.

#	Variable	Loadings
44.	Living arrangement # at exit from Casey care	0.23 [0.85]
45.	Total living arrangements away from both parent	[0.76]

Factor 4 Variables:

#	Variable	Loadings
15.	(Interaction) Sex of child X Sexual molestation	[-0.90] -0.23
17.	(Interaction) Sex X sexual molestation X phys. abuse	[-0.90] -0.22
18.	(Interaction) Sexual molestation X physical abuse	[-0.75] 0.37
19.	A. Sexual molestation?	[-0.69] 0.50

Factor 5 Variables:

#	Variable	Loadings
21.	Index: Hostile-Negativ., Maladjusted Personality	0.22 -0.28 [-0.28]
29.	Index: Adaptation to Casey Foster Care	[-0.40]
46.	Years in Casey placements	0.21 [-0.40] -0.69
47.	Total years out of home at exit from Casey care	0.86 [-0.26] -0.22
48.	Index: Condition & Adjustment of Child at Exit	0.34 [-0.61]
49.	Casey exit (1 = emancip, 2 = parents, 3 = runaway or court)	[0.94]
50.	Casey exit: Return to court or referral agency	[0.90]

Factor 6 Variables:

#	Variable	Loadings
1.	Age at 1st Casey placement	-0.82 [0.86]
2.	Age 1st separated from parents	-0.22 [0.33]
12.	Foster home came with child as "package" arrngmt	[0.37]
35.	Index: Drug Involvement in Casey Care	0.46 [-0.25] -0.28
36.	Index: Wetters and Soilers in Casey Care	[0.56]
46.	Years in Casey placements	0.21 -0.40 [-0.69]

Factor 7 Variables:

#	Variable	Loadings
14.	Sex: 1 = male; 0 = female	[-0.87]
16.	(Interaction) Sex of child X physical abuse	[-0.50]
18.	(Interaction) Sexual molestation X physical abuse	-0.75 [0.37]
19.	A. Sexual molestation?	-0.69 [0.50]
31.	Index: J.D.-Destructive Behavior in Casey Care	0.39 0.22 [0.27]

TABLE 8.2 (Continued)

	Factors								
	1	2	3	4	5	6	7	8	9
Factor 8 Variables:									
25. Index: Child in Conflictual Situation w. Family								0.34	0.21
38. Index: Family Attachment While in Casey Care		−0.26						−0.74	
41. Mothers role in childs life while in Casey care								−0.78	
42. Fathers role in childs life while in Casey care								−0.68	
Factor 9 Variables:									
5. % of pre-Casey out-of-home time in foster care			0.21						0.31
7. Number returns to parents pre-Casey			0.52						0.26
9. Number of adoption failures before Casey		0.50							−0.48
13. Ethnicity: 1 = white; 0 = non-white		−0.24						−0.21	−0.74
35. Index: Drug Involvement in Casey Care	0.46								−0.28
Factor 10 Variables:									
5. % of pre-Casey out-of-home time in foster care						−0.25			0.31
24. Index: Child with Developmental Disability			0.21						
39. Index: School Peformance in Casey Care	0.35								
Factor 11 Variables:									
28. #Non-Casey gp/inst care between Casey placements							−0.23		
33. Index: J.D.-Acting Out Behavior in Casey Care	0.64								
40. Index: Psychiatric or Psychological Evaluation	0.20					0.21			
43. Total number of placements while in Casey care	−0.20								
44. Living arrangement # at exit from Casey care			0.85						
45. Total living arrangements away from both parents		0.23	0.76						
Factor 12 Variables:									
5. % of pre-Casey out-of-home time in foster care									0.31
10. Child placed in gp ho/rtc/inst care before Casey			0.21						
11. Child placed in correctional inst care pre-Casey			0.33						
12. Foster home came with child as "package" arrngmt						0.37			
22. Index: History of Juvenile Delinquency	0.30					−0.22			

Factor 13 Variables:

Variable								
16. (Interaction) Sex of child X physical abuse						-0.50		
18. (Interaction) Sexual molestation X physical abuse						0.37		
20. B.Physical abuse?			-0.75					

Factor 14 Variables:

Variable								
6. First separation from both parents		-0.44						-0.22
23. Index: Child with Mental Illness in Background	0.46							
35. Index: Drug Involvement in Casey Care					-0.25			-0.28
42. Fathers role in childs life while in Casey care							-0.68	

Factor 15 Variables:

Variable								
5. % of pre-Casey out-of-home time in foster care								0.31
12. Foster home came with child as "package" arrngmt			0.21		0.37			
21. Index: Hostile-Negativ., Maladjusted Personality		-0.28		-0.28				
29. Index: Adaptation to Casey Foster Care	0.22			-0.40	0.22			
31. Index: J.D.-Destructive Behavior in Casey Care	0.39					0.27		
37. Moody or depressed				-0.61				
48. Index: Condition & Adjustment of Child at Exit	0.34							

Factor 16 Variables:

Variable								
5. % of pre-Casey out-of-home time in foster care			0.21					0.31
12. Foster home came with child as "package" arrngmt					0.37			
27. Non-Casey gp/inst care purchased by Casey								
31. Index: J.D.-Destructive Behavior in Casey Care	0.39				0.22	0.27		

Factor 17 Variables:

Variable								
25. Index: Child in Conflictual Situation w. Family						0.34		
40. Index: Psychiatric or Psychological Evaluation	0.20		0.21		0.21			
48. Index: Condition & Adjustment of Child at Exit	0.34			-0.61				

Factor Summary:

	Total								
Unshared Factor Loadings	23	3	2	2	2	2	1	1	1
Shared Factor Loadings	27	6	6	2	5	4	4	3	4
Highest Factor Loadings	50	6	5	4	3	3	1	3	1

Table 8.2 (*Continued*)

					Factors			
	10	*11*	*12*	*13*	*14*	*15*	*16*	*17*

Factor 1 Variables:

	10	11	12	13	14	15	16	17
22. Index: History of Juvenile Delinquency			0.37					
30. Index: Acting Out, Delinquent in Casey Care				0.23				
31. Index: J.D.-Destructive Behavior in Casey Care						-0.25	-0.20	
32. Index: J.D.-School Expulsion Etc. in Casey Care						-0.38	-0.37	
33. Index: J.D.-Acting Out Behavior in Casey Care		0.36						
34. Index: J.D.-Sociopathic, Lying & Stealing in Casey						-0.24	-0.23	
35. Index: Drug Involvement in Casey Care					0.33			
39. Index: School Performance in Casey Care	-0.68					-0.26		
48. Index: Condition & Adjustment of Child at Exit								-0.25

Factor 2 Variables:

	10	11	12	13	14	15	16	17
2. Age 1st separated from parents								
3. Years in non-Casey living arrangements								
4. % of pre-Casey time away from both parents								
6. First separation from both parents								
8. Total living arrngmts away from parents pre-Casey					-0.64			
9. Number of adoption failures before Casey								
38. Index: Family Attachment While in Casey Care								
47. Total years out of home at exit from Casey care								

Factor 3 Variables:

	10	11	12	13	14	15	16	17
7. Number returns to parents pre-Casey					0.24			
8. Total living arrngmts away from parents pre-Casey								
10. Child placed in gp ho/rtc/inst care before Casey			-0.75					
21. Index: Hostile-Negativ., Maladjusted Personality				0.24		-0.52		
26. Living arrangement # of first Casey placement								
44. Living arrangement # at exit from Casey care		-0.43						
45. Total living arrangements away from both parents		-0.51						

Factor 4 Variables:

Variable						
15. (Interaction) Sex of child X Sexual molestation						
17. (Interaction) Sex X sexual molestation X phys. abuse						
18. (Interaction) Sexual molestation X physical abuse						
19. A. Sexual molestation?		-0.29				

Factor 5 Variables:

Variable						
21. Index: Hostile-Negativ., Maladjusted Personality		0.24		-0.52		
29. Index: Adaptation to Casey Foster Care				-0.65		
46. Years in Casey placements				-0.24		
47. Total years out of home at exit from Casey care						
48. Index: Condition & Adjustment of Child at Exit		-0.26		-0.26		
49. Casey exit (1 = emancip, 2 = parents, 3 = runaway or court)						-0.25
50. Casey exit: Return to court or referral agency						

Factor 6 Variables:

Variable						
1. Age at 1st Casey placement		0.26				
2. Age 1st separated from parents			0.33			
12. Foster home came with child as "package" arrngmt	0.20			-0.37	0.27	0.21
35. Index: Drug Involvement in Casey Care						
36. Index: Wetters and Soilers in Casey Care	-0.23			-0.24		
46. Years in Casey placements						

Factor 7 Variables:

Variable						
14. Sex: 1 = male; 0 = female						
16. (Interaction) Sex of child X physical abuse		-0.75				
18. (Interaction) Sexual molestation X physical abuse		-0.29				
19. A. Sexual molestation?						
31. Index: J.D.-Destructive Behavior in Casey Care			-0.37	-0.38		

Factor 8 Variables:

Variable						
25. Index: Child in Conflictual Situation w. Family						
38. Index: Family Attachment While in Casey Care			-0.37			-0.55
41. Mothers role in childs life while in Casey care		-0.31				
42. Fathers role in childs life while in Casey care	0.22					

TABLE 8.2 (Continued)

				Factors				
	10	11	12	13	14	15	16	17
Factor 9 Variables:								
5. % of pre-Casey out-of-home time in foster care	0.28		0.35		0.25	-0.29	0.32	
7. Number returns to parents pre-Casey					0.24			
9. Number of adoption failures before Casey								
13. Ethnicity: 1 = white; 0 = non-white					0.33			
35. Index: Drug Involvement in Casey Care								
Factor 10 Variables:								
5. % of pre-Casey out-of-home time in foster care	0.28		0.35		0.25	-0.29	0.32	
24. Index: Child with Developmental Disability	-0.73							
39. Index: School Peformance in Casey Care	-0.68							
Factor 11 Variables:								
28. #Non-Casey gp/inst care between Casey placements		-0.80						
33. Index: J.D.-Acting Out Behavior in Casey Care		0.36						
40. Index: Psychiatric or Psychological Evaluation		0.26						
43. Total number of placements while in Casey care		-0.84				-0.22		-0.65
44. Living arrangement # at exit from Casey care		-0.43						
45. Total living arrangements away from both parents		-0.51						
Factor 12 Variables:								
5. % of pre-Casey out-of-home time in foster care	0.28		0.35		0.25	-0.29	0.32	
10. Child placed in gp ho/rtc/inst care before Casey			-0.75					
11. Child placed in correctional inst care pre-Casey			-0.81					
12. Foster home came with child as "package" arrngmt	0.20		0.26			-0.37	0.27	
22. Index: History of Juvenile Delinquency			0.37	0.23				0.21
Factor 13 Variables:								
16. (Interaction) Sex of child X physical abuse				-0.75				
18. (Interaction) Sexual molestation X physical abuse				-0.29				
20. B.Physical abuse?				-0.92				

Factor 14 Variables:

Variable			
6. First separation from both parents		−0.64	
23. Index: Child with Mental Illness in Background	0.24	0.51	−0.21
35. Index: Drug Involvement in Casey Care		0.33	
42. Fathers role in childs life while in Casey care		−0.31	0.22

Factor 15 Variables:

Variable				
5. % of pre-Casey out-of-home time in foster care	0.35	0.25	−0.29	0.32
12. Foster home came with child as "package" arrngmt	0.26		−0.37	0.27 0.21
21. Index: Hostile-Negativ., Maladjusted Personality	0.24		−0.52	
29. Index: Adaptation to Casey Foster Care			−0.65	
31. Index: J.D.-Destructive Behavior in Casey Care			−0.38	−0.37
37. Moody or depressed			−0.66	
48. Index: Condition & Adjustment of Child at Exit			−0.26	−0.25

Factor 16 Variables:

Variable				
5. % of pre-Casey out-of-home time in foster care	0.28	0.25	−0.29	0.32
12. Foster home came with child as "package" arrngmt	0.20		−0.37	0.27
27. Non-Casey gp/inst care purchased by Casey	−0.23	0.26		0.73
31. Index: J.D.-Destructive Behavior in Casey Care			−0.38	−0.37

Factor 17 Variables:

Variable		
25. Index: Child in Conflictual Situation w. Family	0.26	−0.55
40. Index: Psychiatric or Psychological Evaluation	−0.22	−0.65
48. Index: Condition & Adjustment of Child at Exit	−0.26	−0.25

Factor Summary:

									Total
Unshared Factor Loadings	1	1	2	1	1	1	1	0	23
Shared Factor Loadings	2	4	4	2	3	6	3	3	27
Highest Factor Loadings	2	4	2	2	2	4	1	2	50

(especially the physical abuse of a boy) enter the factor. In its largest form, measures of turbulence in living arrangements are associated with delinquent behavior while in care.

The physical abuse of a child (.28), especially the physical abuse of a boy (an additional .32 for boys for a total loading of .60 for boys), is associated with a greater degree of delinquency while in Casey care. In addition, a child who was hostile and negative at entry (.55) was more extensively associated with delinquent behavior while in care. A child who had a history of delinquent behavior (.43) was more involved in delinquent behavior while in care.

The basic grouping of delinquent behaviors reported above continued to hold. In addition, the extent of psychopathic behavior, i.e., lying and stealing while in Casey care (.57) and the extent of depression while in care (.37), were associated with a greater degree of delinquent behavior in Casey care. These in turn were associated with poorer condition at exit from care (.67), emancipation status: return to family (.42), and leaving Casey to enter group care (.44).

Factor 2: Percentage of Pre-Casey Time Away from Both Parents and Degree of Attachment to Family

The second eigenvalue is also large, 5.24, indicating another obvious pattern. The variable with the largest loading in the 17–factor solution was the percentage of the child's time before entry into Casey care that the child spent away from both natural parents (.93) with the variable years in non-Casey program living arrangements having a loading nearly as large (.91). Many of the associations suggested in this factor are logically necessary.

These structural relations indicate that a child who was older when first separated from both natural parents (.82) spent on average a lesser percentage of pre-Casey time away from both parents, that a child who had more living arrangements before the first separation from both parents (.44) spent on average a lesser percentage of pre-Casey time away from both parents, and that a child who spent more years in non-Casey living arrangements spent a greater percentage of pre-Casey time away from both parents. There were additional structural relations with the other major variable in the factor.

A slightly more interesting association was that a child who had more adoption disruptions (.50) spent more years in non-Casey living arrangements and a greater percentage of pre-Casey time away from both parents. A child who spent a greater percentage of pre-Casey time away from both parents had a lesser attachment to the natural family (.26), a marginal association. None of these associations are surprising, and none of these variables appear in more than one other factor.

When we reduce the number of factors included in our solution, the nature of this factor changes very little. The second factor of the two-factor solution is essentially the same as reported above. As the number of factors in the solution is reduced, some possible linkages become apparent. The ethnicity variable is marginally related to this factor, with the nature of the association being that minority children spend more time in foster care once they have entered the system. The association is, however, weak.

There was a thread of associations that was first pulled off when the eight-factor solution was used. A child who was older when first separated from both natural parents was more involved in a conflictual relationship with the family, was more attached to the family, and had a mother who assumed a greater role in the child's life while the child was in Casey care.

A less substantive association was pulled off in the five-factor solution. A child who was older when first separated from both parents spent a smaller percentage of pre-Casey placement in foster homes, was less involved in bed wetting and soiling, and spent fewer years in Casey care. These relationships can be deduced a priori.

The history of juvenile delinquency index was marginally associated with this variable. A child who was older when first separated from both parents tended to have a greater extent of prior involvement in juvenile delinquency. A child who was older when first separated from both parents was more likely to be returned to parents. These associations were split from this factor early on (in the four-factor solution) and are not a strong part of this picture.

Although this factor is largely structural, it has some interesting aspects in associations that are pulled off when a larger number of factors is used. A child who was older when first separated from both parents was more attached to the natural family, more involved in conflictual relationships with the family, and more likely to be returned to the natural family. There are aspects of this factor that support the conventional approach of working to reunify a child with the natural family even when there is considerable discord as long as there is a family available for the child.

Factor 3: Living Arrangement Number of First Casey Placement.

The third eigenvalue is 3.41, indicating a fairly strong factor. The largest loading was with the number of living arrangements prior to the first Casey placement (0.95). A child who had a large number of living arrangements before first placement in Casey care had a large number of returns to the natural parents and a large number of total living arrangements away from both parents. Such a child tended to have had at least one group care placement before the first Casey placement and tended to be more hostile and negativistic when first placed in Casey care. Of course, such a child would have more living arrangements enumerated when leaving Casey care and more total living arrangements away from both parents.

As the number of factors is reduced, this factor preserves its essential structure up to and including the three-factor solution. When the number of factors is reduced to two, this factor is largely combined with the second factor. Some of the interesting aspects are that as the number of factors is reduced, this factor picks up a positive association between the number of living arrangements for the child before entry and the indicator whether a child was placed in a correctional institution before entry, the age at which the child was first separated from both parents, the number of adoption disruptions before entry, and the age of the child at entry. These associations may strike the reader as quite obvious

A child who experienced more living arrangements prior to entry went on to experience a greater number of Casey placements, suggesting that the Casey program also had trouble finding a stable living arrangement for the child.

When the number of factors is reduced to three, a more interesting structure emerges. A child who had a greater number of living arrangements before entry into Casey care tended to have a greater extent of earlier history of mental disturbance at entry, greater extent of a conflictual relationship with parents, greater likelihood of having been physically abused, greater likelihood of having been exposed to a disturbing sexual event, and was in poorer condition at exit.

Factor 4: Abuse of Boys

The fourth eigenvalue is 2.99, indicating a strong but not overwhelming factor. In the 17–factor solution, this factor concentrated on the boy's having been exposed to a disturbing sexual event before entry ($-.90$). A boy who had been exposed to a disturbing sexual event was also likely to have been physically abused as well. Put another way, a child who was physically abused and who had been exposed to a disturbing sexual event was more likely a boy. We first discussed these associations in chapter 3. This pattern of associations was remarkably stable and first appears in the four-factor solution as the fourth factor and is the fourth factor in all solutions with a greater number of factors. When the number of factors is reduced to three, this pattern of association largely links up with the factor dealing with the number of living arrangements that the child experienced prior to entry. When the number of factors is reduced to two, this pattern links up with the violence factor.

Factor 5: Return of Children to Families

The fifth eigenvalue is 2.65, again indicating a strong but not overwhelming factor. The largest loadings are with variables indicating whether the child was returned to the natural family (.93) or whether the child was emancipated to group care (.90). The core structure of associations was that a child who was hostile and negativistic at entry tended to adapt poorly to Casey care. Such a child spent fewer years in Casey care and was in poorer condition at exit. The end result association was that such a child was more likely to leave the Casey program to be returned to the family or to be placed in a non-Casey group care setting, most often because the child could not be well served in foster family care.

The nature of this factor is not sensitive to the solution used. As the number of factors in the solution is reduced, the factor picks up an association with delinquent behavior and mode of exit from Casey. A child who engaged in destructive juvenile delinquent behavior was more likely to be returned to family or wind up in residential care via a return to the court that referred the child. Further reduction in the number of factors in the solution confirms this pattern by picking up associations with the other delinquency indices.

A child in a package placement was less likely to be returned to family or residential care. Further reduction finds the association with the percentage of pre-Casey out-of-home time in foster care negatively associated with return to family or discharge to residential care.

Children who were physically abused and physically abused boys more than physically abused girls were more likely to be returned home or to be discharged to residential care. This could reflect rehabilitation of the abusing parent or the violent behavior patterns of physically abused boys.

In sum, the fifth factor picks up some interesting patterns. It focuses on the mode of exit from Casey care. The core pattern is that a child who was hostile and poorly adapted at entry was less likely to be emancipated and more likely to be returned to family or discharged to residential care. In particular, the factor concentrates on juvenile delinquent behavior while in Casey care as the core issue in determining whether the child was returned home or discharged to residential care. Abused children seem more likely to be returned home. The data do not contain information to resolve whether any rehabilitative efforts of the parents have been successful. The factor suggests that some of the success of the Casey program in achieving emancipation is capitalization on successful placements arranged by another agency and labeled here as a package placement.

Factor 6: Age of Child When Entering Care

The sixth eigenvalue is 2.23, indicating a moderately strong pattern. In each solution with six or more factors (up to and including the seventeen factor solution), the age of the child at entry had the largest loading. As the number of factors in the solution increased, the nature of the factor changed somewhat.

The age of the child at entry was part of the second factor discussed above that centered largely on technical associations with the child's age and length of time in Casey care. In the six factor solution, the age of the child at entry was separated as a clearly important subtheme and remained so for all more complex solutions. In the six-factor solution, this factor included some interesting subthemes. A child who was older at first Casey placement also tended to be older when first separated from both parents. Boys tended to be younger at entry and younger when separated from both parents. The variable indicating whether a child was a physically abused boy also appeared in this factor for this solution. A child who was older at entry and who was older when first separated from both parents was more likely to have been exposed to a disturbing sexual event. A girl was more likely to have been exposed to a disturbing sexual event. A child who had been exposed to a disturbing sexual event was less involved in destructive delinquent behavior but more involved in drugs. A boy who was physically abused was more involved in destructive delinquent behavior while in Casey care and was less involved in drugs while in Casey care. Finally, there were the a priori associations that a child who was older at entry spent fewer total years in Casey care, whereas a child who was older when first separated from both parents spent fewer total years out of the home.

We were surprised that the factor selected out that boys who were physically abused were younger when first separated from both parents and younger when they were first placed in the Casey care. Such boys were more often wetters and soilers than other children were. These findings are counterintuitive and contrary to the results of the other analyses. We do not have an explanation for the result.

The nature of the factor changed with a seven-factor solution. The sex of the child, the variable indicating whether a boy was physically abused, and the variable indicating whether a child had been exposed to a disturbing sexual event were separated out into the seventh factor. There was a substitution of history of juvenile delinquency before entry for delinquent behavior while in Casey care. The variable percentage of pre-Casey time in foster care and the variable indicating whether a child had been placed in a correctional facility entered the factor.

As the number of factors in the solution increased, two groups of variables were alternately included in the factor. One was centered on a history of juvenile delinquency before entry and included the variable indicating whether the child had been placed in a correctional facility. The other group centered on the variable indicating whether the child was in a package placement and included the variables destructive delinquent behavior while in Casey care and the extent of psychopathic lying.

Factor 7: A Focus on Boys in Care

The seventh eigenvalue is 1.72, indicating only a moderately strong factor. This factor has appeared earlier, particularly in factor 6 of the six-factor solution. It was split off essentially from this factor. As the seventh factor in the seven-factor solution, the largest loadings of this factor were on the variable indicating whether a boy was physically abused and on the variable indicating the sex of the child. In later solutions, the dominant loading was on the variable indicating the sex of the child. A boy was less likely to have been exposed to a disturbing sexual event before entry than a girl. A boy was more likely to have been physically abused than a girl. The physical abuse of a child was associated with a greater history of juvenile delinquency, and a greater extent of delinquent destructive behavior while in Casey care. There was a much stronger association between a boy's being physically abused and the boy's having had a history of juvenile delinquency and the boy's engaging in destructive delinquent behavior while in Casey care.

The variables describing history of delinquent behavior and destructive delinquent behavior while in Casey care were stripped off this factor when the number of factors was 10 or greater. When the number of factors was 13, the factor reduced to the variables describing the sex of a child and the abuse and molestation variables. When the number of factors in the solution was 16 or 17, the variable describing destructive delinquent behavior while in Casey care again was included in the factor with a marginal loading.

Factor 8: The Family as a Factor in the Child's Life

The eighth eigenvalue is 1.57, indicating only a moderately strong factor. The nature of this factor was essentially stable and unaffected by the number of factors in the solution once there were eight or more factors used. This factor gathers together threads from the two basic factors in the study results. In the eight-factor solution, the largest loadings are with the variables describing the extent of the mother's role while the child was in Casey care and the extent of attachment that the child had to the natural family. As would be expected, a child whose mother had a larger role in the child's life while in Casey care had a stronger attachment, on average, to the natural family. A child who had a stronger attachment to the family was returned to the parents more times before the first Casey placement. A child who had a greater attachment to the parents was more extensively involved in conflictual situations with the parents. A child whose mother had a greater role in the child's life while the child was in Casey care tended to have a father who was more involved with the child while the child was in Casey care. A child who had a greater attachment to the natural family spent fewer total years out of the home.

As the number of factors in the solution increased, the variables included in this factor were somewhat reduced, but there always remained a core of variables: number of returns to parents before entry, the extent of involvement in conflictual situations, the attachment of the child to the family, and the role of the mother and father in the child's life while in Casey care.

*Factor 9: Ethnicity and Percentage of Pre-Casey Time Spent in
Foster Boarding Home Care*

The ninth eigenvalue is 1.50, indicating only a moderately strong
factor. The structure of this factor is one that is somewhat sensitive to
the number of factors in the solution used. When it first appears, the
percentage of pre-Casey time spent in foster care had the largest
loading (.64). A large percentage of pre-Casey time in foster care was
negatively associated with the number of disrupted adoptions experienced by the child, a rather natural association. A high percentage of
pre-Casey time spent in foster boarding home care was associated
with a greater probability of the child's being in package placement,
suggesting again that the placement that the Casey program made
permanent was really a relatively secure placement that had a long
history of working out well. A child with a greater percentage of pre-
Casey time in foster boarding home care was more likely to be a
minority child. A minority child was more likely to have been in a
package placement. A child with a greater percentage of pre-Casey
time in foster boarding home care was less hostile and negativistic at
entry and was less involved in conflictual situations with the parents.
A child with a greater percentage of pre-Casey time in foster boarding
home care tended to have a better adaptation to foster care and
tended to be less moody and depressed. Children with disrupted adoptions tended to adapt less well and to be more moody and depressed.

When the number of factors in the solution reached 13, there was a
split of this factor. The percentage of time in foster boarding home
care before entry was no longer the variable with the largest loading
in factor 9 of this solution, but its loading was relatively large (.43).
The loading of this variable was large in factor 12 and factor 13. These
two factors contained many of the associations discussed above.

The reduced factor 9 (in the 13-factor solution) had its largest
loadings for the variables number of disrupted adoptions and ethnicity. A white child in this population was more likely to have a disrupted adoption than a minority child, possibly reflecting that minority children are less likely to be adopted in the first place and hence
at less risk of a disrupted adoption. The factor also included the
variables indicating whether the child was in a package placement,
the number of times the child was returned to the parents before
entry, and the percentage of pre-Casey time spent in foster boarding
home care.

When the number of factors in the solution was increased to 14, the
percentage of time in foster boarding home care before entry again

had a relatively large loading on three distinct factors. Two of these (12 and 14) we discuss later For factor 9, the variables representing measures of the extent of hostile negativistic behavior, extent of a child's background of mental illness, and involvement with drugs while in Casey care were also included in the factor with marginal loadings.

The nature of this factor in the 15-factor solution was interesting in its own right. Both the percentage of pre-Casey time spent in foster boarding home care and the variable indicating whether the placement was a package placement home had large loadings, but the largest loading was on the variable adaptation to foster care. The extent of destructive delinquent behavior, the extent of moodiness or depression, and the condition of the child at exit were in this factor reflecting the structure that was apparent when the factor first appeared.

When the number of factors was increased to 16, the nature of the factor changed. Again, factors were split off from the original sequence Four other factors had relatively large loadings for the variable percentage of pre-Casey time spent in foster boarding home care. The ninth factor consisted of the associations between percentage of pre-Casey time in foster boarding home care, the number of returns to the parents before entry, the number of adoption disruptions, the ethnicity of the child, and the extent of the child's involvement in drugs. The direction of the associations remained constant. The largest loading was with the ethnicity of the child.

Factor 10: Developmental Disability

The tenth and subsequent eigenvalues are less than 1.5. We continue our interpretation into regions beyond that used by most analysts because of the continuing value of the associations suggested. The core of this factor is the developmental disability measure derived from the intake section of the case record. When the number of factors in the solution is 13 or more, this factor consists of the developmental disability and school performance measures. A child who was developmentally disabled on average did not do as well in school. A less important variable is the percentage of time prior to entry that the child spent in foster boarding home care. A developmentally disabled child spent a greater percentage of pre-Casey time in foster boarding home care on average.

This factor was largely split off from the ninth factor discussed above. When it first appeared, the variables with the largest loadings were the variable indicating whether the child had been placed in a congregate care setting, whether the child had been placed in a correctional facility, the extent to which the child had a history of juvenile delinquent behavior, and the extent of the child's developmental disabilities. Children placed in group care or in a correctional facility tended to have a greater extent of involvement in delinquent behavior. They tended to be more involved in school related delinquency while in Casey care and in psychopathic behaviors such as lying and stealing while in Casey care.

When the number of factors in the solution was increased to 12, the nature of the factor changed slightly. The largest loadings were on the measure of developmental disability and school performance, but there were notable loadings on whether the child was physically abused, the extent to which the child was hostile and negativistic at entry, the measure of the mental illness of the child, the child's adaptation to foster care, and the extent of moodiness or depression in the child. A child who was developmentally disabled was more hostile and negativistic at entry on average and was more moody and depressed. A child who was physically abused tended to be more moody and depressed and tended to adapt more poorly to foster care while in Casey care.

Increasing the number of factors in the solution led to the core set described above. The other relations are highlighted in factor 13 of the 13–factor solution.

Factor 11: Number of Non-Casey Group Care Placements and Total Number of Placements While in Casey Care

This factor is exceptionally stable, and its associations are ones that would be expected to occur a priori. It was split off from the first factor, the one that essentially dealt with aspects of violent behavior in the child. Factor 11 in the 13–factor solution is the most interesting of this group. The largest loading is on the total number of placements while in Casey care, and a somewhat smaller loading holds for the number of non-Casey group care placements purchased by the Casey program.

A child who had experienced more Casey placements had on average more non-Casey group care placements purchased. A child with more Casey placements was engaging in a greater extent of sexual acting-out behavior while in Casey care and was more likely to be exposed to psychiatric or psychological evaluation while in Casey care. A child with more Casey placements has had a greater number of living arrangements upon finally leaving the Casey program and had a greater total number of living arrangements away from both parents.

These associations are relatively obvious, and many hold by definition. As the number of factors in the solution is increased to 17, the variable indicating whether the child had been in a non-Casey group placement purchased by Casey is stripped from this factor and merged with factor 16, in which it has the largest loading.

Factor 12: Whether the Child Had a Youth Correctional Placement Before Entry

This factor was pulled from factor 10 discussed above and essentially maintains its identity for all solutions with 12 or more factors. In the 12–factor solution, the largest loading is on the variable indicating whether a child had been placed in a correctional institution ($-.75$) with a large loading on whether the child had been placed in group care prior to entry ($-.67$). A child who had been placed in a correctional facility or in a group care placement prior to entry had spent less time before entry in foster boarding home placements and was less likely to be in a package placement. A child who had been in a correctional facility or in a group care placement had a greater history of involvement in delinquent behavior before entry and tended to have a greater degree of mental illness. A minority child was somewhat more likely to have been placed in a correctional facility or in a group care placement than a white child.

Factor 13: Physical Abuse

The core of this factor appeared when the number of solutions was 16 or 17. The largest loading was on whether the child was physically abused ($-.92$). A child who was physically abused was more likely to be a boy, and a child who was physically abused was more likely to be both physically abused and to have been exposed to a disturbing sexual event.

When the number of factors in the solution is reduced to 15, more interesting associations appear. A child who was physically abused before entry was more hostile and negativistic at entry than a child who was not abused. A child who was physically abused was involved in a conflictual relation with the parents to a greater degree than a child who was not abused.

When the number of factors in the solution is reduced to 13, the factor changes its nature somewhat. Although the loading on the variable indicating whether the child was physically abused is large (−.36), the largest loading is on the child's measure of depression while in Casey care (.58). When the number of factors in the solution goes to 14, the depression associations go largely into factor 14. Consequently, here we discuss only the associations with the physical abuse of the child. A child who was physically abused spent, on average, a lesser percentage of pre-Casey time in foster boarding home placements, was more likely a boy, was more hostile and negativistic at entry , had a greater degree of mental illness, was more poorly adapted to foster care, was more moody and depressed, was more apt to be exposed to evaluation by a psychiatrist or psychologist while in Casey care, and was in poorer condition at exit.

Factor 14: Children with Mental Illness in Backgrounds

This factor was split off from factor 13 discussed above. The core of this factor is the association between the number of living arrangements that the child experienced prior to separation from both parents (with a loading of −.58 in the 16–factor solution) and the extent to which a child experienced problems indicative of mental illness prior to entry (.39).

A child who experienced a greater number of living arrangements prior to first separation from both parents showed a greater likelihood of problems associated with mental illness prior to entry. A child with a greater number of living arrangements prior to the first separation from both parents would naturally spend a lesser percentage of pre-Casey time in foster boarding home placements. A child with a greater number of living arrangements prior to the first separation from both parents was involved in a more conflictual relation with the parents, was more involved with drugs while in Casey care, and was more likely to require evaluation by psychologists and psychiatrists while in Casey care. A child who spent more time in foster boarding home care tended to be one less likely to have a pre-Casey history of mental illness, less involved in conflictual relations with parents before entry, and less involved in drugs while in Casey care.

The fourteenth factor in the 14-factor solution presented a richer picture of associations. The largest loading was on the depression variable while the number of living arrangements that the child experienced prior to first separation from both parents had only a moderate loading (−.29). The child's history of mental illness was less strongly evident than in the other solutions discussed here (.44).

In addition to the associations already discussed, a child who experienced a large number of living arrangements prior to the first separation from both parents was more hostile and negativistic at entry, was more poorly adapted to foster care, was more involved with drugs while in Casey care, was more moody and depressed, was more likely to be evaluated by a psychologist or psychiatrist, and was in poorer condition at exit. Parallel associations hold for the other variables in the factor.

Factor 15: The Well-Adapted Child

This factor remains essentially stable in solutions with 16 and 17 factors. Although the genealogy of this factor is not obvious, its nature is clear enough for discussion based on factor 15 in the 16–factor solution. The measure of the adaptation of the child to care while in Casey care has the largest loading ($-.65$). A child who spent a greater percentage of pre-Casey time in foster home placements was more likely to have been in a package placement. Such a child was less hostile and negativistic and better adapted to foster care. A child who was better adapted to foster care was less involved in acting-out behaviors while in Casey care, was less involved in destructive delinquent behavior, was less moody or depressed while in Casey care, and was in better condition at exit.

Factor 16: Non-Casey Group Care Purchased for Child

This factor appeared in the 9–factor solution and remained stable in both solutions that it could have appeared in. The variable indicating whether the child received non-Casey group care purchased by Casey had the largest loading (.73). A child who spent a greater percentage of pre-Casey time out of the home in foster boarding home care was more likely to receive non-Casey purchased group home care. A child with more pre-Casey time in foster boarding home placements was more likely to have been in a package placement. A child with non-Casey group care purchased by Casey was more involved in destructive delinquent behavior.

Factor 17: Children Receiving Psychiatric or Psychological Evaluation

We cannot judge the stability of this factor. The largest loading ($-.65$) was on the variable identifying the child's having received a psychiatric or psychological evaluation by professionals, an indication of the concern of staff about the child's adjustment. A child who was more involved in a conflictual situation with the biological parents was likely to be referred for psychiatric or psychological evaluation and tended to be in poorer condition at exit.

SUMMARY COMMENTS

An examination of the published research literature using exploratory factor analysis as a basic tool for data analysis almost always finds the authors presenting the results of a single solution. We have in this chapter departed from this practice and have discussed all the solutions produced by the computer, from the seventeen-factor solution to the two-factor solution. Our concern has been to avoid exploiting a single solution since such a choice might reflect a bias of the investigators. On the other hand, coping with all of the solutions presents the reader with an embarrassment of riches. It is not our expectation that the reader can retain in memory the plethora of associations discussed. Rather, it is our hope that some of the important associations will be retained.

Four major themes can be traced over the life spans of the subjects studied here: (1) a theme of deviance—early delinquent behavior prior to entry, continuity of such behavior in Casey care, and subsequent deviant behavior in the adult years; (2) a theme of conventional adjustment unrelated to deviant behavior describing the degree of oppositional behavior shown by the child at entry, quality of adaptation in Casey care, circumstances surrounding the exit from care, and the adjustment of the child at the time of departure; (3) structural patterns characterizing the placement histories of the children, i.e., when the child was first separated from parents, number of returns to parents, number of placements before entry; and (4) physical abuse of a boy associated with undesirable outcomes.

CHAPTER NINE

Into the Adult Years;
Further Exploratory Factor Analyses

This chapter is based on the results of the factor analysis including index scores from the follow-up interviews. We thus extend the time span covered by the analysis reported in chapter 8 by an additional seven years on average. This factor analysis combines the ratings and index scores obtained from the closed case reading study with the index scores describing the child as an adult. As in chapter 8, we organized the observed patterns as a sequence of solutions, each solution with an increasing number of factors included.

While we devote most of our attention to the eleven-factor solution, we were rather surprised, from a technical point of view, that we could extend the number of solutions even further to explore the intricacy of the factorial structure of our data and still find our data interpretable in most details. We have chosen the eleven-factor solution to display the major substantive findings while sparing the reader the task of sorting through an overly elaborated set of findings. We show the list of variables included in our analysis in table 9.1 and the varimax rotation results for the eleven-factor solution in table 9.2.

The "interpretability" requirement for a factor must be taken with due caution.[1] There is no intrinsic value to any of the factors: they represent theoretical construct variables postulated to exist so that a relatively simple relationship among them holds, calculated so that as few exist as are mathematically necessary to describe the variance covariance matrix observed and such that they reproduce the observed variance covariance matrix as accurately as possible. The

TABLE 9.1   Variables Included in the Factor Analysis of
Birth-to-Follow-up

Pre-Casey Variables:

1. Age of child at first Casey placement
2. Age first separated from parents
3. Years in non-Casey living arrangements
4. Percent of pre-Casey time away from both parents
5. Percent of pre-Casey out-of-home time spent in foster care
6. Placement number when first separated from both parents
7. Number of pre-Casey returns to parents after first separation
8. Total pre-Casey living arrangements away from both parents
9. Adoption disruptions before Casey
10. Child placed in group home, residential center, or institution pre-Casey
11. Child placed in institution for delinquent children pre-Casey
12. Prior foster home came to Casey with child (package placement)
13. Ethnicity (1 = white; 0 = minority)
14. Sex (1 = male; 0 = female)
15. Interaction of sex of child and indication of pre-Casey exposure to a disturbing sexual event
16. Interaction of sex of child and pre-Casey indication of physical abuse
17. Interaction of sex of child, indication of pre-Casey exposure to a disturbing sexual event and physical abuse
18. Interaction of indication of pre-Casey exposure to a disturbing sexual event and pre-Casey physical abuse
19. Indication of pre-Casey exposure to a disturbing sexual event
20. Indication of pre-Casey physical abuse

Variables 21–25: Index scores for children as seen at intake to Casey

21. I: Hostile-Negativistic Personality (7 items)
22. II: History of Juvenile Delinquency (6 items)
23. III: History of Mental Illness in Background (3 items)
24. IV: Child with Developmental Disability (3 items)
25. V: Child in Conflictual Situation with Parents (2 items)

Casey Variables:

26. Placement number of first Casey placement
27. Non-Casey care purchased by Casey
28. Number of non-Casey group/institutional placements between Casey placements
29. Challenge presented by child to foster parents at entry

30. Child at age-appropriate school grade level at entry into Casey care

Variables 31–42 Index scores for children reflecting Casey care experience

31. I: Adaptation to Foster Care (11 items)
32. II: Acting Out, Delinquents (12 items)
33. III: Juvenile Delinquent—Destructive (3 items)
34. IV: Juvenile Delinquent—Expelled from School (3 items)
35. V: Juvenile Delinquent—Acting Out (3 items)
36. VI: Juvenile Delinquent, Psychopathic—Lying and Stealing (3 items)
37. VII: Drug Involvement (3 items)
38. VIII: Wetters and Soilers (3 items)
39. IX: Moody or Depressed (2 items)
40. X: Family Attachment (3 items)
41. XI: School Performance (5 items)
42. Psychiatric or Psychological Evaluation (2 items)
43. Mother's role in child's life while child in Casey care
44. Father's role in child's life while child in Casey care

Exit Variables:

45. Total number of placements of child while in Casey care
46. Casey placement number at exit from Casey care
47. Total living arrrangements away from both parents at exit from Casey care
48. Years in Casey placements
49. Total years out of home at exit from Casey care
50. Index of Adjustment at Departure from Casey Care (2 items)
51. Emancipation status at exit from Casey care (1 = emancipated at 18, 2 = emancipated at less than 18, 3 = returned to family, 4 = remanded to court or public agency)
52. Exit from Casey destination: residential care

Follow-up Variables:

53. Time interval between exit from Casey care and follow-up interview

Variables 54 through 72: Index scores reflecting follow-up information

54. Index of Adequacy of Housing and Neighborhood (3 items)
55. Index of Adequacy of Finances (9 items)
56. Index of Job Stability and Satisfaction (4 items)
57. Index of Quality of Social Relationships (4 items)
58. Index of Family Building/Dependents (3 items)

59. Index of Employment Situation (3 items)
60. Index of Educational Achievement and Satisfaction (8 items)
61. Index of Physical Health Status (3 items)
62. Index of General Well-Being (37 items)
63. Index of Emotional Disturbance (6 items)
64. Index of Friendship Patterns (4 items)
65. Index of Drinking Problems (2 items)
66. Index of Substance Abuse Problems (9 items)
67. Index of Involvement in Crime-Related Activities (10 items)
68. Index of Involvement in Serious Crime/Armed Robbery (2 items)
69. Index of Attachment to Foster Family (4 items)
70. Index of Treatment by Foster Family (10 items)
71. Index of Relatedness of Social Worker (8 items)
72. Index of Caring of Social Worker (4 items)

number of subjects interviewed is relatively small, and there is not a contrasting group of less deprived children to compare the Casey subjects with. Consequently, there are genuine difficulties with putting our findings in the perspective of a more general theory.

RESULTS OF THE ELEVEN FACTOR SOLUTION

We have chosen to cite variables with a loading of .35 or greater in absolute value as a general guide although sometimes we cite variables with somewhat smaller loadings because of their substantive significance. Although in chapter 8 we cited variables with loadings of .25 or higher, here we use a larger loading because of the relatively smaller size of the follow-up group (N = 106).

Factor 1: Placement History Linked to Delinquent Behavior That Continues into Adulthood.

This factor gives evidence of the continuity of delinquent trends in a foster child's life. The largest eigenvalue is 9.97, indicating a very strong pattern in the data of the follow-up study. The nature of the factor was consistent through solutions with from two to twenty-four factors. It brings together information about the propensity of the child to become engaged in delinquent behavior while in Casey care and information about the placement career of the child.

On the positive side of the descriptive continuum, the highest loading is shown for the variable Index of Acting Out—Delinquent Behav-

TABLE 9.2 Varimax Factor Rotations Descriptive of Subjects from Birth to Follow-up: Eleven-Factor Solution (N = 106)

						Factor					
	1	2	3	4	5	6	7	8	9	10	11
Factor 1 Variables:											
27. Non-Casey gp/inst care purchased by Casey	−0.41						0.35				
28. #Non-Casey gp/inst care between Casey placements	−0.52										
29. Challenge to foster parents- first year	−0.37										−0.48
31. Index: Adaptation to Casey Foster Care	0.43										0.45
32. Index: Acting Out, Delinquent in Casey Care	0.83										
33. Index: J.D.-Destructive Behavior in Casey Care	0.69						0.33				
35. Index: J.D.-Acting Out Behavior in Casey Care	0.65						0.30				
36. Index: J.D.-Sociopathic, Lying & Stealing in Casey	0.69						0.31				
42. Index: Psychiatric or Psychological Evaluation	0.55										
45. Total number of placements while in Casey care	−0.81										
46. Living arrangement # at exit from Casey care	−0.61		0.71								
47. Total living arrangements away from both parents	−0.66		0.62								
50. Index: Condition & Adjustment of Child at Exit	0.47				−0.43				0.32		
60. FU Index: Educational Achievement & Satisfaction	0.36				−0.43						

Factor 2 Variables:

Variable						
2. Age 1st separated from parents		0.81	−0.32			
3. Years in non-Casey living arrangements		−0.87				
4. % of pre-Casey time away from both parents		−0.91				
6. First separation from both parents		0.41				
9. Number of adoption failures before Casey		−0.46				
24. Index: Child with Developmental Disability		0.35				−0.32
40. Index: Family Attachment While in Casey Care	−0.32	0.44				
43. Mothers role in childs life while in Casey care		0.40		0.35		
49. Total years out of home at exit from Casey care		−0.85				

Factor 3 Variables:

Variable						
7. Number returns to parents pre-Casey		0.37			−0.33	
8. Total living arrngmts away from parents pre-Casey		0.83				
10. Child placed in gp ho/rtc/inst care before Casey		0.48			−0.31	
26. Living arrangement # of first Casey placement		0.90				
46. Living arrangement # at exit from Casey care	−0.61	0.71				
47. Total living arrangements away from both parents	−0.66	0.62				

TABLE 9.2 (Continued)

	Factor										
	1	2	3	4	5	6	7	8	9	10	11
Factor 4 Variables:											
1. Age at 1st Casey placement				-0.84							
37. Index: Drug Involvement in Casey Care				0.44							
38. Index: Wetters and Soilers in Casey Care				-0.65							
48. Years in Casey placements				0.78							
64. FU Index: Friendship Patterns				0.41							-0.39
Factor 5 Variables:											
50. Index: Condition & Adjustment of Child at Exit	0.47				-0.43						
54. FU Index: Adequacy of Housing and Neighborhood	0.34				-0.56				0.32		
55. FU Index: Adequacy of Finances					-0.77						
57. FU Index: Quality of Social Relationships					-0.52						
60. FU Index: Educational Achievement & Satisfaction	0.36				-0.43						
61. FU Index: Physical Health Status					-0.59						
62. FU Index: General Well-Being					-0.79						
Factor 6 Variables:											
5. % of pre-Casey out-of-home time in foster care						0.42					
15. (Interaction) Sex of child X sexual molestation						0.59					
17. (Interaction) Sex X sexual molestation X phys. abuse						0.71					
18. (Interaction) Sexual molestation X physical abuse						0.67					
19. A. Sexual molestation?		0.30				0.59	0.35				

Factor 7 Variables:

#	Variable						
14.	Sex: 1 = male; 0 = female				-0.72		
16.	(Interaction) Sex of child X physical abuse				-0.70		0.36
19.	A. Sexual molestation?				0.35	0.59	
20.	B. Physical abuse?				-0.43		0.34
23.	Index: Child with Mental Illness in Background				-0.35		
27.	Non-Casey gp/inst care purchased by Casey	-0.41			0.35		
34.	Index: J.D.-School Expulsion Etc. in Casey Care	0.30			0.49		
65.	FU Index: Drinking Problems		-0.33		0.47		
66.	FU Index: Substance Abuse Problems				0.36		
67.	FU Index: Involved in Crime-Related Activities	0.34			0.62		

Factor 8 Variables:

#	Variable						
43.	Mothers role in childs life while in Casey care			0.40	0.35		
53.	Time at follow-up since left Casey care				-0.57		
58.	FU Index: Family Building/Dependents				0.46		
69.	FU Index: Attachment to Foster Family				0.55	-0.35	
70.	FU Index: Treatment by Foster Family				0.48	-0.33	
71.	FU Index: Relatedness of Social Worker				0.52		
72.	FU Index: Caring of Social Worker				0.52		-0.34

$$\text{TABLE 9.2} \quad (Continued)$$

						Factor					
	1	2	3	4	5	6	7	8	9	10	11
Factor 9 Variables:											
11. Child placed in correctional inst care pre-Casey				−0.33					−0.51		
22. Index: History of Juvenile Delinquency			−0.30	0.33					0.36		
51. Casey exit (1 = emancip, 2 = parents, 3 = runaway or court)									−0.79		
52. Casey exit: Return to court or referral agency	−0.31								−0.75		
63. FU Index: Emotional Disturbance									0.42		0.34
Factor 10 Variables:											
16. (Interaction) Sex of child X physical abuse							−0.70			0.36	
30. Child at age-appropriate grade level at entry										−0.71	
41. Index: School Performance in Casey Care										−0.73	

Factor 11 Variables:

Variable					Factor 11
12. Foster home came with child as "package" arrngmt		–0.32		0.31	0.39
13. Ethnicity: 1 = white; 0 = non-white					–0.62
29. Challenge to foster parents- first year	–0.37				–0.48
31. Index: Adaptation to Casey Foster Care	0.43				0.45
39. Moody or depressed	0.35				0.55
64. FU Index: Friendship Patterns		0.41			–0.39

Unused Variables:

Variable					
21. Index: Hostile-Negativ., Maladjusted Personality		–0.34	–0.35		
25. Index: Child in Conflictual Situation w. Family					
44. Fathers role in childs life while in Casey care	0.34				
56. FU Index: Job Stability and Satisfaction					
59. FU Index: Employment Situation		–0.32	–0.30		
68. FU Index: Involved in Serious Crime/Armed Robbery				0.34	

Factor Summary:	Total											
Unshared Factor Loadings	55	7	8	4	4	5	4	7	6	5	2	3
Shared Factor Loadings	11	3	1	1	1	1	1	1	0	0	0	2
Highest Factor Loadings	66	10	9	5	5	6	5	8	6	5	2	5

ior based on the experiences of the child while in Casey care. The loading (.83) indicates that a child who avoided sexual acting-out behavior tended to have experienced fewer placements on average while in Casey care (loading .80). This confirms the finding in chapter 7 that a large number of Casey placements was associated with sexual acting-out behavior. As would be expected, the child showing problematic behavior had more placements on average.

The subcomponent scores based on the delinquency items were consistent with this information: Index of Destructive Delinquent Behavior (loading .69), Index of Acting Out Delinquent Behavior (loading .64), Index of Delinquent Sociopathic Behavior, i.e., lying and stealing, (loading .69). A child who avoided the delinquent pattern was assessed as having adapted well to Casey care; the Index of Adaptation showed a loading of .43. In keeping with this description, such a child was assessed as presenting less of a challenge to the foster family with whom the child was placed than other, more problematic children (loading − .37). The action of the agency to secure psychiatric or psychological evaluation of the child tended to take place less frequently for such a child (loading .55).

The child not showing delinquent types of behavior was less likely to be placed in non-Casey group care purchased by the program (loading − .41), or to have experienced a group placement while in Casey care (loading − .52). Such nondelinquent children tended to be less involved with their natural families while in Casey care (loading − .31).

A nondelinquent child tended to leave Casey care under more normal aging out circumstances and was rated as adjusting well at exit (loading .47). Such a child tended to be emancipated to self-responsibility at exit rather than be referred back to the courts (loading − .31).

In adulthood, the self-reports of the subjects of this type indicated that they felt they had achieved more in education (loading .36) and tended to avoid involvement in criminal activities (loading .34). Comparatively, they enjoyed better housing and neighborhood conditions as an adult (loading .34).

Factor 2: Child's Separation History

The second eigenvalue is 5.89. We observe a priori relations as the strongest associations found in the factor. On one side of the continuum there is described a child coming into Casey care after extended living experience with the birth parents. High loadings are shown for the variables specifying the percentage of pre-Casey time the child has spent away from both parents (loading − .91) and the number of years in non-Casey foster care placements (loading − .86). Children with more extensive and intensive involvements with their natural families experienced a first separation from both parents at an older age (loading .81). At exit from Casey such a child typically had experienced less total years out of the parents' home (loading − .84). These children were more extensively involved with their families while in Casey care (loading .43). Their mothers played a more active role in their lives during the period of Casey care (loading .39), and this was true of their fathers as well (loading .34).

Children who experienced more extended separations from their families were less likely to have experienced a disrupted adoption (loading − .46). There was also a higher proportion of these children reported to be free of developmental disabilities at entry (loading .35).

Overall, we observe that this factor does not produce noteworthy linkages to the "outcome" variables represented by the follow-up study index scores.

Factor 3: Volatility of Placement History

The third eigenvalue is 4.11. Like factor 2, this factor reflects the degree of stability in the child's life. The variable with the highest loading describes on one side of the continuum a child whose entry into Casey care was the latest of relatively many placements (loading .90). The phenomenon is also associated with a high total of living arrangements in the pre-Casey life course history of the child (loading .83). We remind the reader that "placements" experienced by a child are a subset of the count of all "living arrangements" that child has experienced. Upon exit from Casey care, such a child showed a comparatively large number of past placements (loading .70) and past living arrangements (loading .62). Clearly, the variables with high loadings here are structurally related. After being exposed to separation from both birth parents, the child experienced relatively more movements back and forth to the parental home. Such a child showed a tendency to be more oppositional in behavior at entry (loading − .33). Such a child was less likely to have been in a package placement.

Factor 4: Younger Children with More Extended Casey Experience

The fourth eigenvalue is 3.28. The meaning of the factor is dominated by the age of the child when entering the program by and phenomena one would expect to be associated with age. It is clear that age at entry into Casey plays a role in shaping the character of the experience of the child. A child who tended to be younger (loading − .84) tended to have been separated from both parents at a younger age (loading .32) and tended to stay in the program longer (loading .77). Such a child had a less extensive history of juvenile delinquency before entry (loading .33) and was less frequently exposed to care in an institution serving delinquent children (loading − .33).

Related to the age-at-entry variable, younger children showed more extensive wetting and soiling while in Casey care (loading − .65). In keeping with the common sense understanding that the older a child is when entering care, the broader the repertoire of potential antisocial and aggressive behaviors available to the child, we find that the younger children had less extensive use of drugs while in Casey care (loading .43). The only link to the follow-up situation was the increased likelihood that such a child (younger at entry) was not isolated and had a more extensive network of friends as an adult (loading .41).

Factor 5: Child's Life Course Adjustment Into Adulthood

The fifth eigenvalue is 3.19. The factor shows its largest loadings on variables that describe the condition of the subjects at the time of adulthood with an overall picture of how their lives are being played out in a variety of life areas. It is simplest to view the phenomena dealt with in the proper time sequence. A child who was more hostile and oppositional at entry (loading − .34) was more poorly adapted to Casey care (loading − .27) and left Casey care in poorer condition and under more serious conditions (loading − .43). Such a child showed a strong likelihood of revealing an overall sense of malaise and impaired sense of well-being when interviewed as an adult (loading - .78). Such a subject was less well-off financially (loading − .77), in poorer health (loading − .59), reported poorer housing and neighborhood circumstances (loading − .56), poorer educational attainment and dissatisfaction with educational achievement (loading − .43), poorer social relations (loading − .52), and less satisfactory employment conditions (loading − .31). Such subjects showed more pronounced drinking problems (loading − .33). They had larger families (loading − .52). From a life course perspective, the continuity of patterns of adjustment from childhood into adulthood is impressive. The factor also shows the summarization power of condition at exit.

Factor 6: Children Who Were Physically Abused or Exposed to a Disturbing Sexual Event

The sixth eigenvalue is 3.07. The factor deals with the physical abuse and exposure to a disturbing sexual event prior to entry. The factor is structurally determined and reflects the coding operations in which a number of interaction variables were created linking physical abuse, exposure to a disturbing sexual event, and gender of the child. We observe that boys who were both physically abused and exposed to a disturbing sexual event is the variable with the highest loading on this factor (loading .71). The next highest loaded variable identifies children—both boys and girls—who experienced a combination of physical abuse and exposure to a disturbing sexual event (loading .67). Exposure to a disturbing sexual event also has a fairly high loading (.59). A physically abused child tended to have experienced a higher proportion of pre-Casey time in foster care (loading .42). The only follow-up outcome variable in this factor indicates that children who were physically abused or exposed to a disturbing sexual event were doing more poorly with respect to employment as adults (loading − .30).

Factor 7: Abused Boys Continue Delinquent Trend Into Adult Crime

The seventh eigenvalue is 2.87. This factor holds considerable interest because of its substantive content. In a nutshell, the factor shows males as more likely to be physically abused, and abused males had a more extensive history of juvenile delinquency, more extensive sexual acting out in Casey care and more extensive school delinquency, and more extensive adult involvement in criminal activities and had a more serious drinking and substance abuse problem as adults. In our discussion we reverse the signs shown in table 9.2 in order to place the spotlight on the boys. The variable with the highest loading is the child's sex (.71). Next in order of strength of loading was the variable representing physically (that is, the interaction variable of gender and history of physical abuse with loading .69).

It is noteworthy that the factor does not pick up the extent of hostility and negativity at entry as significantly involved in the overall picture. The child's history of juvenile delinquent behavior comes through in more muted fashion than one would expect (loading − .27).

The child's adjustment while in Casey care clearly shows the issue of delinquency as being prominent in the life course pattern revealed by this factor. The Index of Sexual Acting Out Behavior shows a loading of −.33, indicating that abused boys are behaving in nonconformist fashion in Casey care. Expulsion from school fleshes out the portrait of such delinquent-prone children (loading −.48) as well as sociopathic behavior involving lying and stealing (loading −.31) and destructive delinquent behavior (loading −.30). While in Casey care, such children were apt to have interim group or institutional care purchased by the program (loading −.35).

The loadings for the follow-up index scores include a clear tie-in with the presence or absence of adult criminality (loading −.62) and to a somewhat lesser degree with problematic drinking behavior (loading −.46) and substance abuse problems (loading −.36). The life course pattern revealed here has obvious implications for practice and for society at large: the physical abuse of boys who wind up separated from their families appears to have grave consequences extending from childhood into adulthood.

Factor 8: The Casey Experience from a Distance of Time

The eighth eigenvalue is 2.40. A pattern is shown whereby the more recently discharged subjects spoke at follow-up with greater warmth and fondness about the foster family that had last cared for them and the social worker to whom they related. The closer the experience in time, the greater the emphasis on positive aspects of the placement experience, suggesting the possibility that time serves to erode ties between substitute parents and children. It is also possible that those who have grown up in foster care might eventually want to get the experience behind them or that the early Casey practice of avoiding the child's natural family generated considerable hostility in the children.

Specifically, there is a link between the variable accounting for the time since the subject left Casey care (loading −.57) and the extent to which the former Casey child reported positive ongoing attachment to the last Casey foster family in which the child was placed (loading .55) and spoke positively about the kind of treatment received in the foster home (loading .48). Such subjects also reported that the social worker served them well and was available when needed (loading .51) and felt that the social worker really cared about how the subject was getting along (loading .51). These positively oriented former wards of the program had a natural mother who was more involved with her child when the child was in the Casey program (loading .35). This suggests that a foster child whose mother had not permanently removed herself from the picture, as was true of so many mothers in the population studied here, was able to accept other parental figures more easily.

Factor 9: Mode of Exiting Casey Care and Troubled Adulthood in the Years To Follow

The corresponding eigenvalue is 2.34. This factor has its largest loadings on mode of exit information. The dominant theme is that the most positive outcomes are associated with situations in which a child can be sustained in the program until emancipated to independent living. Expressed in the positive version of the factor is the fact that a child who has been emancipated from The Casey Family Program as opposed to either returning to the family or being returned by the agency to the courts with likely placement in a more restrictive group care setting (loading −.78) was in better condition at exit (loading .32). Such a child had a less extensive history of juvenile delinquency before entry (.36) and experienced less "coming and going" with the natural parents after the first separation from both parents (loading -32). Such a child was more likely to have been in a package placement (loading .30).

The follow-up information picked up by this factor highlights the more extreme outcomes in adulthood: emotional disturbance and serious crime. As an adult, a subject who managed to stay with the program until reaching the "aging-out" milestone, i.e., 17 or 18 years of age, reported less extensive adult emotional disturbance (loading .42) and less involvement in serious crime such as armed robbery (loading .33).

Factor 10: School Performance

The corresponding eigenvalue is 2.09. This factor deals with school performance issues. A child rated poorly in the Index of School Performance while in Casey care (loading −.73) was one who was further behind the age-appropriate grade level at entry (loading −.71). Such a child was identified as having a developmental disability at entry (loading −.31). That is to say, a child who is developmentally disabled was further behind the age-expected grade level at entry and performed less well in school while in Casey care. There was modest linkage between educational performance while the subject was in Casey care to the subject's reports of educational attainment and satisfaction at follow-up (loading −.25).

Abused children performed less well in their school work while in Casey care (loading .33), and abused boys were especially poor in their performance (loading .36).

Factor 11: The Minority Child in Casey Care

The corresponding eigenvalue is 1.86. Factor 11 emphasizes contrasting information about minority and white children in Casey care. The minority child (identified by a loading of $-.61$) was more likely to have been in a package placement (loading .39). It occasions no surprise that this combination of factors is further linked to the minority child's being rated as showing less of a challenge to the foster parents during the first year in Casey care (loading $-.48$). The minority child was more often rated as adapting well to care (loading .44) and less apt to be described as moody or depressed (loading .54). The minority subjects reported less evidence of emotional disturbance when seen at follow-up (loading .33). However, the minority children appeared to be more socially isolated when seen at follow-up, reporting fewer close friends and fewer social contacts (loading $-.38$). They also tended to describe their social workers as playing a less involved role in their lives while they were in Casey care (loading $-.34$).

SUMMARY OF MAJOR FINDINGS FROM EXAMINATION OF OTHER FACTOR SOLUTIONS

A large number of factor solutions were run, and much computer printout was available for our examination. The factors associated with the largest eigenvalues were generally very stable and meaningful. The factors associated with the smaller eigenvalues shifted somewhat over the various solutions. Hence, we began by considering the factors associated with the smallest eigenvalues. If the associations suggested in this loading made "sense" in the context of foster care issues and the mechanisms underlying the experience of children in The Casey Family Program, we kept that factor and all factors with larger eigenvalues. If that factor were clearly irrelevant, we stepped down to the solution with one less factor. We then examined the smallest factor in the reduced solution as described above. We continued until we found a solution in which the factor with the smallest eigenvalue was "interpretable" and used that one. Of course, we included all factors with larger eigenvalues in our analyses.

The result of the eleven-factor solution we have described is of course only one of many produced by us. Because of limits of space and the tolerance of many readers, it is not possible to provide the full results of the many computer runs carried out. We have decided instead to summarize for the reader our impressions of the stability across factor solutions of certain important themes in the lives of foster children.

The Abuse of Boys and the Tie-in with Adult Criminal Behavior

The association between a history of physical abuse experienced by boys and the report of criminal behavior in adult life was strong and the association held from two- to twenty-four-factor solutions. That is, the two variables consistently showed high loadings in the same factor no matter how many factors were in the solution, as shown in table 9.3 below.

Continuity of Behavior

The clearest pattern shown in the follow-up data was one of continuity. The chain of associations was that a child who had fewer living arrangements was associated with a less extensive history of juvenile delinquency prior to entry and a less hostile or negativistic behavior at entry. Such a child then developed into one who was relatively well behaved while in Casey care and adapted well to Casey foster care. Such a child left Casey care in good shape and developed into an adult who did not abuse drugs or alcohol. Of course, the converse pattern of associations held as well: a child who was hostile and negativistic at entry or who had a history of juvenile delinquency did not adapt well to Casey foster care on average and engaged in delinquent behavior while in Casey care. Such a child was not in good shape when he left Casey care and developed into an adult who did abuse drugs and alcohol. Although this pattern is entirely expected and not surprising, our readers should remember that there is all the difference in the world between what we have shown and what we think we know.

Major Predictor of Adult Success Is Condition at Exit

The next most obvious pattern may seem superficially obvious, but it has a subtle implication that we feel has interest for practice. The chain of associations in this factor is that a child who was well adjusted at exit from the Casey program was on average a more successful and healthy adult. That is, the subject described current

TABLE 9.3   Loadings of Variables Defining Pre-Casey
Physical Abuse of Subjects by Gender and Extent of Self-
Reported Criminal Behavior as Adults Over a Sequence
of Factor Analysis Solutions

Number of Factors	Factor Loading: Gender/Abuse	Factor Loading: Adult Criminal Behavior
Two	.415	.563
Three	.358	.486
Four	.507	.621
Five	.646	.692
Six	.640	.673
Seven	.683	.658
Eight	.760	.628
Nine	.763	.598
Ten	.746	.610
Eleven	.696	.623
Twelve	.810	.423
Thirteen	.602	.687
Fourteen	.808	.463
Fifteen	.852	.602
Sixteen	.826	.641
Seventeen	.811	.709
Eighteen	.855	.588
Nineteen	.871	.597
Twenty	.871	.603
Twenty-one	.879	.584
Twenty-two	.866	.542
Twenty-three	.858	.552
Twenty-four	.658	.690

life circumstances indicating the achievement of better housing conditions, more stable and satisfactory income, more satisfying social
relationships, better physical health, and a much stronger sense of
emotional well-being. The factor does not include in its chain of
associations major links with variables determined before the point
of exit from the Casey program.

In table 9.4 we show the loadings from the rotated factor solutions
going from a five-factor solution to a 24–factor solution linking (1) the
condition and adjustment of the child at exit; (2) Index of Well-Being;

TABLE 9.4   Loadings of Variables Defining Condition of Subjects at Exit and Follow-up Study Indexes Measuring Well-Being, Health, Housing, Finances, and Education Over a Sequence of Factor Analysis Solutions

Factor Solutions	Condition at Exit	Well-Being	Health	Housing	Income	Education
	(loadings for each solution presented horizontally)					
Five	.342	.626	.481	.539	.533	.492
Six	.410	.744	.591	.535	.661	.520
Seven	.382	.742	.624	.548	.705	.490
Eight	.364	.752	.617	.493	.677	.503
Nine	.391	.770	.604	.469	.716	.498
Ten	.417	.795	.604	.556	.757	.427
Eleven	.431	.787	.593	.565	.772	.433
Twelve	.423	.760	.585	.595	.776	.422
Thirteen	.422	.790	.581	.583	.770	.449
Fourteen	.435	.769	.581	.548	.747	.441
Fifteen	.443	.792	.602	.574	.780	.425
Sixteen	.440	.773	.576	.610	.784	.412
Seventeen	.424	.816	.679	.511	.788	.447
Eighteen	.419	.823	.679	.497	.784	.430
Nineteen	.410	.834	.688	.490	.784	.417
Twenty	.427	.803	.676	.518	.801	.448
Twenty-one	.404	.801	.695	.485	.802	.407
Twenty-two	.393	.794	.740	.453	.792	.397
Twenty-three	.399	.807	.712	.502	.792	.349
Twenty-four	.389	.783	.703	.552	.812	.406

(3) Index of Health Status; (4) Index of Adequacy of Housing and Neighborhood: (5) Index of Adequacy of Finances; and (6) Index of Educational Achievement and Satisfaction.

The suggested implication is that a successful effort to help a Casey foster child become better adjusted has a direct payoff in producing an adult who is more successful financially and healthier physically and emotionally no matter when the effort was made. That is, efforts with older children produce payoff for the child, as well as efforts with younger children. A more subtle pattern in another factor also links the adjustment of the child at exit from the Casey program with educational success as an adult and with a lack of criminal involvement as an adult.

The associations suggest that the condition of the child at exit should be regarded as analogous to financial capital. It does not matter when the capital was accumulated as long as it is there at the time of exit. So too, the time at which The Casey Family Program makes an investment in improving a child's capital of adjustment does not matter. The child's adult success is associated with the capital of good adjustment that the child has at the time of exit.

CHAPTER TEN

Former Foster Children Speak for Themselves

To fill out the picture and to show the human dimensions of the issues being addressed in this study, we present excerpts from the interviews to provide the reader with an opportunity to examine the feelings of the subjects. This qualitative approach to the interviews is possible because a number of open-ended questions had been included in the follow-up interviewing schedule. The interviewers had also been instructed to encourage the subjects to speak freely about their experiences in care.

We review the following areas: (1) positive evaluative statements by the subjects when referring to their foster families and the program as a whole, (2) negative criticisms by those who felt poorly served by the experience in Casey care, (3) references about the social workers assigned to their care and their evaluations of the degree to which these professionals were helpful to them, (4) charges by some subjects that they were sexually molested while in care and their descriptions of their experiences, (5) comments of those subjects who described personal involvement in crime as adults or other habituated deviant behavior such as alcoholism or drug abuse, and (6) summary comments by two very thoughtful former foster children.

The excerpts have been chosen because they were viewed as representative of a significant feature of the interviews taken as a whole, although some themes do not necessarily reflect the attitudes of a majority of the subjects. We urge the reader to note what the former foster children have to say since their comments have the authority of the most directly involved actors in the drama of foster care.

1. Many Voice Praise for The Casey Family Program and Foster Parents

As we reported in chapter 6, the large majority of subjects spoke in warm, appreciative terms as they described the caring attitude of the Casey foster parents who served them. They saw themselves as being rescued from adversity and often contrasted the treatment they had received in the Casey homes with the brutality and indifference that they received in other substitute care settings and within their own families. A similar emotional response was shown when they described the meaning it had for them as children living in adversity to be able to count on the agency as a force in their lives even when things did not seem to be going well. They might have outlived their welcome in a foster home, but the Casey worker was ready to try again with another placement. While the glowing praise of the subjects might sometimes read as fulsome, it is necessary to keep in mind the fact that these former foster children had often experienced many disruptions in living arrangements before coming to Casey care and, by contrast, saw their new situations as offering surcease from their oppressive circumstances. The flavor of the responses can be seen in the following quotations.

(*"Please tell me in your own words what it was like to be in this foster home."*)

They were very good to me, and loved me very much. It was like finding a piece of heaven. They were very affectionate and caring. Best home I had in my life (A).[1]

Felt as if I were born there. I was accepted and comfortable (B).

Knowing that somebody was there when I was sick — someone who loved me for who I was. I don't know how to describe it — it's just a warm feeling. Tried to make it look like any other ordinary family. They treated me like one of their own children. If I had to go through all this again, I'd go back with FC and MC (C).

Felt good — there's somebody taking care of me. I felt secure. I wasn't out in the orchard looking for apple cores to eat. I had clean clothes and wasn't out in the street. Someone cared for me — that's it. My natural parents didn't want me (D).

Great—greatest parents ever. I love them more than my biological family (E).

It felt good—provided necessary living arrangement, schooling, felt loved, cared for me more than they needed to (F).

They were the best parents I ever had—they were of a different religion but they were good (G).

Good, very good. FH and MH were the most positive experience up to that time. From them I learned what a normal family was all about. I feel that I have more in common with them than I do with my bio-family (H).

("What was the most gratifying experience while in foster care with The Casey Family Program?")

They were able to find a family that was good for me, and I was good for them (I).

Knowing that no matter how many foster families I lived with, there was still someone who I could turn to for help with anything (J).

I knew I could depend on the Casey program to fulfill my needs. Also, Casey paid for my education even overseas. It is the best program around (K)!

Casey gave me one more chance to straighten up (L).

("Do you have any other comments?")

They have all the bases covered—this is the best program there is for foster kids. If Casey hadn't gotten me, I'd either be dead or in prison. I wish I could have been different—I was an ornery case to begin with (M).

They (foster parents) are comfortable people with a great sense of humor. Their love was constant. I could lean on them as well as be independent. No matter what happened, they loved me. I felt I was lucky in the way that they knew me and wanted to be my folks, whereas a lot of my friends couldn't choose their folks. . . . When I first came to them, I was pretty rebellious; and I'm sure I caused them many headaches, but they always talked with me and we worked through some pretty heavy problems. The normal everyday things of growing up. I could talk with them about myself, my family. Its hard for parents to take in a teenager; it's bound to involve severe testing.

I think I asked a lot of them, and they of me, but it had mostly to do with trying to make sure they cared for me. And they did (N).

("What suggestions do you have to improve foster care services in The Casey Family Program?")

Don't have any. I think it is the best program in the United States They care about your welfare, schooling everything. Very different from state home to Casey (O).

I was involved for a short time really, and I did not have any unpleasant experiences while in The Casey Family Program. Everything they did was good as far as I could see — they really cared about you and wanted you to go as far as you could. I don't know of any agency like it (P).

2. Brickbats from Some—the Pain Persists

A minority of the subjects did not fare well in Casey foster care placements and were quite vocal and often biting in their criticisms. Their complaints about their foster families were varied and included physical abuse, molestation, favored treatment of own children, harsh discipline, unrealistic expectations of what the subjects could accomplish, and sheer incapacity to understand troubled children.

("Please tell me in your own words what it was like to be in this foster home.")

Being beaten by the foster parents (leather belt like the ones barbers use). They beat me up pretty regularly—I thought it was unnecessary (Q).

Extremely painful—to this day it makes me angry. I entertain thoughts of vengeance. There's lots of hate involved in thinking about that family.

[Interviewer's comments: This 26–year-old white male has numerous emotional difficulties—most of which stem from feelings of abandonment and distrust of others. He is hypertensive and taking medication for high blood pressure. He is somewhat grandiose in that he envisions himself as becoming a millionaire when he gets his mind right—but also is unwilling to spend money to go into therapy which he says he needs. He was initially guarded in talking about his relationships with women

but did open up with gentle prodding. He stated he was slave labor for the family and abused, and he was intimidated by them and fearful to tell what was happening to him until he was 15 and "broke out of prison." He had some hostile feelings for social workers who allied themselves with foster families and did not have private talks with him. He stressed over and over the need for careful screening—he suggested foster parents needed to take psychological tests for manipulation, lying, and sadistic behaviors and be weeded out before they are given children to care for] (R).

Felt physically secure but didn't fit with family interests, lifestyle, etc. Great at first, lots of kids in same situation—but no sons, only four daughters, and later it was not so comfortable—marital problems and no male activities like watching football, sports on TV; no support to do anything from foster father; wasn't supportive of anything I did (S).

At times it was good but they did not trust me. Plus they expected me to be what I was not (T).

I didn't like the foster mother. I was a city girl put in the countryside. I got a kick out of getting Mrs. MU angry. I was removed. I had no respect for the parents. I thought they played games with the agency. They were making sex in the same room as their children (U).

Awful. They wouldn't speak to us. I couldn't go out as often as I wanted. They were never nice to us. They didn't help us at all. They caused us more problems, I was suicidal by the time I left. They affected my sense of whether I was a worthwhile person. I was insecure. I always felt threatened. I couldn't do anything right. I felt like I was a slave They were too young. Still dealing with their own problems (V).

It was a good environment, but too much pressure for me to be the way they wanted me to be—career oriented, family oriented—wanting so much for me to be part of the family. The biggest burden was that they wanted me to be a success, continue my education, having friendships, having boyfriends, to be very active socially. That one word "pressure" describes it all for me. I felt I wasn't ready or didn't want some of the things they wanted me to be. I felt I let them down, let the program down, but on the other hand I didn't do anything I didn't want to do (W).

("Looking back, what was the most unpleasant experience while in The Casey Family Program? Why?")

Leaving the program. I didn't feel I'd lived up to the foster parents' expectations. I felt I'd let the program down. I hadn't completed it successfully. The relationship with the foster parents wasn't good. I had lost all trust in the counselor (Casey). The counseling—the things I told her in counseling and her opinions of me—this information got back to the foster parents (W).

The following subject had a different reaction to each of two foster homes in which he had been placed:

(Last foster home) It was a high point for me there, I really enjoyed it. The only thing I did differently was not to get very close to them this time. (Previous foster home) No understanding or love for us kids compared to their own. Mistreated. Different rules for us. Abusive. We were threatened that if we left their home we would never live in a home again and that we would be split up and sent to youth centers. We didn't belong there. They were not and should not have been foster parents. We were abused physically and mentally (x).

("Overall, what was the most gratifying experience while in The Casey Family Program?")

My second foster home (X).

("What was the most unpleasant experience?")

My first foster home (X).

("Suggestions for improving service?")

Find people who can recognize a problem in a home and communicate with the kids to reassure them that they can be honest and tell the truth to them without a threat of harm in any way (X).

For some children, the Casey foster families were experienced as benign and there were good things to say about them. However, the loss of the biological families made it difficult to accept the substitute care arrangement.

("Please tell me in your own words what it was like to be in this foster home.")

Good, wonderful; its just normal, right. Did not feel strange—finished growing up; they are my current family (Y).

("What was the most gratifying experience?")

The attention they gave; they care about you, where you are, your well-being (Y).

("What was the most unpleasant experience?")

None unpleasant; still regret, however, not knowing original family or circumstances (Y).

("Suggestions for improving service?")

None—for me not knowing of my family was disappointing but not bad; for other kids, maybe they shouldn't be told how bad their real families are (Y).

[This 22 year old single black man received some 15 years of foster care through Casey in a home which ultimately adopted him. He had a number of non-Casey foster homes—of which he has little or no recall—from the time of birth. Subject Y sees himself as able, confident, hard working, and is optimistic about his future. He reports specific skills and goals and is very content with his personal life. He expresses awareness of his foster care/adoptive history, but in no other regards sees himself as different. His adoptive family is his natural family, past, present and future. I perceived Y as very secure and appropriately confident — due undoubtedly to the strength of his family support. He is aware of his good fortune and does not dwell on setbacks. Though Y is dyslexic, he had special help and does not appear to manifest particular sensitivities in this regard (Y).

3. Social Workers in the Lives of Foster Children

For those subjects who felt that they had been well served by their social workers, there was clearly a sense that they attached great meaning to the relationship that had been established.

(Comment by subject about social worker.) My worker wasn't perfect, but my worker cared and had time for me. He saw me through some very hard times and appreciated my pain, my struggle and my growth (Z).

("Overall, what was the most gratifying experience while in foster care in The Casey Family Program?")

Sharing with the social worker at the agency. I used to look forward to those moments—To find out how I was doing. About the only person I had contact with was WAA so I am not sure what the others were like. I felt that the things he said or did for/to me was for my own good. It did take me quite a while before I learned to trust him (which I'm sure made him upset at times), but when I did things started looking up for me (AA).

("Overall, what was the most gratifying experience while in foster care in The Casey Family Program?")

Getting to know my worker—WAB—and how she helped me through the tough times then and now (AB).

Having such a nice case worker, who was truly interested in me as a person (AC).

When negative criticism was voiced, more help with personal problems, the issue of privacy for the child to talk to the social worker, and confidentiality about what was discussed emerged as important themes.

("What suggestions do you have to improve foster care services in The Casey Family Program?")

I didn't have much contact with case worker. Caseworker had contact with foster family. I could have used help from caseworker regarding emotional and situational problems. For example, could have used caseworker's help in mediating my relationship with foster mom (AD).

("What suggestions do you have to improve foster care services in The Casey Family Program?")

Case worker to have closer contact with child and listen to child and check out story (AF).

("What suggestions do you have to improve foster care services in The Casey Family Program?")

Have unexpected visits so worker can see the true environment — not just hear about it — it makes it hard to believe without seeing for themselves (AG).

("Any additional comments?")

Want to know if there can be retreat or gathering of foster care kids who went through Casey because they have similar experiences. Once when I was 11 or 12 they did; I would like another gathering to share (AB).

("Did you feel secure in this home?")

I never knew why I was a foster child. I didn't know if my parents were dead or alive.

("What suggestions do you have to improve foster care services in The Casey Family Program?")

Screening the foster parents better. Closer contact with the social worker (AG).

("What suggestions do you have to improve foster care services in The Casey Family Program?")

Screen their homes more carefully; social workers should ask more questions when they come out to check; I was never told when my worker was coming out so I was never prepared to open up and talk (AH).

("What suggestions do you have to improve foster care services in The Casey Family Program?")

Tell the kids what's going on with their lives. And find someone to spend quality one on one time with the kids (AC).

("Do you find yourself feeling bitter about the way things have turned out for you?")

Yes, very often (AI).

("What generally causes you to feel this way?")

If counseling had gone further I wouldn't have had emotional problems later. I received counseling while in one foster home, just prior to entry into Casey program. Never received counseling while in Casey Program (AI).

("What was your experience in foster care like prior to coming to The Casey Family Program?")

Very unsatisfactory. I had emotional troubles and didn't receive help. There was lack of stability in my life because I got kicked out when things got tough. In a number of homes, lack of emotional help created more extensive problems that affected my life (AI).

("What suggestions do you have to improve foster care services in The Casey Family Program?")

Better counseling for kids. Counselling for foster parents. I see the counseling as a crucial factor in my adjustment. When kids get in trouble, it's not necessarily because they are bad. Get them counseling before problems become so big that person ends up in judicial system (AI).

("What suggestions do you have to improve foster care services in The Casey Family Program?")

More privacy in talking with foster child. Worker would talk to me in the presence of the foster parents. Felt that I couldn't talk. I needed someone also who could talk my language. I felt I couldn't tell the worker "I don't want to stay here" (AJ).

("Any additional comments?")

Maybe kids could be observed regularly in receiving homes or foster homes, and it would be known soon when the home isn't right at all or for that kid. And give more opportunities and specific knowledge about what it would be like in "outside world" such as how to get a job, how to present yourself on interview, etc. and give more information on alcohol and drug abuse (AK).

As far as we are aware, the follow-up study of former foster children reported here has only one recent broad-based parallel effort involving direct quotations from foster children about their concerns about the roles of social workers. Festinger (1983) reports direct quotes from subjects in her follow-up study of former foster children in New York City that closely approximate what was told us by former wards of The Casey Family Program.

Some subjects were critical of the fact that social workers did not deal with core issues in their lives such as their feelings about loss of their parents, their difficulty in getting over a disrupted adoption, dealing with unrealistic expectations of foster parents, and so forth.

("Of things that happened in the past, what was the most unhappy time of your life? Why?")

Some discomfort hearing information about childhood from other sources instead of foster parents or social worker; not knowing full history; my sisters were told, but not me (general past discomfort). Also finding out never actually adopted—or not being told; I wasn't when the other kids were (AL).

("Additional comments?")

Was happy that Casey wasn't always "patrolling" and let families handle it themselves. Some exceptions where Casey not involved enough with foster parent expectations, e.g., a 16 year old will not "perform" like a 5–year old (AL).

("Why was this an unhappy time in your life?")

Because no one seemed to think I was of any importance. Because no one could try to understand the importance of who I came from and where. Every time I asked questions I was made to feel guilty. I've constantly been told I was selfish, manipulative, and no good. Even today these things haunt me. No one really seemed to care how I thought or felt. I was categorized as a liar or an outsider and consequently was considered by family, foster family, and people in "authority" as an uncooperative person (AM).

("Of things that happened in the past, what was the most unhappy time of your life?")

Confronting the social worker that I was going to my family (AM).

("What suggestions do you have to improve foster care services in The Casey Family Program?")

Get a group where foster kids share their experiences in care (a rap group) so they can find out that they are not alone in the situation they are in. Continue with the "On Your Own Program" and help prepare for independent living (AA).

("Overall, what was the most gratifying experience while in foster care in The Casey Family Program? Why?")

The social worker helped me to get out on my own. Gave me guidance upon emancipation.

("What suggestions do you have to improve foster care services in The Casey Family Program?")

(1) Talk more to the child (lack of privacy, they always talked to the foster parents). (2) Make sure foster parents are happy with each other (3) Will their own children have a hard time accepting other children (AN)?

("Suggestion for improving service?")

Find people who can recognize a problem in a home and communicate with the kids to reassure them that they can be honest and tell the truth to them without a threat of harm in any way (AO).

("Suggestion for improving service?")

No matter if a kid in foster care has a problem or not, improve on the closeness with the caseworker. The child should have more say over which caseworker he gets. You know better who you could talk to and get along with. That way at least you would have some basis rather than just being stuck with someone you don't care for. As for counseling, I never really dealt with some of the things that I'm dealing with now. We were kind of on the surface level but he was always there if I did have a problem (AO).

4. Tales of Anguish: Alleged Sexual Molestation in Foster Homes

In chapter 6, we reported that 24% of the women and 8% of the men responded affirmatively when asked "Did anyone in the foster home ever try to take advantage of you sexually?" Most often the information provided was quite detailed and the cause of considerable emotional distress, persevering into adulthood.

("What do you think of the most unhappy time of your life? Why?")

Because of the trauma inflicted due to my foster father's sexual advancements. . . . I wasn't sure how to fight back or stop it. . . No one would believe me. Plus I realized that no matter what foster family I was in, there was and always would be a place where the "real" family drew lines and the foster child would always be an outsider (AM).

("Looking back, what was the most unpleasant experience while in The Casey Family Program?")

Being a victim of sexual abuse. From the age of 13 to 19 years Harassment by my foster father (AE).

("What suggestions do you have to improve foster care services in The Casey Family Program?")

Give the child an opportunity to speak privately and in confidence with the worker. Try to make a child feel that he can explain what is happening to him without losing everything he has. Please keep in mind that signs of abuse or body language to indicate all is not well. If I can be of any help, I pray that the case worker will find these signs in children so that other children will not have to go through the pain that I have been through (AE).

("Why do you describe yourself as hard to care for?")

Between MAF and her son who was always trying to make advances, I did have problems. No one would believe me (AF).

("What suggestions do you have to improve foster care services in The Casey Family Program?")

Case worker ought to have closer contact with the child and listen to her and check out story. I was shocked when I heard FAF and MAF had another child after me (AF)!

("Looking back, what was the most unpleasant experience while in The Casey Family Program?")

Being sexually abused, and not knowing what would happen if I were to tell (AC).

("Please tell me in your own words—what was it like to be in this foster home?")

Some really good and really bad things. Nice house, nice people, did anything for me. Divorced while I was in foster care. Mother drank; father made sexual advances and abused me once (sexually). Sexual advances by foster father have had the most lasting impression. Divorce of foster folks —most upsetting at the time because I realized I had no family left (AQ).

[Interviewer's comments: AQ is currently involved in a live-in relationship, has a 2–1/2 year old daughter, and has been divorced six months. She has a steady, full-time job but thinks her skills are not being utilized to the fullest. She is bright and articulate. Although she claims to be having stressful relationship problems now, both she and her live-in were very upbeat and related warmly to each other. He was helpful with household responsibilities during my visit. She may feel a bit trapped because she said she could not support her daughter on her salary alone. She is dependent on her live-in's family for familial relationships. She does consider them family. Sexual abuse in foster care has presented on-going problems for her. Her daughter brings her joy and enables her to feel useful as a parent in providing what she never got. Although AQ has career and education aspirations, she feels somewhat pessimistic about ever achieving them, partly due to parenting responsibilities. The day when she will be free to pursue her goals seems too far away to be real.]

("Looking back, what was the most unpleasant experience while in The Casey Family Program?")

My life fell apart when my foster father started having sex with me. I felt awful. I finally left a year later. I couldn't take it anymore.

("What suggestions do you have to improve foster care services in The Casey Family Program?")

Spend more time. Look at the movements, reactions and way of talking, way of dressing and how it changes. Like I gave up how I looked after FAR molested me. I didn't want to be pretty (AR).

[Interviewer's comments: This 31 year-old woman is a very passive, attractive, and likable woman. She is struggling still to overcome her abusive childhood experiences. The degree of her passivity is such that she still protects her parents and the foster father who sexually molested her. She has not been able to become angry or resolve her victimization. Her interview took four hours and was the first time she had really opened up to anyone about her abuse, both in her own family and in the foster home. She is currently a gentle and nurturing mother and faithful wife. Luckily she did not marry an abusive man. She was a case in which schools continually passed her to the next grade and yet she is functionally illiterate. Consequently, her self-esteem is very low] (AR).

It was lousy—they didn't love me they only wanted me to be their slave and get my money—they lied to me—he molested me and he was my payee for SSI and he kept taking my money (AS).

5. Precursors to Crime: Abusive Parents in the Backgrounds of the Subjects[?]

("What was your experience in foster care like before coming to The Casey Family Program?")

My hand was burned by adults because I had been playing with matches—I am still scarred—I can't remember if it was by mom or foster parent. I was placed in a children's center—didn't like it there; but it was o.k. as a place. I liked doing things my own way, which led to problems. I have a foggy recollection of what was foster care and what was mom's care. I'm foggy in general.

("Why do you describe yourself as hard to care for?")

I was a sneak and headstrong. I was going to do things my way, no matter what. You could consider me "independently headstrong." I was removed from the foster home for throwing a bottle through window; I guess I threatened and defied foster mom. The foster parents were actually good people. It would probably have turned out well if they had been given a child who gave them less problems" (AT).

[Interviewer's comments: AT has been incarcerated since 1980 and was moved to the current correctional facility two weeks ago. He was friendly, quite talkative, and outgoing. Although he presents a quality of self-assurance, he has a somewhat negative self-concept, e.g., "I've always known I'm crazy," "I'm vindictive," "I was a rotten bastard" (in foster care). He kept emphasizing his sense of ethics. However, this translates into retribution or vindication for wrongs that others commit, even if it means AT has to commit illegal acts. He is bright and spoke of himself as being very creative. There was a schizy quality to his talk and thoughts. He often had difficulty giving concrete responses. He struck me as being somewhat of a loner and a lonely person, e.g., he asked if I were single and if I would write to him. He has one close friend, his former Casey worker. And even in this case, AT doesn't share all that's on his mind because he doesn't want to burden this friend. Since he left foster care in 1975, AT has been transient and has not held a job more than six months.]

The subject AT is an example of a boy's downward spiral starting with his early physical abuse that was described quantitatively in the regression analysis of chapters 3, 4, 5 and 6 and our factor analyses.

My parents did not want me; I was told they were cruel — used me as an ashtray. I was malnourished, on critical list for 10 months in a hospital I don't personally remember. At age five, I went to a boy's home. (AL)

("Thinking now about the way things were in the past, what do you think of as the most unhappy time of your life?")

When I tried to kill myself last year (AT).

("Why do you think of that as an unhappy time?")

Nothing I tried helped, nothing I tried worked. I was totally in the dumps. I hold things in and then explode (AT).

("In your own words, please tell me what factors made it necessary for you to be cared for by foster care arrangements.")

The state took me away. Family accused of child abuse — physical. State lawyers thought we were bad people, especially my stepfather (AT).

("What was it like being in the Casey foster home?")

Overall it wasn't bad, but when it was bad it was terrible. When the other kids had motor bikes, I got a bicycle, had to do chores, they got to play, I wasn't allowed to have friends over. Nothing I did was "right"; if it was perfect, "it could be improved." I was made to feel not as good as their kids and I wasn't allowed contact with my real folks (AT).

("Why did you leave the home?")

I ran away; I was blamed for a good many things that went wrong, e.g., if a goat got sick, if a 15–year old lamb died, etc.; the last straw was when a cat was run over. . . . I wasn't even near the car. . . . (AT)

("Looking back, what was the most unpleasant experience while in the program?")

Being yanked out of school bus, being blamed because they ran over the cat, being put on restriction and having to bury the cat. . . . (AT)

("Suggestions for the program?")

Check out the families more carefully — too stern. It wasn't supposed to be a chain gang or being hired as a laborer. There should be more contact with biological family; child should have more information (AU).

[Interviewer's comments: AU is a 30–year-old single white man who received approximately one-and-a-half years of Casey service (age 11–1/2 to 13); he ran away from his foster home. The reason for foster care was repeated physical abuse by his stepfather. AU did not make a very strong or positive impression personally. His scraggly beard, long hair, and marine fatigue hat all seemed to speak of confusion — his life. He has just recently resumed working but this is a dramatic shift from unemployment and his precarious street, flop-house, wino-type life-style. Apparently AU has had a great deal of difficulty after his five years of incarceration and undesirable discharge from the Marines. According to his mother he was innocent of charges and all advocacy efforts failed to release him from a conviction for sexual deviance against a "town father's son." His mother reported that a psychiatrist had finally clarified the misunderstanding that occurred about AU being physically abused as a child. She additionally advises that AU takes poor care of himself and will sit and watch soap operas, and drink two lbs. of coffee and 10 lbs. of sugar a week if left to himself. He had a recent hospitalization for suicide attempt. My impression was that AU could be more successful than he has been and could be making a come-back at long last. He was polite, responsive but very unsophisticated. He was only marginally aware of the Casey program and the brief but negative experiences with foster care and social services] (AU).

A similar picture of personal disorganization is noted by an interviewer in another case situation:

[Interviewer's comments: AV is a confused young man, who probably would not describe himself that way. He uses a lot of bravado and projection to cover up great insecurity and feelings of deprivation. He is in lots of trouble with the law (many warrants against him) and makes light of them. The only thing he doesn't like about it is the inconveniences it creates—e.g., not being able to get a loan and jail time. AV takes great pride in the home and belongings he has acquired for himself, even though it has often been by illegal means. He smokes "weed" daily to maintain a mellow disposition . He described himself as "hyper"] (AV).

The following case illustrates clearly the life course pattern of a very deprived child by presenting the case reader's comments about the child's background first followed by the information from the follow-up interview and comments by the interviewer:

[Case reader's summary comments after reading AW's Casey record at Columbia University: AW was the second of five born to Mr. and Mrs AW. This family was known to the public agency since 1960 when Mrs. AW at 16, gave birth to her first child whom she abused and neglected. She was tested and found to have an IQ of less than 60. She also was an alcoholic, and so was her husband. They both beat all the children Mr. AW also beat Mrs. AW, and the older children beat the younger children. There were allegations of sexual abuse by the paternal grandfather as well. From 1963 until 1970, the family had twelve known address changes. During the period, 1968–1976, there were eleven protective service complaints by school, hospital personnel, and neighbors. The boys committed numerous delinquencies, always together. On March 1, 1973, the children were removed and made excellent progress, but were returned to the parents in June 1974. Delinquencies started again. In 1977, they were placed again, only to be removed when the parents wanted them back. They set fires and ran away. Finally, after committing first- and second-degree burglary, AW was committed for a diagnostic workup in November 1978 and placed with Casey in January 1979 with two of his brothers. They did well, although in this case it may have been better to separate them. Each time they had family contact they became disruptive. This should have been one of the cases where public agency did restrict family contact. After stealing a motor bike in August 1980, they all ran away. In November 1980, the placement broke down. AW was committed to institutional care at that time and a motion to terminate parental rights was put forth] (AW).

The follow-up interview with AW in 1986 revealed that his life course had continued on the path revealed in his case record. He had twice been convicted of crimes since leaving care involving charges of shoplifting and burglary. He had spent 28 months in prison but was now free. His history involved sporadic employment as a dishwasher, laborer and other unskilled jobs. He was currently unemployed. He had fathered a child for whom he took no responsibility. He reported himself as being under strain, anxious, worried and upset (AW).

[Interviewer's comments: This 21–year-old white male (AW) has spent most of his time since leaving the care of The Casey Family Program in

jail. (Last charge for which he was convicted was burglary.) He was guarded, somewhat angry, and participated in the interview only for the money. He appears to be the kind of person who is so impulsive that he is prone to being in trouble no matter what the situation may be. He has two other brothers who are also incarcerated—so the tally is that three out of six boys in the family have prison records. Four of the six have been in foster homes. He describes his mother as "unable to handle us" and was angry at the state social service agency for interfering and taking him and his brothers from his parents. He has no goals or ambitions— just to stay out of jail] (AW).

6. Putting Phenomenon of Foster Care in Perspective

Being cared for by social agencies for most years of one's childhood is an abnormal experience that separates the individual who has been called a "foster child" from other children in a profound way. Most of the subjects were very conscious of this.

What follows is a statement written by AX, a former foster child who chose to respond in writing to a last opportunity to report on his experience when asked at the end of the interview "Do you want to make any additional comments?" In the leisure of his own time and in his own living quarters, he reflected on his experience in foster care and wrote the statement below.

I had to learn how to be accepted as someone's child and always worried if I was succeeding.

The care of a foster child should be done under an umbrella of freedom that allows for development instead of the many restrictions that are placed on him/her as a safeguard, trying to prevent the child from going astray. A child in foster care has a great deal to be concerned about above and beyond the regular task of just growing up. I had to learn how to be accepted as someone's child and always worried if I was succeeding.

There is an important time in a child's life that being and having a friend and being accepted by one's peers becomes substantially more important. I was, for instance, way behind in all categories of normal peer relations behavior. I was being made fun of and being mortified by this and this affected my behavior and development for years afterwards, becoming very self-conscious and un-confident. Chances are very good that any child in their teens will have problems in this area and understanding this is essential for the success of a child in foster care.

For myself, all the things I complained about, and didn't approve of, I would gladly take them if I could only have found some satisfaction, some solace, and some understanding of the problems I was having in school with other kids and the social structure of adolescence.

Also, a philosophy of work-it-out-at-all-costs should be stressed. The methods used in terminating foster care must be closely guarded. The parents here are responsible for a person's future and have a direct influence on how that future is shaped. I never had a chance to review what exactly led up to my expulsion from the foster home and I have written a letter letting them know that they have caused bitterness and much suffering because of how they unloaded me. These effects must be closely examined The manner with which a foster child leaves foster care is far more important than the way a child enters the world of foster care.

Whoever reads this study, and however the results are compiled, the most important aspect of foster care is to safeguard its failure. What happens when a child is rejected? Remember that a child has a difficult time learning and adjusting to the problems of living in a society. It becomes almost impossible to do so without having to suffer through all the mistakes that one will make without learned guidance. Our society is failing today because our parents are not interested or educated enough to educate their children in social behavior. If a child leaves home to try living on his own, if he fails— he has home to fall back on and also possibly he will be able to learn from his parents why he failed. In a foster family, when a child leaves a home he must sink or swim because the foster parents have a choice whether to keep the child afterwards or not.

Also foster children are the results of social failure. In most cases it can be a negative experience and to survive as a decent human being is an achievement above and beyond what is fair in society. Therefore foster children should be treated as a valuable resource to society and should be made to understand life and themselves this way. Do we make for better parents? Or do we just perpetuate the ills of family living in America that brought us to foster care to begin with? Do we make for better citizens? Or are we so adversely affected by our situation that we become infected with socially unacceptable behavior? Foster children should have as much contact with each other as possible. We must not repeat the mistakes that lead our children to abandonment. But even this, as I write these words, I know that our society doesn't care enough. Even with this questionnaire I suspect that its only purpose will serve to demonstrate numbers of success or failure. I hope I am not just being overly skeptical.

"You plant many seeds, they may not all take hold or grow right away but a garden can then replace the barren ground."

A letter was received from AY, a subject who filled out only part of the schedule sent to her at home, a matter of her preference. But her keenly felt comments are illuminating and full of the wisdom of one who has reflected thoughtfully about her experience in care.

As I decided not to fill out or complete the entire form after I got it, as stated on the phone, I was willing to fill out the last two pages as requested. They are enclosed. In addition, some very basic information I am willing to share and that is this: I was in The Casey Family Program for two years. I received scholarship aid to complete my education. I am 35 years old and have been (in professional) work for ten years. I was in a total of 18 placements, four after coming to Casey. In my own home, I had been sexually, physically and emotionally abused. Under the state foster care system, I was emotionally abandoned. While in their care, I had a provider commit suicide and I was confronted with other very difficult situations, which no one had the time to really assist me with because they had caseloads of up to 80 children. Social services has come a long way since then but none of them have the quality of Casey. I know because I was in them.

Despite my not wanting to fill out the questionnaire you sent, not wanting anyone to have that much detailed information again on me, being glad there are no records with my name on them any more (of a personal nature), I wanted you to know this much, because I don't know that Casey truly understands the impact they have. I think some times they have become "too" professional and have forgotten their biggest service to kids: "you plant many seeds, they may not all take hold or grow right away but a garden can then replace the barren ground."

("Overall, what was the most gratifying experience while in foster care in The Casey Family Program?")

(1) That I finally belonged SOMEWHERE. I went through many homes before coming to Casey and after. What was most important to

me is that no matter where I went, I knew I was a Casey Family Program kid. It gave me a positive identity. No matter whom I was living with, on my birthday and on Christmas, I got a card from the program and no matter what happened, I knew my photo was in their office and I had a caseworker (the same one, not different ones like when I was under the state foster care system). Casey did a lot for me but this simple fact, that I belonged, was the most healing. It may not sound like much, but when one grows up in a world of continual crisis and disorganization, it means everything. (2) That I had a chance. They gave me an opportunity to change my life. They gave me hope. I knew I could go to college and I knew, if I did, I could break away from the generational problems of my natural family. For me, that was what they offered and I seized the opportunity. It took more than going to college to learn to live a life that wasn't so damaging, but that was a beginning. I am not sure that without Casey I would have become either professionally successful or personally happy. I make mistakes, I have my problems. . . . but I do not live in the continual hell that my family lives in, even to this day. I truly broke loose and I say it was because someone finally gave me a chance—a real chance, not Band-Aids.

("Looking back, what was the most unpleasant experience while in The Casey Family Program?")

I could say being moved from one home to another but that wasn't anyone's fault. At the time I was too emotionally scarred and damaged to let anyone get very close to me.

("What suggestions do you have to improve foster care services in The Casey Family Program?")

That ALWAYS, no matter whether a child looks like they will stay in one home or not, consider them anyway for placement. When one isn't ready to attach emotionally what becomes healing is to be able to attach to a less threatening entity, such as a program, a program that really cares. Kids need time to heal and I think Casey may rule out some kids because they look too difficult, that may really want to change but need time. They deserve to have the opportunity. Pain is a very strong emotion and kids need the time to heal, even if meanwhile, their behavior isn't great. I doubt by Casey's current standards I would have been accepted today, and yet, it changed my life. Who could ask for more?

CHAPTER ELEVEN

Conclusions and Commentary

Many of the placements of children with The Casey Family Program described in this book would appear to have been hazardous ventures from the start. On average, the subjects came into care as teenagers with six prior living arrangements. It was common for the youngsters to be quite oppositional in their behavioral tendencies upon arrival, often with the proverbial chip on the shoulder. Many children were accepted into care precisely because they would pose a challenge to any foster parents with whom they might be placed. After entry, many youngsters had to be replaced in new foster homes or group care placements as they wore out their welcomes with their foster families. That is to say, the oppositional behavior had its consequences. Yet, these were the very children Jim Casey had in mind when he founded the program.

What is striking as we review the aggregated experience of the 585 subjects is that, despite the negative odds, almost three in five were successfully sustained in the program, some after many replacements, until emancipation. A majority of the emancipated children were showing good adjustment at exit. Only one child in five from this very challenging group had to be returned to a court or a public social service department because of the inability to mobilize a living situation in which the child could be sustained. We have the distinct impression after reading almost six hundred records and being immersed in the analysis of the data that the relative success we found reflects a widespread determination among agency staff and foster parents to keep children in the program. Over and over again, the records revealed that a child was not easily let go even when displaying very difficult behavior. We find such an orientation admirable and, where circumstances permit, worth emulating in other agency settings.

In achieving emancipation, children often overcame the disadvantages of their past backgrounds. Our data are sufficiently positive to suggest that even if there is only a slim chance that a child who has to be removed from a foster home will make a satisfactory adjustment when replaced in a new home, the chance ought to be taken. The follow-up study showed that those who had emancipated at eighteen years of age in relatively good condition were able to go on to adult lives in which they were able to adequately address their income and housing needs, build families, enjoy relative well-being and good health, and obtain satisfaction out of their lives even when their earlier history would have pointed to more negative outcomes. Not all such children were hostage to their troubled life histories.

Given the newness of the program and the fact that the study population includes many cases reflecting start-up activities in the six divisions covered by the study, the degree of success documented here is encouraging. Additionally, defining the study population as the set of closed cases in the study biases the results unfavorably to the program. That is, those children coming into care in recent years at the same time as subjects in the study and who are doing relatively well in care are not reflected in the results because such cases were still open on the defining date of the study population, December 31, 1984.

CONCLUSIONS

1. Traumatic Events Have Impact into Adulthood

Our data permitted us to consider whether six potentially traumatic events had influence on the foster child's development. These were physical abuse before entry into Casey care, severe physical punishment in the Casey home of longest residence, exposure to a disturbing sexual event before entry, adverse sexual experience in the Casey home of longest stay, large numbers of living arrangements, and experiencing a disrupted adoption. There were lasting impacts of physical abuse, especially for boys, of exposure to large numbers of living arrangements, and of abuse in the foster home.

2. The Predictive Power of Physical Abuse

The strongest set of associations found in our study was a direct chain of associations starting from the physical abuse of a boy and ending at adult criminality, especially involving serious crimes. This result strongly confirms repeated findings in the psychiatric literature on more extreme populations that physical abuse of boys and subsequent violent behavior are strongly associated. The simple correlation between physical abuse of a boy and our measure of adult criminality was .55. More impressively, there is a direct set of linkages from physical abuse of a boy to an early history of delinquent behavior, to delinquent behavior in school, to poor educational achievement, and criminality as an adult.

A child who was physically abused before entry into Casey care was more likely to receive severe physical punishment while in Casey care. This finding has the quality of which came first, chicken or egg. We cannot distinguish whether the delinquency of the child caused the physical punishment or whether the physical punishment caused the anger that was expressed in delinquency. The larger point is that under either explanation the use of physical punishment of a delinquent foster child is not associated with a beneficial long-term result. If the foster parents were responding to the child's delinquency with physical punishment, then the results show that there was no long-term benefit. If indeed the physical punishment leads to a bad outcome at adulthood, then it is ipso facto unacceptable.

The implication of these findings for practice is the importance of delinquent behavior in a physically abused boy as indicative of impending major problems. The sequence of problems will be poor school performance and delinquency while in school. In adulthood, the delinquency will escalate into criminality. For workers in foster care, the implications for practice are to make sure that the foster parents of such a child are prepared to deal with the child's reaction to his earlier abuse and to discourage responding to the challenges with corporal punishment.

3. Turbulence in Living Arrangements Has Undesirable Associations

The next most traumatic experience was a sequence of turbulent living arrangements. A large number of living arrangements before entry was associated with more hostility and negativity at entry. The hostility measure was a very good summarization of the implications of the number of living arrangements and was directly associated with adaptation to foster care, which in turn was directly associated with condition at exit. The condition at exit was a very good summarizing variable for predicting such important adult measures as well-being, financial status, housing condition, and educational achievement. A large number of living arrangements while in Casey care was also associated with less satisfactory condition at exit. Both the analysis of the number of pre-Casey living arrangements and the analysis of the number of Casey placements found that an additional ten living arrangements was associated with serious deterioration of the child's condition.

When we combine these findings with our findings about the success rate of a foster home placement controlling for the number of prior Casey placements, a compelling finding emerges. Our results in chapter 7 suggest that a success or failure of a foster care placement is largely a matter of chance. There is no strong evidence that the worker and agency learn the factors related to a failure or the properties of a foster home that are necessary for the success of a placement. Although one has to admire the perseverance of the agency's efforts to find a successful foster home placement, we have to question the larger wisdom of the placement strategies, for we have trouble finding a sign of its effectiveness. Despite the fact that Reid (1959:390) laid out the importance of the foster family in determining the success or failure of the handling of a child, no more is known about the factors associated with a good family placement than was known when he made his comments. There are few, if any, comments about the foster home in the records.

There seems to have been partial failure of the Casey worker to examine the conditions in the foster home thoroughly. One of two major complaints that some former foster children made was that the worker did not have enough private communications with the foster child and was not sensitive enough to the possibility of adverse sexual experiences and excessive physical punishment. These abuses had their own destructive impacts.

4. Number of Living Arrangements—From Birth to Exit from Care

Where has the child been before coming to the agency? When one examines the research literature on foster care, it is rarely found that this question is addressed. Most investigators treat a child's entrance into the care of a given child welfare agency as if it represented the first experience of separation from the birth family. Yet, for the children in this book, multiple placements since birth have been the common experience. A great deal of movement from one residence to another has been characteristic of their life experiences. This instability in living arrangements brought in its wake behavioral tendencies that serve as a challenge to caretakers with whom the child might be placed. We have found that a child who was exposed to more changes in life situations prior to entry was more hostile and negative at entry. While the instability most often derives from the original failure of dysfunctional birth parents, there comes a time when the child's dysfunctional defenses against rejection and associated obnoxious personality traits become a factor in the further disruption of living arrangements. This is well described in a recent study of ten thousand foster children in California:

> Inability to control was a major parental problem for most children. However, as the children got older and penetrated the system further, the "conditions leading to placement" began to shift from "things happening to children" (e.g., abuse and neglect) to "things the children are doing" (e.g., behavioral problems, crimes). Similarly, "presenting problems" shifted from a focus on the child's physical and psychological conditions (e.g., depression, impulsive behavior) to acts by child" (Fitzharris 1985:ix).

We suggest that counts of preplacement living arrangements be routinely made by all agencies serving children in foster care. The data are relatively easy to collect, aggregate, and store and make it possible to compare agencies with respect to the populations of children they are serving, some caseloads reflecting more difficult children than others. It also facilitates charting changes in the characteristics of children coming into care in a given service system over extended periods of time. The objectivity of such a measure as shown by the high interrater reliability makes it a very attractive target variable to collect generally and apply in practice as a measure of the child's potential hostility.

We have made the following observation to the Advisory Committee on Adoption and Foster Care Information established by an act of Congress:

> A child coming into care for his tenth placement faces and presents different problems than the child first coming into care. A child who has been previously placed or who has seen siblings previously placed faces different issues than the child who is placed because the child's mother has a temporary physical illness. The foster care

system has to be sensitive to both the length of time that the child has been in care and the volatility of the child's placement pattern: the total number of living arrangements, the number of different foster parents involved, the number of returns to family, the placement of the child's siblings. There is also the possibility that the child has been in institutional care. The nature of this care can vary widely: a large institution, a small group home, an institution composed of a number of smaller group home structures. Children can move between systems: the child care system, the mental health system, and the correctional system, and the medical system. Each of these moves leaves its own scar. After a while, the child becomes more insecure about his life, and each succeeding move feeds this feeling (Fanshel, Finch, and Grundy 1987).

5. Summarizability, a Chain of Continuity

A sequence of our measures of the condition of a child while in foster care was an effective summarization of the process of a child's development through his foster care experience in the sense that including a measure as an independent variable in a multiple regression led to regression coefficients equal to zero for variables that operated prior to the measure. The sequence of measures was the number of living arrangements prior to entry, extent of hostility and negativity at entry, adaptation to Casey care, and condition at exit from care. The condition of the child at exit was usually the best single predictor of adult outcome measures.

The condition of summarizability suggests viewing these measures as the psychological equivalent of economic capital. It does not matter when or how the child accumulates psychological capital. What does matter is that the child accumulates it. In other words, an investment in therapy or group care that improves a child's condition will bear return profit from that point on.

When we combine this condition with the finding that a child who had a Casey group care placement had an unequivocally improved condition at exit, we have a compelling recommendation for identifying strategies of group care techniques that can be used as an important resource in helping a child adjust.

6. Associations with Conditions in the Last Foster Home and with the Worker

One of the highly interesting parts of our study was the opportunity to have a first look at the associations with foster home conditions and with the worker. We had only four composite index measures representing composites of items and two status variables, reports of excessive physical abuse and adverse sexual experiences. As inadequate as these measures are to describe the complexity of this mechanism and as small as our follow-up group was, there were some powerful associations. Yet again, we are reminded of Reid's quote that appeared in chapter 1. Variables descriptive of the foster home, the foster child, and their interaction together are obviously so important in determining the success or failure of a placement that we wonder and are dismayed that such meager research attention has been paid to these issues—this in spite of the clarity of the research agenda set out so long ago.

Our analysis of the associations with the Casey program's decision to place a child in group care allowed a small glimpse of a part of this mechanism. One important association with the failure of a placement is the sexual acting out of the foster child. We conjecture that programs to train the foster parent to cope with the emerging sexuality of the foster child will reduce the failure rate and increase the viability and effectiveness of placements.

7. Associated Impact of a Disrupted Adoption Small

There was an immediate traumatic association with a disrupted adoption whose magnitude lessened in time. We found no evidence of long-term adult impacts from a disrupted adoption.

8. The Odds Are Against Adoption

Adoption is not likely to be the answer to the instability in living arrangements faced by children such as those described in this study. Some children may require foster care placements until they reach adulthood. This is particularly true of older children who come into care with multiple unsuccessful placement experiences behind them and have problems in trusting parental figures. Kadushin and Martin (1988:606) cite a rather extensive literature about the general difficulties inherent in adoptive placements of older children. They observe that an older child is "likely to face a problem of competing or conflicting loyalties"; such a youngster is more likely to be a "damaged" child and "more likely to suffer from disabilities as an emotionally disturbed child." While adoption is not absolutely ruled out as a possibility, and some agencies, such as Spaulding for Children, have had some success in placing such children for adoption, the odds against succeeding are more formidable than for the younger child.

RESEARCH AGENDA

Our analyses have found some very suggestive associations. Our data are not strong enough to offer definitive conclusions, and additional studies will have to resolve these issues. There are four principal issues that need further attention.

1. Longitudinal Study of Physically Abused Children

A prospective longitudinal study of children who were physically abused would help to determine the sequence of developmental changes of these children and to determine whether a boy who was physically abused and who had initiated delinquent behavior was at greater risk of becoming a criminal as an adult. Although our data did not find a significant set of associations for girls who were physically abused, we hypothesize that the effects on girls must be equally devastating. A prospective longitudinal study would help define the developmental consequences for girls who suffered abuse. In addition, the longitudinal study could include therapeutic interventions for these children and assess whether there were documentable associations with the interventions.

2. Treatment of the Foster Child in the Foster Home

The research agenda should include studies of the conduct of the foster home and of the interaction of the child and the foster parent. This agenda is partially repetitive with the previous point. A major difference is that researchers should investigate foster home placements that are less than ideal to determine what aspects of the treatment of the foster child in the home really matter. Our findings suggest that excessive corporal punishment and adverse sexual experiences in the foster home have a profoundly negative impact on the placement and that there are positive results to kindly and warm treatment in the foster home.

COMMENTARY

1. Dysfunctional Parents in the Lives of Foster Children

The total loss of birth parents through death, surrender for adoption, abandonment, termination of parental rights, incarceration, illness and other factors was the life experience of a majority of the subjects. For these children, coping with the abnormality of the situation of being without parents was an important task to be addressed. Social workers frequently gave witness in the written records to the anguish that can be experienced by foster children in making peace with the massive loss involved. On the other hand, our data about the children who did not lose contact with their birth parents suggest that their travail was often even more severe. Malignant interaction between parents and their children in care for those who did not experience total loss of their birth parents appears to have contributed to the development of deviant careers and severe emotional disturbance over the life course of the subjects.

The emotional turmoil surrounding loss of parents or ongoing conflict with those who have not been lost is at the heart of clinical tasks to be faced in treating children like these. It is difficult to offer advice about this matter since there is not always a clear picture emerging about the role of parents. For example, we were struck by the fact that in a number of analyses of the follow-up subjects, occasional contact with the birth father would appear to be linked with positive outcomes while intensive interaction with birth mothers or both parents was associated with more disturbance being manifested by the children.

In a prior study of foster children at Columbia University, reported in the book *Children in Foster Care: A Longitudinal Investigation* (Fanshel & Shinn 1978) the loss of contact with parents was found to be associated with the exacerbation of developmental problems in the children. For example, unvisited children suffered significantly more decline in nonverbal IQ scores compared with visited children, and they showed more personality and behavior problems as measured in figure drawing tests and in social workers' ratings of their behaviors. Such children also appeared more problem-prone as reflected in the ratings of their school teachers. Given these findings, the authors strongly advocated that agencies be evaluated in regard to their efforts to keep parents in the picture while children were in care.

The data from the study reported here appear to give a different message from that emerging from the earlier study: children who lost their parents early appear to be relatively better off in a number of instances than those still entangled with their parents. Reconciling these two seemingly contradictory outlooks on parents is a challenge. The following thoughts form part of the context of these findings.

1. Some of the differences in perspectives from the two investigations stem from the fact that the earlier research dealt with a very different

study population than this one. Children were not included in the earlier study if they had ever been in foster care before. As first-time cases, the amount of devastation among the birth families was much less pronounced than in those studied here. The picture at entry described the family well after its initial breakup and showed much more pathological behavior on the part of the parents.

2. Where parental behavior toward the child is not grievously assaultive, the total rupture of the parent-child relationship through abandonment does not serve the child's welfare. In the main, it is better for a youngster to have to deal with a dysfunctional parent than to have to conjure about a missing parent. We have reported positive associations with continued parental contact.

3. Even where a child is involved in very stressful conflict with birth parents, it is rarely a viable solution to seek termination of the relationship. They are too enmeshed with each other. There was ample evidence in the case records that, given the opportunity, a child will seek reunion with the birth parent often on a very unrealistic basis.

4. It is evident that children entangled in a mutually hostile relationship with their parents while in care require help through clinical treatment in coming to terms with their sense of anger and with their fantasies about the nature of the relationship. This basic problem in the lives of such distressed children almost always leads to the children's relating to foster families with a pervasive lack of trust and unreasonable expectations. A relearning experience is possible in living in the more wholesome environment of a foster family but the historically based anguish about the original failure of the birth family to provide an abiding home is almost always present as a factor potentially undermining the ability to accept the better circumstances of the current substitute home.

5. Once a child has lived in many homes, it is not clear whether the internal struggle to deal with the rejection and maltreatment at the hands of parents always involves the birth parents as the referenced parents or whether an amalgam of several parent figures becomes the inner representation of parenthood. Child development theorists do not appear to have dealt with this important theoretical issue.

2. Blaming the Child

Responding to a presentation of findings from the study reported here, some of the social workers who were responsible for these children expressed concern about the almost exclusive focus on predictive variables that measure qualities in the children at various phases in their life course. When placements fail and when children become involved in criminal activities as adults, the predictive factors cited are whether the child was showing oppositional behavior when entering the agency's care, the child's adaptation to the care arrangements, and the child's condition upon exit from care. They raised the questions: Does not this approach essentially blame the children for the negative outcomes? What about the failure of foster families to meet the needs of the children? What about the social workers who might lack the clinical skills to reach them effectively? Could the agency as a whole develop programmatic activities that better meet the needs of the children? This concern is understandable, and we offer the following responses:

1. From our previous longitudinal study of foster children, we have found that the best predictor of what a child will look like at some later point in time after baseline data have been gathered is what the child looked like earlier. Thus, there was a fair amount of constancy in the intelligence test scores of the foster children over a five-year period (Fanshel and Shinn 1978). In the context of the study reported here, the effort to establish stability of child personality and behavioral disposition over extended time meets an obvious research need. The task is not undertaken to establish "blame."

2. There is a conventional wisdom that has emerged from evaluation studies of psychotherapy and related activities: the clients or patients who are in the best condition to begin with get the most benefits out of treatment (Sullivan, Miller, and Smelser 1958). This wisdom applies to foster care programs: the more turbulent the background histories of the children entering care and the more oppositional their behavior, the more likely they will present challenges to caretakers and the more likely their placements will be disrupted. Conversely, we have demonstrated that children in package placements were less oppositional at entry and showed better outcomes. Following through the logic of these circumstances helps us view the outcomes with greater understanding. At the same time, we observe that a fair number of children were emancipated in good condition at age 18 even though their earlier experiences might not have led experts to predict such good results.

3. There is no doubt that careful evaluation of the performance of all the actors involved in providing service to the children, i.e., foster parents, social workers, and the agency program itself, can contribute added explained variance in the outcomes of interest. Such evaluations are, however, almost impossible to carry out in the context of a content analysis of closed case records because information about these phenomena is not well described in the records. There is no doubt that in future studies such variables would provide valuable information. Even under the best of conditions, however, the measurement tasks faced by investigators in such studies are quite formidable and valid execution of such evaluations are likely to be difficult to carry out.

3. Performance of Children in School

A rather critical aspect of how well children fare in foster care concerns their ability to function normally in the school situation and acquire the education needed to survive as adults in an increasingly technological age. It is clear that how children perform in school has strong implications for their future ability to be employed in relatively satisfying work situations and to be self-sustaining. Almost a fourth of the subjects in this study (26%) were identified as showing behavior difficulties in school before entry, and this was linked to their need for care. Further, among the risk factors identified at entry in considering the suitability of a child for placement in the program was the matter of difficulty in adjusting to a normal school situation; more than a third of the subjects (35%) were identified as being at risk because of this factor.

We also learned that about a third of the subjects (31%) were behind their age-appropriate grade levels at the time they entered care, and a similar proportion (32%) were behind at exit from care. Almost a third of those who were behind at entry caught up to an age-appropriate grade level at exit, whereas about 15% of those who were at an appropriate level at entry into Casey care, fell behind by the time they left care. In probing factors contributing to the failure of children in school, we found that about a fifth of the children had school difficulties because of limited mental abilities and an even larger group (52%) could not apply themselves, being restless and being unable to pay attention in class. About 35% of the children showed discipline problems while in Casey care. Almost one in five children experienced expulsion or suspension from school while in Casey care.

In the follow-up study, three fifths of the subjects identified special problems that had prevented them from doing their best while in school and two thirds expressed regrets about failure to accomplish more while in school. Children who had suffered physical abuse in their families before entering foster care showed, on average, less accomplishment in schooling and were more dissatisfied with their performance.

Our data provide ample evidence that the educational needs of the children loom large. One innovation to be considered is to have a full time educational consultant available for children like these who would provide help to individual children. The interplay between emotional problems related to abuse and other forms of trauma and deprivation and cognitive impairment requires that educational

problems be seen from a clinical perspective, as well as an educational one.

4. Policy Implications

A scrutiny of national data suggests that more than a quarter of the
children in foster care in the United States have had such unstable
life histories that the assumptions underlying permanency planning,
as envisioned in The Adoption Assistance and Child Welfare Act of
1980 (Public Law 96–272), are not particularly applicable. Allen and
Knitzer (1983) observe that the intent of this landmark legislation is
strictly permanency oriented:

> P.L. 96–272 redirects federal fiscal incentives toward the develop-
> ment of preventive and reunification services and adoption subsi-
> dies. It requires that any increased funds for the Title IV- program
> (over the 56.5 million appropriated in Fiscal Year 1979) be targeted
> for the development of these alternative services. It prohibits the
> use of these funds for such services as foster care board payments or
> employment-related day care (120–121).

If attention is focused on teenaged children in foster care who have
spent a good part of their lives away from their biological families,
reunification or adoption by others becomes a remote expectation.
Although the prevention of such a turbulent life experience for a child
is and should be the first priority, we must have a contingency plan
for the children who have fallen through our putative safety nets and
subsequently had turbulent life experiences. We estimate that between 25% and 30% of the children currently in foster care in the
United States have been in three or more placements.[1] For the teenaged group, such as this population, the average number of living
arrangements experienced is much higher.

If the children have experienced particularly unstable life histories
with many moves back and forth within their biological families and
have also run the course of multiple placements with diverse agencies, it is not realistic that "permanence" and "reunification" are the
primary goals for them. Rather, the prevention of full-blown deviant
careers in the form of mental illness, criminality, teenaged pregnancy,
drug and alcohol abuse, suicide, and an adult life of economic dependency ought to be the main agenda items of the service system for
these children. A panoply of services may be required to prevent the
emergence of a socially crippled adult, and among these, group care
facilities are unquestionably extremely important.

In the general population of children in foster care, some 300,000 in the United States at any one time, institutional care has been a declining mode of care.[2] In terms of the numbers of children involved, institutional placements do not begin to approach foster families as a resource for children needing care. When, however, one considers the subset of foster children who are older and have had unstable life histories, such as those served by The Casey Family Program, institutional care looms large as a needed mode of care at some time in the child's history as a recipient of out-of-home care. Since institutional care and other forms of group care are relatively expensive compared with foster family care, it has become increasingly difficult for communities to maintain such facilities. There is need for a national policy that provides a second funding stream to insure maintenance of group care facilities by recognizing the resource needs of foster children such as described in this report.

Our review of the Casey experience shows that group care placements, when used carefully and when directed to the child's individual needs, are generally positive in their implications for these children.

RESEARCH PERSPECTIVES

We emerge with the following perspectives about research methodology.

1. Content Analysis: We endorse Allen-Mearas' affirmation (1981) of content analysis as part of the repertoire of investigative techniques useful to the study of social work. Content analysis worked very well for us. We were able to extract a large amount of useful information that allowed us to approximate a longitudinal study of foster children without having to operate within a real time data gathering venture. The latter would have required a much longer period to accumulate the data, and such an effort would have been very expensive to carry out. We were able to create a number of multi-item indexes reflecting the nature of the child at entry, during care, and at exit from care. Many of these showed quite acceptable internal and interrater reliabilities. The strongest measures reflected the in-care experience and the circumstances of discharge because these were the most fully described in the case records. We were pleased to find strong validation of our measures when these were correlated with the self-descriptions of our subjects in the followup study. The firm connection between what the subjects told us and what their social workers had written about them years earlier has served to strengthen our positive view of the decision to use the method of content analysis.

2. Research Design: In matters of design we are concerned with the basis on which groups of subjects can be compared. The situation in which claimed group differences are likely to have the greatest validity is the experimental one in which subjects have been randomly assigned to experimental and control groups. Whatever characteristics they might bring with them into the treatment situation would be present in relatively equal measure in the experimental and control groups. One would be on firm ground in making claims about the consequences of the Casey experience for the children exposed to the program's care if the study were carried out as a randomized experiment. We cannot, however, conceive any circumstance in which a situation could be created in which children would be randomly assigned to one program or to another. The design we are permitted here involves what has been referred to by some researchers as an "internal analysis" (Lipset, Trow, and Coleman 1956:425–427). Using this approach, we seek to account for differences in "outcomes" among the subjects through statistical analysis of variables we are interested in—for example, whether or not the subjects report in the follow-up study that they have been involved in serious crime—by determining the background factors that contribute significantly in predicting such adult behavior. The solidity of the findings can be determined by the strength of the associations we report and by subsequent replication in studies carried out by other investigators of similar populations. This is not to rule out the possibility that a program might choose in the future to carry out experiments testing new procedures for meeting the needs of children accepted into its care.

3. Former Foster Children Speaking for Themselves: Like Festinger (1983), we have developed a strong positive view of the importance of giving former wards of agencies providing foster care services to children an opportunity to provide feedback to the agency and to the researchers about the nature of their experiences in care and the course of their lives as adults. The great majority of the subjects were very positive about participating in the research interviews, and the act of talking about their experiences met a deeply felt emotional need. Even when there was painful material to report and occasions in the interviews in which anger and criticism was directed at the practices of foster parents and social workers, the ability to talk about these phenomena seemed to serve as a healthy emotional release. Very often, they needed to say how much they cared about and felt connected with people who had been good to them—individual foster parents, social workers and the agency as a whole. Most important, they were able to share the child's perspective about the world created for them by social service systems.

From a research standpoint, we are impressed with the solid measures we were able to create from the research interview data and feel that the interview schedule we created for the study might be utilized by other agencies contemplating follow-up studies. We would urge agencies to carry out routinely follow-up interviews of samples of former wards well into adulthood. In a study such as we report, we have only begun to scratch the surface in trying to develop knowledge of how children who have been exposed to early trauma and instability in their life course carry disabilities derived from these experiences into their twenties and thirties. For example we were impressed to find traces of the effects of physical abuse some seven years, on average, after the subjects had left care. One wonders whether such traces would continue to be manifested when the subjects are in their forties or even in their fifties.

4. Measurement Issues: The reader will recall that factor analysis was the method employed, followed by conventional index construction procedures, to organize multi-item measures from the many items included in our content analysis schedule and our follow-up interview questionnaire. We need to be cautious that the concepts from which the items were originally derived in the construction of the research instruments are reflected in these central measures and that the latter are useful in dealing with major issues of concern in studying the life course development of foster children. We are mindful of a recent admonition from those reviewing measurement techniques in the social sciences: "Measurement remains problematic in the social sciences. The existence of readily available computer programs for doing even the more complex types of scaling has made it possible to produce indices of this or that concept without ever giving a thought to the violence one may be doing to the concept" (Anderson, Basilevsky, and Hum 1983:233).

Two major dimensions of foster child description have been a feature of our overall measurement package and have allowed us to characterize the pre-Casey placement histories of our subjects. Similar dimensions emerged in our study of the Casey care experience and in the follow-up study in Seattle and Yakima: (a) general aspects of personality and behavior and (b) delinquency proneness and criminal behavior. While there were many more multi-item measures in each of the foster care phases covered by our study these two measurement thrusts allowed for establishment of continuity of core behavioral dimensions over the subject's life course.

5. Static and Noise About Molestation: In discussions with the staff, we have been impressed with the frequency with which we have heard the view expressed that in the recent period more children are coming into foster care with adverse sexual experiences in their backgrounds. There is obvious need for agencies to monitor the frequency of occurrence of such events and to develop means of preventing them, as well as of dealing with their consequences for the children when not prevented.

However, the issue of sexual molestation and its emergence as a factor in the lives of foster children poses some problems of research methodology. As noted in our report of preplacement data, we found a reliability problem in comparing the reports of two readers of the same case records about molestation experiences of the children before coming into Casey care.

The Casey Family Program as a Voluntary Sector Service Organization

It is important to note some of the special advantages of this program that might have enhanced its ability to serve children well.

1. The caseload of each division is relatively modest, 60 to 75 in most divisions, and close to 100 in the present-day Seattle division. Many of the subjects in this study were in placement when the divisions were even smaller. The average social worker's caseload was relatively manageable, varying from about 12 to 15 children over the course of the years covered by the study. The small scale of operations helps support the awareness of individual identities among the children, and most youngsters tend not to get lost in the proverbial shuffle. Located in quite attractive buildings, some custom designed by architects, the offices are congenial, so that the foster child usually finds visiting a potentially warming experience. When these sites are contrasted with the grim-looking offices of public child welfare agencies frequently found in large urban centers where very large caseloads are associated with high staff turnover rates, one tends to be supported in the view that "small is good" when it comes to foster care services.

2. A relatively stable staff who tend to be better paid than most social workers in other child welfare agencies has given the children who are wards of the agency relative continuity of professional service that appears to have meant a great deal to them. A sense of appreciation for the continued support of the social workers, especially when foster homes were being disrupted, was frequently voiced by the subjects in the follow-up study.

3. In selected cases, the availability of funds has meant that the special needs of the children could be met with respect to such areas as tutoring for children with school problems, psychotherapy with locally based professionals in private practice, medical care, and purchased residential treatment care, often quite expensive.

Closing Comment

The determination of Jim Casey, the founder of a very successful and respected business enterprise, has led to a very promising organization caring for children from deprived circumstances. His approach to solving the problems of child foster care were a modification of his approach to solving business problems and, we suspect, his approach to life in general. He decided that he wanted to offer direct help to oppressed children and was instrumental in securing substantial foundation funds to underwrite a program offering a well-known and fairly conventional form of substitute care for children. He did not choose an exotic idea that reflected new programmatic conceptions in child welfare. He chose instead to support a service arrangement that is commonly found throughout the United States: foster family care. This was in keeping with his stated understanding of what went into the transformation of a company "that was born in a basement and reared in an alley":

> We did not invent any gadget on which we held a patent. We didn't have any scheme upon which we had exclusive rights. We merely took a sound idea and tried to work out the details necessary for its successful conclusion.

His organization has devoted itself to this mission and has cared for many children found in exactly the life circumstances Jim Casey saw as most destructive. The last testimony from chapter 10 is an important comment on the program from one who was helped,

> In my own home, I had been sexually, physically, and emotionally abused. Under the state foster care system, I was emotionally abandoned. While in their care, I had a provider commit suicide and I was confronted with other very difficult situations, which no one had the time to really assist me with because they had caseloads of up to 80 children.
>
> ...I wanted you to know this much, because I don't know that Casey truly understands the impact they have. I think some times they have become "too" professional and have forgotten their biggest service to kids: "you plant many seeds, they may not all take hold or grow right away but a garden can then replace the barren ground."

Case No. _____

C A S E   R E A D I N G   S C H E D U L E

R E C O R D   S U R V E Y

T H E   C A S E Y   F A M I L Y   P R O G R A M   S T U D Y

David Fanshel, Director
John F. Grundy, Research Associate
          and Computer Programmer
Stephen J. Finch, Statistical Consultant
January 23, 1985

CHFACE   Case No._____   -1-   TCFP 9/ 7/84

CHILD'S FACE SHEET

CASE NO. ____   DIVISION: __   SS#: ___-__-___

Name: _____   aka:_____
            (Last,   First   Middle)   (Nicknames, etc.)

Sex: _   Race: __   Health: __   Height: _" Weight: ___ Lbs

Grade: __   Last School Attended: _____

Court of Jurisdiction: _____   Status: __

Referral Date: __/__/__ Agency: _____   Worker: _____

 Closure Date: __/__/__ Destination: __ Reason: __

Most recent
Address: _____, _____, _____
            (Street)   (City)   (State)
       Country (if not U.S.) _____   _____(ZIP)

Birthdate: __/__/__ Birth place: ___, _____ _____
            (yy mm dd)   (St) (City or Town) (Country)

Religion: __ Marital status: __ Occupation: _____

 If deceased, Date: __/__/__

   USUALLY THIS INFORMATION SHOULD REFLECT SITUATION
   AS IT PREVAILED AT TIME OF INTAKE.

          Case Reader _____   Date __/__/__

   Date for which Face Sheet information applies:

   ____ Intake

   ____ Other (Date: _____)

   Time spent: ____ Hours ____ Minutes

PLACEMENT   Case No._____   -2-   TCFP 9/ 7/84

CHILD'S FACE SHEET - PLACEMENT HISTORY

(Begin with Birth to Last known location.)

LOCATION	RELATION or FACILITY	BEGIN DATE	END DATE	REASON MOVED
_____	_____	__/__/__	__/__/__	_____
_____	_____	__/__/__	__/__/__	_____
_____	_____	__/__/__	__/__/__	_____
_____	_____	__/__/__	__/__/__	_____
_____	_____	__/__/__	__/__/__	_____
_____	_____	__/__/__	__/__/__	_____
_____	_____	__/__/__	__/__/__	_____
_____	_____	__/__/__	__/__/__	_____
_____	_____	__/__/__	__/__/__	_____
_____	_____	__/__/__	__/__/__	_____
_____	_____	__/__/__	__/__/__	_____
_____	_____	__/__/__	__/__/__	_____
_____	_____	__/__/__	__/__/__	_____
_____	_____	__/__/__	__/__/__	_____
_____	_____	__/__/__	__/__/__	_____
_____	_____	__/__/__	__/__/__	_____
_____	_____	__/__/__	__/__/__	_____
_____	_____	__/__/__	__/__/__	_____
_____	_____	__/__/__	__/__/__	_____
_____	_____	__/__/__	__/__/__	_____
_____	_____	__/__/__	__/__/__	_____
_____	_____	__/__/__	__/__/__	_____

FAMILY   Case No._____   -3-   TCFP 8/ 1/84

F A M I L Y   D I R E C T O R Y

Name: _____ Sex: _ Relation: ____

Address: _____, _____,' __ ____
                (Street)   (City)   (St) (Zip)
         Country (if not U.S.) _____

Birthdate: ___/___/___ Birth place: ___, _____ _____
           (yy mm dd)   (St)   (City or Town) (Country)

Religion: __ Marital status: __ Occupation: _____

 If deceased, Date: ___/___/___

Name: _____ Sex: _ Relation: ____

Address: _____, _____,' __ ____
                (Street)   (City)   (St) (Zip)
         Country (if not U.S.) _____

Birthdate: ___/___/___ Birth place: ___, _____ _____
           (yy mm dd)   (St)   (City or Town) (Country)

Religion: __ Marital status: __ Occupation: _____

 If deceased, Date: ___/___/___

Name: _____ Sex: _ Relation: ____

Address: _____, _____,' __ ____
                (Street)   (City)   (St) (Zip)
         Country (if not U.S.) _____

Birthdate: ___/___/___ Birth place: ___, _____ _____
           (yy mm dd)   (St)   (City or Town) (Country)

Religion: __ Marital status: __ Occupation: _____

 If deceased, Date: ___/___/___

THIS INFORMATION SHOULD BE MOST RECENT FOR
SIGNIFICANT FAMILY MEMBERS.

FAMILY-2   Case No._____   -4-   TCFP 9/ 7/84

CHILD'S FAMILY SYSTEM

Family Members (Last name, First)

Parents:

	Identity	Religion	Birthdate (yy/mm/dd)	Ethnicity	Location at Child's Entrance Into Care	Location at Child's Departure From Care
1. Mother			__/__/__			
2. Father#1			__/__/__			
3. Father#2			__/__/__			
4. Father#3			__/__/__			
5. Other (Specify)			__/__/__			

Children (in birth order) (Circle child in this case.)

	Sex	Father # (Circle)	Paternity	Father's Relation to mother
1. Child#1		1 2 3 4		
2. Child#2		1 2 3 4		
3. Child#3		1 2 3 4		
4. Child#4		1 2 3 4		
5. Child#5		1 2 3 4		
6. Child#6		1 2 3 4		
7. Child#7		1 2 3 4		
8. Child#8		1 2 3 4		

Location Code:

Adults:
1. Own home: case addr
2. Own home: other
3. Hospital
4. Mental institution
5. Penal institution
6. Deceased
7. Other
8. Unknown

Children:
1. Parent's domicile
2. Relative's domicile
3. Independent domicile
4. TCFP foster family
5. Non-TCFP foster family
6. Residential group care
7. Institutional care
8. Other
9. Unknown

Ethnicity Code:
W = White
B = Black
M = Mexican, Chicano
P = Puerto Rican
H = Other Hispanic
A = Native American
O = Oriental
E = Other East Asian
X = Unknown
Y = Other

Paternity Status:
1. Paternity acknowledged
2. Identity of father known
3. Identity of father not known
4. Not ascertainable
5. Other

Father's Relation to Child's Mother at Birth
1. Married
2. Married after birth
3. Common law (Consensual union)
4. Unrelated
5. Not ascertainable
6. Other

REFERRAL   Case No._____   -5-   TCFP 7/20/84

REFERRAL SOURCE

A. Name of referral source:_____

B. Category of Referral Source

   1. ☐ Self-referral
   2. ☐ Parent
   3. ☐ Relative
   4. ☐ Voluntary agency
   5. ☐ Public social service agency
   6. ☐ School
   7. ☐ Hospital
   8. ☐ Mental health facility
   9. ☐ Private psychiatrist
   10. ☐ Family Court
   11. ☐ Juvenile Court
   12. ☐ Police court / Jail
   13. ☐ Police
   14. ☐ Other (Specify: _____

If case was not self-referred or referred by family or friend:

C. How long had child and family been known to the referral
   source?

   1. ☐ Under one month
   2. ☐ Two to six months
   3. ☐ Seven months to one year
   4. ☐ More than one year (_____ years, _____ months)
   5. ☐ Unknown

D. Referral Source's Past Relationship to Child and Family
   (Prime service provided to child and/or family)

1. ☐ Provided foster family care service

2. ☐ Provided small group home care

3. ☐ Provided residential treatment service

4. ☐ Provided residential care (delinquent)

5. ☐ Provided emergency shelter care

6. ☐ Provided hospital care (mental)

7. ☐ Provided hospital care (general hospital)

8. ☐ Provided hospital care (developmental disability)

9. ☐ Provided family protective services (child abuse and neglect investigation and treatment)

10. ☐ Treated child for emotional problems (out-patient)

11. ☐ Treated family for relationship problems

12. ☐ Treated parent for drug abuse

13. ☐ Treated parent for alcoholism

14. ☐ Treated parent for mental illness

15. ☐ Adjudicated abuse or neglect petition

16. ☐ Adjudicated termination of parental rights petition

17. ☐ Other (Specify: _____

E. What best characterizes the referral source's reason(s) for seeking out the Casey Family Program for this child? (Write brief narrative.)

REASON:CHILD   Case No._____   -7-   TCFP 9/ 7/84

FACTORS RELATED TO THE CHILD'S NEED FOR CARE

Factors Related to the Child	Reasons for Placement			
	++	+	-	DNA
1. Ready to leave institutional care	☐	☐	☐	☐
2. Unable to remain in adoptive home	☐	☐	☐	☐
3. Showing anti-social behavior (e.g., stealing)	☐	☐	☐	☐
4. Showing behavioral difficulty at school	☐	☐	☐	☐
5. Unable to remain in last foster home	☐	☐	☐	☐
6. Severe personal adjustment problem: depression	☐	☐	☐	☐
7. Severe personal adjustment problem: other	☐	☐	☐	☐
8. Limited intellectual ability	☐	☐	☐	☐
9. Resistant to adult authority	☐	☐	☐	☐
10. Abuse of drugs/alcohol	☐	☐	☐	☐
11. Withdrawn	☐	☐	☐	☐
12. Hostile, negativistic	☐	☐	☐	☐
13. Distrusting of adults	☐	☐	☐	☐
14. Other (Specify:_____	☐	☐	☐	☐
15. Other: (Specify:_____	☐	☐	☐	☐

Narrative:

REASON:MOTHER   Case No._____   -8-   TCFP 9/ 7/84

FACTORS RELATED TO THE CHILD'S NEED FOR CARE

Factors Related to the Child's Mother

Reasons for Placement

	++	+	-	DNA
1. Deceased	☐	☐	☐	☐
2. Parental rights terminated	☐	☐	☐	☐
3. Surrendered child	☐	☐	☐	☐
4. Whereabouts unknown	☐	☐	☐	☐
5. Abandoned child	☐	☐	☐	☐
6. Mentally ill, hospitalized	☐	☐	☐	☐
7. Mentally ill, other	☐	☐	☐	☐
8. Physically ill, hospitalized	☐	☐	☐	☐
9. Physically ill, other	☐	☐	☐	☐
10. Mentally retarded, institutionalized	☐	☐	☐	☐
11. Mentally retarded, other	☐	☐	☐	☐
12. Arrested/ detained	☐	☐	☐	☐
13. In prison (convicted)	☐	☐	☐	☐
14. Physical abuse by parent	☐	☐	☐	☐
15. Sexual abuse by parent	☐	☐	☐	☐
16. Neglectful parent	☐	☐	☐	☐
17. Unable to cope (incompetent)	☐	☐	☐	☐

REASON:MOTHER-2   Case No._____   -9-   TCFP 9/ 7/84

FACTORS RELATED TO THE CHILD'S NEED FOR CARE

Factors Related to the Child's Mother

	Reasons for Placement			
	++	+	-	DNA
18. Without housing	☐	☐	☐	☐
19. Inadequate housing	☐	☐	☐	☐
20. Inadequate finances for basic needs	☐	☐	☐	☐
21. Parent-child conflict	☐	☐	☐	☐
22. Drug abuse	☐	☐	☐	☐
23. Alcoholism	☐	☐	☐	☐
24. Prostitution	☐	☐	☐	☐
25. Other criminal activity	☐	☐	☐	☐
26. Marital difficulty	☐	☐	☐	☐
27. Severe personal adjustment problem: depression	☐	☐	☐	☐
28. Severe personal adjustment problem: other	☐	☐	☐	☐
29. Child rearing / child care practices	☐	☐	☐	☐
30. Poor management of home	☐	☐	☐	☐
31. Other (Specify: _____	☐	☐	☐	☐

Narrative:

REASON:FATHER   Case No._____   -10-   TCFP 9/ 7/84

FACTORS RELATED TO THE CHILD'S NEED FOR CARE

Factors Related to the Child's Father	Reasons for Placement			
	++	+	-	DNA
1. Deceased	☐	☐	☐	☐
2. Parental rights terminated	☐	☐	☐	☐
3. Surrendered child	☐	☐	☐	☐
4. Whereabouts unknown	☐	☐	☐	☐
5. Abandoned child	☐	☐	☐	☐
6. Mentally ill, hospitalized	☐	☐	☐	☐
7. Mentally ill, other	☐	☐	☐	☐
8. Physically ill, hospitalized	☐	☐	☐	☐
9. Physically ill, other	☐	☐	☐	☐
10. Mentally retarded, institutionalized	☐	☐	☐	☐
11. Mentally retarded, other	☐	☐	☐	☐
12. Arrested/ detained	☐	☐	☐	☐
13. In prison (convicted)	☐	☐	☐	☐
14. Physical abuse by parent	☐	☐	☐	☐
15. Sexual abuse by parent	☐	☐	☐	☐
16. Neglectful parent	☐	☐	☐	☐
17. Unable to cope (incompetent)	☐	☐	☐	☐

REASON:FATHER-2   Case No._____   -11-   TCFP 9/ 7/84

FACTORS RELATED TO THE CHILD'S NEED FOR CARE

Factors Related to the Child's Father

	Reasons for Placement			
	++	+	-	DNA
18. Without housing	☐	☐	☐	☐
19. Inadequate housing	☐	☐	☐	☐
20. Inadequate finances for basic needs	☐	☐	☐	☐
21. Parent-child conflict	☐	☐	☐	☐
22. Drug abuse	☐	☐	☐	☐
23. Alcoholism	☐	☐	☐	☐
24. Prostitution	☐	☐	☐	☐
25. Other criminal activity	☐	☐	☐	☐
26. Marital difficulty	☐	☐	☐	☐
27. Severe personal adjustment problem: depression	☐	☐	☐	☐
28. Severe personal adjustment problem: other	☐	☐	☐	☐
29. Child rearing / child care practices	☐	☐	☐	☐
30. Poor management of home	☐	☐	☐	☐
31. Other	☐	☐	☐	☐

(Specify: _____

Narrative:

INTAKE   Case No._____   -12-   TCFP 7/20/84

INTAKE

A. When the child was first referred to the Casey Family Program,
   was the initial response to the referral source that he/she was
   not an appropriate candidate for the program?

   ☐ No, referral accepted without prior rejection (Go to B.)

   ☐ Yes, referral source told child could not be served by
         Casey Family Program

      a. On what grounds was referral not accepted?

      b. When did the Casey Family Program change its
         decision (how many months did it take to arrive
         at a decision to accept the child?)

      c. Why was there a reversal of the decision?

INTAKE-2   Case No._____ -13-   TCFP 9/ 7/84

B. What risk factors were identified at intake that needed to be taken into account in the decision to accept or reject the referral of the child?

	Risk Factor	Some Mention	No Mention
1. Child's having been expelled from previous foster homes	☐	☐	☐
2. Child's difficulty accepting separation from natural parent	☐	☐	☐
3. Child's inability to accept the intimacy of family life	☐	☐	☐
4. Child's rebelliousness or inability to accept discipline	☐	☐	☐
5. Child's history of delinquent or semi-delinquent behavior	☐	☐	☐
6. Child's personality problems making him not easy to live with	☐	☐	☐
7. Psychiatric evaluation indicating child's serious emotional problems	☐	☐	☐
8. Child's difficulty adjusting to normal school situation	☐	☐	☐
9. Child's health problems	☐	☐	☐
10. Child's developmental disability	☐	☐	☐
11. Other (Describe:	☐	☐	☐
12. Other (Describe:	☐	☐	☐

PRE-PLACEMENT   Case No._____ -14-   TCFP 9/ 7/84

PRE-PLACEMENT EVENTS

Before coming into care in the Program did the child experience
any of the following phenomena?

A. Sexual molestation?

☐ No indication of this   ☐ Yes

                                       Describe: _____

B. Physical abuse?

☐ No indication of this   ☐ Yes

                                       Describe: _____

C. Runaway episode(s)?

☐ No indication of this   ☐ Yes

                                       Describe: _____

D. Act(s) of juvenile delinquency?

☐ No indication of this   ☐ Yes

                                       Describe: _____

E. Suicide attempt?

☐ No indication of this   ☐ Yes

                                       Describe: _____

F. Cared for in mental hospital?

☐ No indication of this   ☐ Yes

                                       Describe: _____

G. Other noteworthy events in child's life of this character?
   (E.g., abandoned, extreme rejection, etc.)

☐ No indication of this   ☐ Yes

                                       Describe: _____

A. Itemize the salient features of the mother's maternal career
   with this child.

   1. Ways in which she fulfilled her maternal responsibilities

      a.

      b.

      c.

      d.

      e.

      f.

   2. Ways in which she was impaired or otherwise limited in
      fulfilling her responsibilities:

      a.

      b.

      c.

      d.

      e.

      f.

PARENTCARE-2   Case No._____   -16-   TCFP 7/20/84

B. Itemize the salient features of the father's paternal career
   with this child.

   1. Ways in which he fulfilled his paternal responsibilities:

      a.

      b.

      c.

      d.

      e.

      f.

   2. Ways in which he was impaired or otherwise limited in
      fulfilling his responsibilities:

      a.

      b.

      c.

      d.

      e.

      f.

CFPHISTORY   Case No._____ -17-   TCFP 7/20/84

CHILD'S PLACEMENT HISTORY IN CASEY FAMILY PROGRAM

Placement No. 1

Date entered placement: _____

Facility:

☐ 1. Foster Home

☐ 2. Therapeutic foster home

☐ 3. Support facility

☐ 4. Residential setting (Name: _____

Describe TCFP's involvement in placement if child is in
residential setting

_____

_____

If foster home:

Name of Foster Father: _____

Name of Foster Mother: _____

Address: _____

Number of own children in household: _____

Number of other TCFP foster children in household: _____

Number of other non-TCFP children in household: _____

Past experience of foster parents in care of agency-placed
children

_____

_____

Date child left foster home: _____

FOSTERHOME   Case No._____ -18-   TCFP 7/20/84

FOSTER HOME No. 1

A. At the time the child entered the care of the Casey Family Program was he/she aready living in this foster home?

1. ☐ No (Skip to D.)

2. ☐ Yes

B. Had this foster home been affiliated with another agency?

1. ☐ No

2. ☐ Yes (Name of agency _____)

C. Was this the home of a relative of the child or a non-related caretaker enlisted to care for him/her?

1. ☐ No

2. ☐ Yes (Describe: _____
_____

D. Describe in brief fashion the positive attributes of the foster family mentioned in the record that motivated the choice of the home for this child.

_____
_____
_____
_____

E. Describe any negative factors or reservations cited in the record.

_____
_____
_____
_____

F. Were any of the following possible attributes of foster
   families cited in the record as a motivating factor in the
   choice of the foster home for this child?
   (Check all that apply.)

   1. ☐ Family being able to tolerate aggressive children

   2. ☐ Family being rural/out in the country and having lots
         of space

   3. ☐ Family having much experience raising children

   4. ☐ Family having tolerance for emotionally disturbed
         children

   5. ☐ Family being religious

   6. ☐ Family having worked well with the Casey Family
         Program

   7. ☐ Other: _____

   8. ☐ Other: _____

G. Were there any reservations expressed about the foster family
   when the home was selected

   1. ☐ No

   2. ☐ Yes (Give details:_____

_____

Additional Perspectives on Foster Parents

H. Record any unusual features that are identified about this
   foster home as relates to the ability to care for this child:

(Use separate pages for additional foster homes.)

CHALLENGE   Case No._____   -20-   TCFP 7/20/84

CHALLENGE TO CARETAKERS WHILE IN FOSTER CARE

To what extent was the child difficult to care for while in placement, i.e., what challenge did he present to the foster parents?

1. No difficulty - presented almost no problems for caretakers in the living situation.

2. Slight difficulty - presented an occasional minor problem, but usually complied and got along well.

3. Moderate difficulty - presented an occasional major problem, constant or frequent minor problems.

4. Substantial difficulty - presented serious almost constant problems for caretakers, e.g., markedly withdrawn, extreme acting out, noncompliance, demanding excessive attention, etc.

5. Other

6. Unable to determine from record

Calendar Year (Foster Home Ident.)	1st Year (o.)	2nd Year (o.)	3rd Year (o.)	4th Year (o.)	5th Year (o.)	6th Year (o.)	7th Year (o.)
1. No difficulty							
2. Slight difficulty							
3. Moderate difficulty							
4. Substantial difficulty							
5. Other							
6. Unable to determine from the record							

COMMENTS:

FOSTER HOME RATING   Case No._____   -21-   TCFP 7/20/84

SUMMARY RATING OF CHILD'S FOSTER HOMES

Over the course of the child's placement with this foster family, what evaluative assessment of the home and its suitability for the child is indicated by the record? Check in the box below the scale points which correspond to the assessment of each foster family at different points in time for which you can make an assessment.

1. Strongly positive, enthusiastic comment
2. Positive comment
3. Mixed or neutral
4. Some reservations expressed.
5. Strong reservations expressed.
6. Not Ratable

Calendar Year (Foster Home Ident.)	1st Year (No.)				2nd Year (No.)				3rd Year (No.)				4th Year (No.)				5th Year (No.)				6th Year (No.)				7th Year (No.)			
Quarter:	1	2	3	4	1	2	3	4	1	2	3	4	1	2	3	4	1	2	3	4	1	2	3	4	1	2	3	4
1. Strongly Positive																												
2. Positive																												
3. Mixed or Neutral																												
4. Some Reservations																												
5. Strong Reservations																												
6. Not Ratable																												

COMMENTS:

INTERRUPTIONS   Case No._____   -22-   TCFP 8/ 1/84

<u>INTERRUPTED FOSTER HOME PLACEMENT</u> (Foster Home No. ____)

Factors associated with the child's departure from the foster
home (Where placement in home was deemed no longer viable.)
(Check all that apply.)

☐ Child ran away

☐ Foster parents experienced illness or death

    (Describe: _____

    _____

☐ Foster parents moved out of state

☐ Foster parents experienced family problems

    (Describe: _____

    _____

☐ Foster parents asked for child's removal because of
    his/her behavior
    (Describe: _____

    _____

☐ Agency removed child because his/her needs were not well
    met in the home
    (Describe: _____

    _____

☐ Other

    (Describe: _____

    _____

(Use separate pages for additional foster homes.)

REFERS TO A FOSTER HOME PLACEMENT THAT IS INTERRUPTED -- AN
UNPLANNED TERMINATION OF THE PLACEMENT THAT REPRESENTS A
DISRUPTION IN THE CHILD'S LIVING EXPERIENCE. THIS DOES NOT
REFER TO EMANCIPATION OR PLANNED CHANGE IN CHILD'S LIVING
STATUS (e.g., ADOPTION OR RETURN TO PARENT.)

ADJUSTMENT   Case No._____   -23-   TCFP 7/20/84

SUMMARY RATING OF CHILD'S ADJUSTMENT WHILE IN FOSTER CARE

Check in the box below the scale points which correspond to the child's adjustment at different points in time for which you can make an assessment.

1. Child made an excellent adjustment in all spheres of his/her life; problems shown were relatively minor.

2. ___

3. Child made an adequate adjustment overall; some difficult times, but strengths outweighed the weaknesses shown.

4. ___

5. Child made a mixed adjustment. Generally, the problems displayed were serious; living experience characterized by almost even mixture of satisfactory adjustment and troubled periods.

6. ___

7. Child made a poor adjustment. Problematic behavior dominated the placement experience. Child came across as very troubled.

Calendar Year (Foster Home Ident.)	1st Year (No.)				2nd Year (No.)				3rd Year (No.)				4th Year (No.)				5th Year (No.)				6th Year (No.)				7th Year (No.)			
Quarter:	1	2	3	4	1	2	3	4	1	2	3	4	1	2	3	4	1	2	3	4	1	2	3	4	1	2	3	4
1. Excellent																												
2.																												
3. Adequate																												
4.																												
5. Mixed																												
6.																												
7. Poor																												
Not Ratable																												

COMMENTS:

ADAPTATION   Case No._____   -24-   TCFP 7/20/84

RATINGS COVERING CHILD'S ADAPTATION TO FOSTER CARE

Check the time period for this rating:

a. ☐ the first year in care

b. ☐ at a mid-point in the foster care experience (if in care more than two years)

c. ☐ during the last year in care (if in care more than one year)

	Very Much	Moder- ately	A Little	Not at All	Does not Apply	No Basis for Rating
A. Status in Foster Care						
1. Expressed resistance to being in foster care	☐	☐	☐	☐	☐	☐
2. Was anxious to return to natural parent	☐	☐	☐	☐	☐	☐
3. Felt at home in setting	☐	☐	☐	☐	☐	☐
4. Showed positive attachment to own mother – desires to her	☐	☐	☐	☐	☐	☐
5. Showed positive attachment to own father – desires to him	☐	☐	☐	☐	☐	☐
6. Ties to foster family were very close	☐	☐	☐	☐	☐	☐
B. General Behavior Care						
1. Was resistant to adult supervision	☐	☐	☐	☐	☐	☐
2. Tended to be moody or depressed	☐	☐	☐	☐	☐	☐
3. Tended to be secure, free of anxiety	☐	☐	☐	☐	☐	☐
4. Tended to be hostile and belligerant	☐	☐	☐	☐	☐	☐
5. Showed difficulty in controlling behavioral impulses	☐	☐	☐	☐	☐	☐
6. Tended to be relaxed and at ease	☐	☐	☐	☐	☐	☐
7. Was friendly and outgoing in social life	☐	☐	☐	☐	☐	☐
8. Was able to make close intimate friendship ties	☐	☐	☐	☐	☐	☐
9. Showed low tolerance for frustration of desires	☐	☐	☐	☐	☐	☐
10. Showed poor concentration, had short attention span	☐	☐	☐	☐	☐	☐
11. Was easy for foster parents to discipline	☐	☐	☐	☐	☐	☐
12. Was usually cheerful and happy	☐	☐	☐	☐	☐	☐
13. Tended to be rowdyish	☐	☐	☐	☐	☐	☐
14. Experimented with drugs	☐	☐	☐	☐	☐	☐
15. Tended to drink alcohol to excess	☐	☐	☐	☐	☐	☐

ADAPTATION-2   Case No._____   -25-   TCFP 8/ 1/84

C. SOCIAL CONDUCT

During the child's placement experience with the Casey Program, did he/she exhibit any of the following problems?

	Never	One Occa- sion	Several Occa- sions	Often	Un- known
1. Had run away	☐	☐	☐	☐	☐
2. Had stolen petty items (e.g., small radio, shoplifting)	☐	☐	☐	☐	☐
3. Had stolen major item or money (e.g., TV, automobile)	☐	☐	☐	☐	☐
4. Had stayed away overnight without permission	☐	☐	☐	☐	☐
5. Had engaged in destruction of property	☐	☐	☐	☐	☐
6. Had been involved in activities of delinquent gang	☐	☐	☐	☐	☐
7. Had been defiant of caretaker in a major way	☐	☐	☐	☐	☐
8. Had engaged in behavior dangerous to own physical safety	☐	☐	☐	☐	☐
9. Had used hallucinogenic drugs (Specify:_____)	☐	☐	☐	☐	☐
10. Had gotten into difficulty because of sexual behavior (Specify:_____)	☐	☐	☐	☐	☐
11. Other: _____	☐	☐	☐	☐	☐

INDICATE WHEN IN THE CHILD'S PLACEMENT HISTORY EVENT(S) OCCURED. BRIEFLY DESCRIBE EVENTS.

ADAPTATION-3   Case No._____   -26-   TCFP 8/ 1/84

D. SYMPTOMATIC BEHAVIORS

During the course of the child's placement with the Casey Family
Program were the following behavioral symptoms reported in the
record?

	None Recorded	Single Incident	Occasional Incident	Frequent
1. Disturbing dreams	☐	☐	☐	☐
2. Telling lies	☐	☐	☐	☐
3. Soiling self	☐	☐	☐	☐
4. Wetting self--daytime	☐	☐	☐	☐
5. Wetting self--night	☐	☐	☐	☐
6. Sleep disorder	☐	☐	☐	☐
7. Destructive	☐	☐	☐	☐
8. Poor appetite	☐	☐	☐	☐
9. Nail biting	☐	☐	☐	☐
10. Nervous tics	☐	☐	☐	☐
11. Stomach disorders	☐	☐	☐	☐
12. Sucking thumb	☐	☐	☐	☐
13. Afraid or shy	☐	☐	☐	☐
14. Allergy or skin disorder	☐	☐	☐	☐
15. Colds	☐	☐	☐	☐
16. Moody or depressed	☐	☐	☐	☐
17. Excluded by children	☐	☐	☐	☐
18. Over or underweight	☐	☐	☐	☐
19. Too sensitive	☐	☐	☐	☐
20. Too serious	☐	☐	☐	☐
21. Under strain	☐	☐	☐	☐
22. Accident prone	☐	☐	☐	☐
23. Bizarre behavior	☐	☐	☐	☐
24. Other	☐	☐	☐	☐

INDICATE AT WHAT AGE CHILD SHOWED SUCH BEHAVIOR(S)

ADAPTATION-4   Case No._____   -27-   TCFP 8/ 1/84

E. ACHIEVEMENTS/ASSETS

Did child reveal any special interest and or talents or skills
while in the Casey Program?

	No Mention	Some Interest	Strong Interest	Some Achieve- ment	Out- standing Achieve- ment(a)
1. Music	☐	☐	☐	☐	☐
2. Sports	☐	☐	☐	☐	☐
3. Art(painting, sculpture, etc.)	☐	☐	☐	☐	☐
4. Mechanical	☐	☐	☐	☐	☐
5. Crafts	☐	☐	☐	☐	☐
6. Dance	☐	☐	☐	☐	☐
7. Debate	☐	☐	☐	☐	☐
8. Computers	☐	☐	☐	☐	☐
9. Science	☐	☐	☐	☐	☐
10. Creative writing	☐	☐	☐	☐	☐
11. Community participation	☐	☐	☐	☐	☐
12. 4-H clubs/ Animal care	☐	☐	☐	☐	☐
13. Dramatics	☐	☐	☐	☐	☐
14. Clothing design, sewing	☐	☐	☐	☐	☐
15. Other hobbies (Specify:	☐	☐	☐	☐	☐

a) Please describe any outstanding achievements _____
_____

b) Did child reveal any special interests, talents or
   skills before entering Casey Family Program?

☐ Not mentioned   ☐ Yes
   in the record
                         Describe: _____

SCHOOL   Case No._____   -28-   TCFP 8/ 1/84

SCHOOL PERFORMANCE

A. Was the child at the age-appropriate grade level when he/she entered care?

   1. ☐ Yes

   2. ☐ No (_____ Years behind; _____ Years advanced)

B. Overall, how did this child perform as a school student in his/her academic work while in the Casey Family Program? Summarize how the record seems to characterize the child.

   1. ☐ Below Average

   2. ☐

   3. ☐ Average

   4. ☐

   5. ☐ Above Average

   6. ☐ Other:_____

C. At the time the child left care (through emancipation or otherwise) what grade level had he/she achieved? (Circle highest year completed.)

   Grade school 1   2   3   4   5   6   7   8

   High school   9 10 11 12

   College   1   2   3   4

D. Was the child at the age-appropriate grade level when he/she left care?

   1. ☐ Yes

   2. ☐ No (_____ Years behind; _____ Years advanced)

SCHOOL-2   Case No._____   -29-   TCFP 8/ 1/84

SCHOOL PERFORMANCE

E. If the child was behind the appropriate grade level, were any
   of the following factors infuential in causing him/her to be
   behind?

   1. ☐ Limited mental abilities (I.Q. if available:_____)

   2. ☐ Unable to apply self to academic work (e.g., failed
          to study and do homework)
   3. ☐ Expelled or suspended because of behavior

   4. ☐ Truancy

   5. ☐ Physical illness causing absence

   6. ☐ Other (Specify: _____)

F. Does the record reveal any test results related to the child's
   intelligence?

   ☐ No   ☐ Yes

                           a) Give details of the test given,
                              IQ, and date of each test

   _____

   _____

                           b) Is there any indication that IQ
                              represents child's potential?

   ☐ No   ☐ Yes

G. Does the record reveal any results related to the child's
   academic achievement?

   ☐ No   ☐ Yes

                              Give details: _____

   _____

   _____

SCHOOL-3   Case No._____   -30-   TCFP 8/ 1/84

SCHOOL PERFORMANCE

H. Did child show any of the following school related problems
   while in placement with the Casey Family Program?
   (Check all that apply.)

   ☐   1. Discipline problem

   ☐   2. Emotional problems (phobia, nervousness, etc.)

   ☐   3. Poor academic performance

   ☐   4. Under-achiever

   ☐   5. Other problem (Describe:

   Give details for any category checked above:

   _____

   _____

I. Did child attend a special/modified school program while in
   the care of the Casey Family Program?

   ☐   No indication of   ☐   Yes
       of this

   If yes, did he/she attend any of the following?

   ☐   1. Program for emotionally disturbed/social maladjusted
           children
   ☐   2. Reading school

   ☐   3. Classes for emotionally disturbed in regular public
           school
   ☐   4. Classes for retarded children

   ☐   5. Classes for physically handicapped children

   ☐   6. Classes for "slow learners"

   ☐   7. Other (Describe: _____

HEALTH   Case No._____   -31-   TCFP 8/ 1/84

Child's Health While in Care

A. Indicate whether the child experienced health problems in the following areas:

Conditions	Before coming into care		While in care	
	Major Problem	Minor Problem	Major Problem	Minor Problem
1. Weight problem, overweight	☐	☐	☐	☐
2. Weight problem, underweight	☐	☐	☐	☐
3. Vision impairment	☐	☐	☐	☐
4. Hearing deficit	☐	☐	☐	☐
5. Skin disorders	☐	☐	☐	☐
6. Musculo-skeletal	☐	☐	☐	☐
7. Respiratory problem	☐	☐	☐	☐
8. Cardiovascular problem	☐	☐	☐	☐
9. Nervous system disorder	☐	☐	☐	☐
10. Stature (problems in normal growth)	☐	☐	☐	☐
11. Diabetes	☐	☐	☐	☐
12. Anemia	☐	☐	☐	☐
13. Tuberculosis	☐	☐	☐	☐
14. Congenital anomalies	☐	☐	☐	☐
15. Nutritional/metabolic disorder	☐	☐	☐	☐
16. Other (Specify: _____	☐	☐	☐	☐

HEALTH-2   Case No._____   -32-   TCFP 8/ 1/84

Child's Health While in Care

B. Were there ways in which the child's health condition impaired his/her functioning?

☐ No indication   ☐ Yes
  in the record
                       Describe: _____

C. Did this child show evidence of being prone to illness?

☐ Yes   ☐ Somewhat   ☐ No

D. Was it necessary for the Casey Family Program to mobilize any non-routine medical treatment on behalf of the child?

☐ No indication   ☐ Yes
  in the record
                       Describe: _____

E. Did any medically significant incidents occur while this child was in the Program (e.g., accidents, need for surgery, etc.)

☐ No indication   ☐ Yes
  in the record
                       Describe: _____

F. In general what is the view of the child's health revealed by the record?

☐ Good health (robust, good specimen)

☐ Fairly good health (Some minor problems)

☐ Moderate health (Some fairly serious problems)

☐ Poor health (Serious health problems)

☐ Other (Describe: _____

G. Did this child have any moderate or major dental problems while in care?

☐ No indication   ☐ Yes
  in the record
                       Describe: _____

PSYCHIATRIC   Case No._____   -33-   TCFP 7/20/84

PYCHIATRIC EVALUATION AND TREATMENT

Did the child receive an evaluation of his/her mental health status and the nature of his/her emotional problems while under the care of the Casey Family Program?

☐ No indication of this   ☐ Yes
  (Go to p. 41)

If yes, record information covering each distinct occasion in which a psychiatric evaluation took place.

A. When did the evaluation take place? (Date: _____)

B. Describe the circumstances which prompted the recourse to such an evaluation.

C. Briefly summarize the diagnostic appraisal of the child offered by the psychiatrist.

PSYCHIATRIC-2   Case No._____   -34-   TCFP 7/20/84

PYCHIATRIC EVALUATION AND TREATMENT

D. Indicate whether any of the following DSM-III diagnostic codes
(of the American Psychiatric Association) are reflected in the
diagnostic appraisal presented to the Casey Family Program.

	Enunciated by Diagnostic Statement	Suggested by Diagnostic Statement	Not Mentioned
1. Attention deficit disorder	☐	☐	☐
2. Conduct disorder	☐	☐	☐
3. Anxiety disorder	☐	☐	☐
4. Schizoid disorder	☐	☐	☐
5. Oppositional disorder	☐	☐	☐
6. Identity disorder	☐	☐	☐
7. Eating disorder	☐	☐	☐
8. Pervasive developmental disorder	☐	☐	☐
9. Affective disorder: major depression	☐	☐	☐
10. Disorders of impulse control	☐	☐	☐
11. Adjustment disorder	☐	☐	☐
12. Other (Specify: _____	☐	☐	☐
13. Other (Specify: _____	☐	☐	☐

PSYCHIATRIC-3   Case No._____   -35-   TCFP 8/ 1/84

PYCHIATRIC EVALUATION AND TREATMENT

E. Conditions not attributable to a mental disorder that are designated as a focus of attention or treatment.

	Enunciated by Diagnostic Statement	Suggested by Diagnostic Statement	Not Mentioned
1. Malingering	☐	☐	☐
2. Borderline intellectual functioning	☐	☐	☐
3. Anti-social behavior	☐	☐	☐
4. Academic problem	☐	☐	☐
5. Uncomplicated bereavement	☐	☐	☐
6. Parent-child problem	☐	☐	☐
7. Other interpersonal problem	☐	☐	☐
8. Psychological factor affecting child's physical condition	☐	☐	☐

F. If additional psychiatric evaluations are reported, summarize the results below.

Date of Psychiatric Evaluation: _____

Summary:

PSYCHIATRIC-4   Case No._____   -36-   TCFP 7/20/84

<u>PYCHIATRIC EVALUATION AND TREATMENT</u>

F. Did the child receive psychiatric treatment while in the care
   of the Casey Family Program?

   ☐ No indication of this   ☐ Yes

   If <u>yes</u>, give summarized description of the nature of
   treatment, the quality of the child's involvement, and any
   benefits that he/she appeared to derive from the
   experience.

   _____

   _____

   _____

   _____

   _____

   _____

   _____

   _____

   _____

   _____

   _____

   _____

   _____

   _____

   _____

   _____

   _____

PSYCHOLOGICAL   Case No._____   -37-   TCFP 7/20/84

PYCHOLOGICAL DIAGNOSTIC ASSESSMENT AND TREATMENT
BY A PSYCHOLOGIST (and others)

A. During the period of care provided by the Casey Family
   Program, was the child seen for testing by a psychologist?

   ☐ No indication of this   ☐ Yes
     (Go to p. 43)

   If yes

   1. Give brief summary of reasons for testing the child.

   2. Summarize briefly, the findings of the examination.

   3. Was there on-going treatment with the psychologist?

      ☐ No indication of this   ☐ Yes

      If yes, describe treatment and any indication of results of
      treatment.

PSYCHOLOGICAL-2   Case No._____   -38-   TCFP 7/20/84

PYCHOLOGICAL DIAGNOSTIC ASSESSMENT AND TREATMENT
BY A PSYCHOLOGIST (and others)

B. Was child referred for treatment of emotional   problems
   (without testing as a precursor) to a psychologist?

   ☐ No   ☐ Yes

   If yes, summarize purposes of treatment and the nature of
   the experience and apparent results.

C. Was child referred for treatment of emotional problems by a
   professional (other than a psychiatrist or psychologist?)

   1. ☐ No

   2. ☐ Yes

   If yes, give details.

DIRECT   Case No._____   -39-   TCFP 8/ 1/84

Direct Child Treatment by Casey Family Program Staff

A. Does the record indicate effort by the social worker assigned to the case to offer casework treatment services to the child? For example, seeking to help him/her in accepting foster family care, with his continuing relationships with members of his own family and with other persons, or with problems of social functioning?

☐   1. Reference to fairly continuous and intense work with the child

☐   2. Reference to time limited or episodic work on a relatively intense basis

☐   3. Reference to moderate work activity on a continuous basis

☐   4. Reference to relatively episodic, occasional work on a moderate basis

☐   5. No reference to such work in the record

☐   6. Other

B. If there is discussion of direct casework with the child briefly describe the phenomena that are the focus of attention, and the quality of the child's responsiveness.

_____

_____

_____

C. Did child receive treatment services from other Casey Family Program staff (e.g., support services)?

☐ No indication of   ☐ Yes
of this

If <u>yes</u>, describe briefly.

_____

_____

_____

ADOPTION   Case No._____   -40-   TCFP 7/20/84

<u>ADOPTION AS A FACTOR IN THE CHILD'S HISTORY</u>

A. When this child entered care with the Casey Family Program had
   he/she previously been placed in an adoptive home?

   1. ☐ No (Skip to B.)

   2. ☐ Yes (Give details:_____

   _____

B. When this child entered care with the Casey Family Program had
   he/she been surrendered for adoption or otherwise designated
   as someone for whom adoption might be considered?

   1. ☐ No (Skip to p. 45)

   2. ☐ Yes, surrendered (Give details: _____

   _____

   3. ☐ Yes, adoption was considered as a possible goal
         (Give details: _____

   _____

C. Was a foster family with whom the child was placed while in
   the Casey Family Program ever approached to consider adoption
   for the child?

   1. ☐ No indication of this in the record (Skip to p. 45)

   2. ☐ Yes _____ family was approached
             (Name)
             Date: _____

             Response of foster family: _____

   _____

D. Was the child legally adopted by the foster family?

   1. ☐ No (Reason: _____)

   2. ☐ Yes   Date: _____

INCIDENT   Case No._____ -41-   TCFP 8/ 1/84

INCIDENT REPORT

Date of incident: _____
Description: _____

_____

_____

Classification of Incident:

1. ☐ Runaway
2. ☐ Truancy
3. ☐ Expulsion from school
4. ☐ Failure to be promoted in school
5. ☐ Act of delinquency, stealing
6. ☐ Act of delinquency, substance abuse
7. ☐ Act of delinquency, violence
8. ☐ Act of delinquency, other
9. ☐ Suicidal attempt
10. ☐ Serious challenge to foster parents
11. ☐ School dropout
12. ☐ Teenage pregnancy
13. ☐ Other

Agency actions (Check all that apply.)

1. ☐ Psychiatric evaluation
2. ☐ Staff conference
3. ☐ Child removed from foster home and replaced in another foster home
4. ☐ Child removed from foster and placed in other facility
   (Specify: _____)
5. ☐ Other (Specify:_____

Information is to be recorded by the case reader as an "incident" if in the course of the child's placement experience with the Program an event occurs which significantly disturbs the equilibrium of the child's life and/or the foster care arrangements, and gives indication of an adjustment problem of fairly serious proportions. The phenomena to be subsumed under the rubric of "incident" include behavioral episodes such as running away, stealing, fire setting, suicidal threat or attempt, truancy from school, etc. Acts of delinquency bringing the child to the attention of the authorities (Police, juvenile court, etc.) should be noted in an incident report. Expulsion from school, failure to be advanced to the next grade, or abandonment of an educational objective are also to be reported. Minor or middle-ranged occurences need not be treated as "incidents" although note will be made of these in other ratings of the adjustment of the child. An "incident" can usually be identified because the recording displays the concern of social work staff and/or foster parents and leads to such phenomena as staff assessment conferences, psychiatric evaluation or replacement of a child.

VISITING   Case No._____   -42-   TCFP 7/20/84

PARENTAL CONTACT

A. What persons did the child see while in care?
   (Check all that apply.)

| | 1st Year in Care | | | |
	Never	Occa-sion-ally	Some-times	Often
1. Mother	☐	☐	☐	☐
2. Father	☐	☐	☐	☐
3. Stepmother	☐	☐	☐	☐
4. Stepfather	☐	☐	☐	☐
5. Sibling(s)	☐	☐	☐	☐
6. Maternal grandmother	☐	☐	☐	☐
7. Maternal grandfather	☐	☐	☐	☐
8. Paternal grandmother	☐	☐	☐	☐
9. Paternal grandfather	☐	☐	☐	☐
10. Other relative(s)	☐	☐	☐	☐
11. Other non-related person	☐	☐	☐	☐

| | 2nd Year in Care | | | |
	Never	Occa-sion-ally	Some-times	Often
1. Mother	☐	☐	☐	☐
2. Father	☐	☐	☐	☐
3. Stepmother	☐	☐	☐	☐
4. Stepfather	☐	☐	☐	☐
5. Sibling(s)	☐	☐	☐	☐
6. Maternal grandmother	☐	☐	☐	☐
7. Maternal grandfather	☐	☐	☐	☐
8. Paternal grandmother	☐	☐	☐	☐
9. Paternal grandfather	☐	☐	☐	☐
10. Other relative(s)	☐	☐	☐	☐
11. Other non-related person	☐	☐	☐	☐

(Use additional pages if in care more than 2 years.)

VISITING-2   Case No._____   -43-   TCFP 7/20/84

PARENTAL CONTACT

B. Where did contact between parent and child tend to take place?
(Respond to each item.)

Mother	Never	Some-times	Often	Always	DNA	Un-known
1. Child visited parent's home	☐	☐	☐	☐	☐	☐
2. Mother visited in foster home	☐	☐	☐	☐	☐	☐
3. Mother visited in agency office	☐	☐	☐	☐	☐	☐
4. Mother took child elsewhere	☐	☐	☐	☐	☐	☐
5. Other _____	☐	☐	☐	☐	☐	☐

Father	Never	Some-times	Often	Always	DNA	Un-known
1. Child visited parent's home	☐	☐	☐	☐	☐	☐
2. Father visited in foster home	☐	☐	☐	☐	☐	☐
3. Father visited in agency office	☐	☐	☐	☐	☐	☐
4. Father took child elsewhere	☐	☐	☐	☐	☐	☐
5. Other _____	☐	☐	☐	☐	☐	☐

VISITING-3   Case No._____   -44-   TCFP 7/20/84

PARENTAL CONTACT

C. Characterize the parents' tendency to visit their child while in care with the Casey Family Program.

Mother	First Year in Care	Second Year in Care	Third Year in Care	Fourth Year in Care	Fifth Year in Care	Six + Year in Care
1. Never visited	☐	☐	☐	☐	☐	☐
2. Rarely visited	☐	☐	☐	☐	☐	☐
3. Infrequently visited	☐	☐	☐	☐	☐	☐
4. Occasionally visited	☐	☐	☐	☐	☐	☐
5. Visited fairly regularly	☐	☐	☐	☐	☐	☐
6. Visited regularly	☐	☐	☐	☐	☐	☐
7. Other	☐	☐	☐	☐	☐	☐

_____

Father	First Year in Care	Second Year in Care	Third Year in Care	Fourth Year in Care	Fifth Year in Care	Six + Year in Care
1. Never visited	☐	☐	☐	☐	☐	☐
2. Rarely visited	☐	☐	☐	☐	☐	☐
3. Infrequently visited	☐	☐	☐	☐	☐	☐
4. Occasionally visited	☐	☐	☐	☐	☐	☐
5. Visited fairly regularly	☐	☐	☐	☐	☐	☐
6. Visited regularly	☐	☐	☐	☐	☐	☐
7. Other	☐	☐	☐	☐	☐	☐

_____

VISITING-4   Case No._____   -45-   TCFP 7/20/84

PARENTAL CONTACT

D. Was there any contact between parents and child other than through in-person visits? (Check if any contact in this manner indicated in record.)

Mother	First Year in Care	Second Year in Care	Third Year in Care	Fourth Year in Care	Fifth Year in Care	Six + Year in Care
1. Telephone calls	☐	☐	☐	☐	☐	☐
2. Letters	☐	☐	☐	☐	☐	☐
3. Cards (holidays and birthdays)	☐	☐	☐	☐	☐	☐
4. Gifts	☐	☐	☐	☐	☐	☐
5. Other (Specify) _____	☐	☐	☐	☐	☐	☐

Father	First Year in Care	Second Year in Care	Third Year in Care	Fourth Year in Care	Fifth Year in Care	Six + Year in Care
1. Telephone calls	☐	☐	☐	☐	☐	☐
2. Letters	☐	☐	☐	☐	☐	☐
3. Cards (holidays and birthdays)	☐	☐	☐	☐	☐	☐
4. Gifts	☐	☐	☐	☐	☐	☐
5. Other (Specify) _____	☐	☐	☐	☐	☐	☐

VISITING-5   Case No._____   -46-   TCFP 7/20/84

PARENTAL CONTACT

E. Had the Program attempted to increase parental visiting of the
   child in care through any of the following measures?

	1st Year in Care		2nd Year in Care	
	Mother	Father	Mother	Father
1. Not applicable, parent was not permitted to visit	☐	☐	☐	☐
2. Not applicable, parent visited frequently	☐	☐	☐	☐
3. Advising the parent of the child's need for such visiting	☐	☐	☐	☐
4. Providing funds for travel costs	☐	☐	☐	☐
5. Providing funds to pay for babysitter arrangements for other children	☐	☐	☐	☐
6. Other forms of encouragement of visiting (Specify:_____	☐	☐	☐	☐

	3rd Year in Care		4th Year in Care	
	Mother	Father	Mother	Father
1. Not applicable, parent was not permitted to visit	☐	☐	☐	☐
2. Not applicable, parent visited frequently	☐	☐	☐	☐
3. Advising the parent of the child's need for such visiting	☐	☐	☐	☐
4. Providing funds for travel costs	☐	☐	☐	☐
5. Providing funds to pay for babysitter arrangements for other children	☐	☐	☐	☐
6. Other forms of encouragement of visiting (Specify:_____	☐	☐	☐	☐

(Use additional pages if in care more than 4 years.)

VISITING-6   Case No._____ -47-   TCFP 7/20/84

PARENTAL CONTACT

F. Were any of the following factors operating to explain the lack of contact between parent and child? (Check all that apply.)

	Mother	Father
1. Identity of parent was unknown	☐	☐
2. Had not acknowledged paternity		☐
3. Had never lived with child	☐	☐
4. Had surrendered child	☐	☐
5. Had expressed intention of surrendering child	☐	☐
6. Parent lived out of state*	☐	☐
7. Parent's whereabouts were unknown **	☐	☐
8. Parent was institutionalized (Type of inst.___	☐	☐

Mother _____

Father _____

| 9. Other (Specify _____ | ☐ | ☐ |

_____

* Where did parent live? _____

** For how long a period were whereabouts unknown?

Mother _____

Father _____

VISITING-7   Case No._____   -48-   TCFP 7/20/84

PARENTAL CONTACT

G. Had the Program ever found it necessary to restrict or prohibit a parent from having contact with the child? (Check response that applies.)

	Mother	Father
1. No, contact never restricted or prohibited	☐	☐
2. Yes, for a limited time (from _____ to _____) (date) (date)	☐	☐
3. Yes contact was restricted over the full course of the placement	☐	☐
4. Other (Specify _____	☐	☐
5. Unknown	☐	☐

If visiting ever restricted or prohibited, please give details (including whether Court has issued directives restricting or modifying visiting opportunities of parents):

_____

_____

_____

_____

VISITING-8   Case No._____   -49-   TCFP 7/20/84

PARENTAL CONTACT

H. Characterize the degree to which the Program attempted to
   influence parents to visit during the child's years in care.
   (Check appropriate response.)

	1st Year in Care		2nd Year in Care	
	Mother	Father	Mother	Father
1. Parent visited, no special effort required	☐	☐	☐	☐
2. Major effort to get parent to visit	☐	☐	☐	☐
3. Moderate effort to get parent to visit	☐	☐	☐	☐
4. Slight effort to get parent to visit	☐	☐	☐	☐
5. No effort to get parent to visit	☐	☐	☐	☐
6. Other (Specify _____	☐	☐	☐	☐
7. Unknown				

	3rd Year in Care		4th Year in Care	
	Mother	Father	Mother	Father
1. Parent visited, no special effort required	☐	☐	☐	☐
2. Major effort to get parent to visit	☐	☐	☐	☐
3. Moderate effort to get parent to visit	☐	☐	☐	☐
4. Slight effort to get parent to visit	☐	☐	☐	☐
5. No effort to get parent to visit	☐	☐	☐	☐
6. Other (Specify _____	☐	☐	☐	☐
7. Unknown				

Were there any circumstances which have deterred the agency
from exerting greater effort?
parents):

Mother: _____

Father: _____

(Use additional pages if in care more than 4 years.)

SIBLINGS   Case No._____   -50-   TCFP 7/20/84

CHILD'S SIBLINGS

For each sibling (or half-sibling) of the CFP child provide the following information (going from the oldest to the youngest sibling):

A. Sibling number 1: _____
                        (First name)

B. Birthdate: _____   C. Sex: _____

D. Same mother as TCFP child

    ☐ Yes   ☐ No
                  (Give details:_____

E. Same father as TCFP child

    ☐ Yes   ☐ No
                  (Give details:_____

F. To what extent was the sibling raised together with the TCFP child, i.e., raised in the same household?

G. Give approximate periods in which they lived in the same household:

    From: _____ To: _____
            (year)   (year)

H. What living arrangements did the sibling experience (e.g., raised continuously in home of the mother, in foster care, etc.)

I. What contact did the TCFP child have with his/her sibling while in care with the Casey Program?

    ☐ No contact   ☐ Monthly

    ☐ Occasional sporadic contact   ☐ More than once a month

    ☐ About once in six months   ☐ In same foster home

    ☐ About once in three months   ☐ Other
                                       (Specify: _____

J. Indicate what is known from the record about the overall adjustment of the sibling and record any problems or special circumstances mentioned in the record.

(Use separate pages for additional siblings.)

PARENT   Case No._____ -51-   TCFP 7/20/84

WORK WITH CHILD'S PARENTS AND PARENTS' ROLE

A. What was the nature of the effort undertaken by agency staff
   to work with the parents of the child while he was is care?

	First Year in Care	Second Year in Care	Third Year in Care	Fourth Year in Care	Fifth Year in Care	Six + Year in Care
Mother						
1. Parent was not available for service contact	☐	☐	☐	☐	☐	☐
2. No contact between agency and parent; no indication of effort to involve parent	☐	☐	☐	☐	☐	☐
3. No contact; effort made to involve parent but without success	☐	☐	☐	☐	☐	☐
4. Sporadic contact (once or twice a year)	☐	☐	☐	☐	☐	☐
5. Contact at least bi-monthly	☐	☐	☐	☐	☐	☐
6. Other	☐	☐	☐	☐	☐	☐

	First Year in Care	Second Year in Care	Third Year in Care	Fourth Year in Care	Fifth Year in Care	Six + Year in Care
Father						
1. Parent was not available for service contact	☐	☐	☐	☐	☐	☐
2. No contact between agency and parent; no indication of effort to involve parent	☐	☐	☐	☐	☐	☐
3. No contact; effort made to involve parent but without success	☐	☐	☐	☐	☐	☐
4. Sporadic contact (once or twice a year)	☐	☐	☐	☐	☐	☐
5. Contact at least bi-monthly	☐	☐	☐	☐	☐	☐
6. Other	☐	☐	☐	☐	☐	☐

PARENT-2   Case No._____   -52-   TCFP 7/20/84

C. Briefly describe the content of agency service contacts with the parents.

   Mother:

   Father:

D. Characterize the image contained in the record of the parents' role in the child's life while he was in care with the Casey Family Program.

                                                      Mother Father

   1. Essentially out of the picture; parent   ☐   ☐
      totally absent

   2. Parent a peripheral   figure;   presence   ☐   ☐
      rarely manifested

   3. Parent   in   the   picture,   sometimes   ☐   ☐
      sporadically

   4. Parent pretty much in the picture;   ☐   ☐
      somewhat significant presence

   5. Parent very much in the picture;   ☐   ☐
      constituted a significant presence

   6. Other: ☐   ☐
      (Specify: _____

EXIT   Case No._____   -53-   TCFP 7/20/84

CHILD'S EXIT FROM CARE

A. At what age did the child cease being a ward of the Casey
   Family program?

   _____ Years

B. What best describes the basis upon which the child ceased
   being a ward of the Casey Family program?

   1. ☐ Child emancipated from care

   2. ☐ Child adopted by foster parents

   3. ☐ Child adopted by others

   4. ☐ Child returned to natural mother and father

   5. ☐ Child returned to natural mother

   6. ☐ Child returned to natural father

   7. ☐ Child went to live with other person

   8. ☐ Child ran away and did not return

   9. ☐ Child was returned to Court by Program

   10. ☐ Child hospitalized

   11. ☐ Child placed with other agency: _____

   12. ☐ Child imprisoned: _____

   13. ☐ Other (Specify: _____

EXIT-2   Case No._____   -54-   TCFP 9/ 7/84

CHILD'S EXIT FROM CARE

C. Overall how would one characterize the circumstances under which the child left care?

   1. ☐   A normal "aging out", emancipatory process -- generally devoid of any sense of conflict or crisis

   2. ☐

   3. ☐   Ending of care arrangement on a positive note but some elements of turbulence and associated problematic behavior shown by child

   4. ☐

   5. ☐   A less than serene ending with considerable evidence of emotional crisis and problematic behavior -- some positive features to the ending phase gives the exit from care a mixed quality

   6. ☐

   7. ☐   An acute crisis in the child's foster care status (e.g., child is being thrust out of home) -- a sense of failure accompanies the ending of care

   8. ☐   Other (e.g., adoption)

D. Did the Program continue to serve child and/or his family in same way after child left care?
(Check all that apply)

   1. ☐   No further service indicated in record

   2. ☐   Continued to offer social services, counseling to child

   3. ☐   Continued to offer social services, counseling to natural parents

   4. ☐   Continued to offer social services, counseling to adoptive parents

   5. ☐   Program financially supported child in his/her educational program

   6. ☐   Other Program involvement after discharge (Specify: _____

EXIT-3   Case No._____   -55-   TCFP 7/20/84

CHILD'S EXIT FROM CARE

E. Child's living arrangements upon emancipation from care

1. ☐ Set up own independent domicile

      (Details: _____

      _____

2. ☐ Remained in home of foster parents

      (Details: _____

      _____

3. ☐ Entered military service

4. ☐ Entered college or other educational institution

      (Details: _____

      _____

5. ☐ Other (Details: _____

      _____

6. ☐ No information in record

EXIT-4   Case No._____   -56-   TCFP 7/20/84

CHILD'S EXIT FROM CARE

F. Overall Adjustment Rating at Termination of Care

Considering the accumulated information available about this child, rate his/her overall adjustment at the time of his leaving the care of the Casey Family Program.

☐ 1. Child was making an excellent adjustment in all spheres of his life

☐ 2.

☐ 3. Child was making an adequate adjustment -- his/her strengths outweighed the weaknesses showed

☐ 4.

☐ 5. Child was making a mixed adjustment -- generally the problems he faced were serious

☐ 6.

☐ 7. Child was making an extremely poor adjustment

☐ No basis for rating.

SCHOLARSHIP   Case No._____   -57-   TCFP 7/20/84

SCHOLARSHIP AID

A. Did the child ever appeal for scholarship aid from the Casey Family Program?

  1. ☐ Yes

  2. ☐ No

If yes, provide the following information:

B. In what year did the child make application? _____

C. Was the request granted by the Program?

  1. ☐ Yes

  2. ☐ No (What was the reason for turning down the request? _____

D. If request was granted, what educational objective did the child wish to pursue?
_____

E. What was the financial outlay by the Program for each year the child received support?

  19____ _____   19____ _____

  19____ _____   19____ _____

F. Did the child ever experience an interruption in his/her educational program?

  1. ☐ No

  2. ☐ Yes (Give details:_____

_____

G. Did the child succeed in completing the educational program embarked upon?

  1. ☐ Yes (What certificate, degree or other symbol of completion did he/she receive? _____)

  2. ☐ No (Give details: _____

_____

SCHOLARSHIP-2   Case No._____ -58-   TCFP 7/20/84

SCHOLARSHIP AID

H. Additional comments about the experience (e.g., relation of training to subsequent employment.)

_____

_____

_____

_____

_____

_____

_____

_____

_____

_____

_____

_____

_____

_____

_____

_____

_____

_____

_____

PURCHASE   Case No._____   -59-   TCFP 7/20/84

PURCHASE OF SERVICES

Reviewing this case as a whole, were there resources brought to
bear on behalf of the child that represented the special capacity
of the Casey Family Program to undertake expenditures not normally
available to other child welfare agencies? Indicate whether there
is evidence of such expenditure in the following areas:

A. Payment for child's care in a residential treatment program.

1. ☐ No indication of this in record

2. ☐ Yes
       Describe the kind of care purchased

       Specify the period the child was in care:

           From: _____ to _____

       Give examples of expenditure amounts shown in
       record covering the purchase of this service

B. Payment for psychotherapeutic or counseling treatment from a
   private practioner (e.g., psychiatrist, psychologist, social
   worker, speech therapist, etc.)

1. ☐ No indication of this in record

2. ☐ Yes
       Describe the problems of the child requiring
       treatment.

       Describe the nature of the treatment offered.

       In general, what did the treatment accomplish?

       Specify the period(s) in which treatment was
       received and the general frequency of contact
       with the child.

       Give examples of the expenditure amounts shown in
       record covering the purchase of services.

PURCHASE-2   Case No._____   -60-   TCFP 7/20/84

PURCHASE OF SERVICES

C. Payment for medical/health care treatment beyond routine
   health supervision.

   1. ☐ No indication of this in record

   2. ☐ Yes
          Describe the kinds of medical care/health
          service provided.

          In general, what did the treatment accomplish?

          Give examples of the expenditure amounts shown
          in record covering the purchase of services.

D. Payment for dental services beyond routine care.

   1. ☐ No indication of this in record

   2. ☐ Yes
          Describe the kinds of dental care provided.

          Give examples of the expenditure amounts shown
          in record covering the purchase of services.

E. Other expenditures (not including student aid) that appear
   noteworthy (e.g., expenditure for travel to bring natural
   parents and child together).

   1. ☐ No indication of this in record

   2. ☐ Yes
          Describe the purpose of the expenditures.

          Give examples of the expenditure amounts shown
          in record covering the purchase of services.

QUESTIONS   Case No._____   -61-   TCFP 8/ 1/84

If there are any salient features about this case not captured by the case reading schedule, please make note of them:

Item 1.

Item 2.

Item 3.

Item 4.

Are there any questions not now included in the case reading schedule that seem useful as added information to be gathered on all cases?

Item 1.

Item 2.

Item 3.

Item 4.

POST-DISCHARGE   Case No._____   -62-   TCFP 7/31/84

Post-Discharge Information

Briefly describe any relatively significant contact after discharge between the Casey Family Program and the child, his family or another source (agency, hospital, prison, employer, etc.) Indicate any change in marital status, accomplishments, any serious incidents, and/or material reflecting upon quality of adjustment.

Date: _____

Date: _____

Date: _____

INQUIRIES   Case No._____ -63-   TCFP 7/20/84

Inquiries or Comments from Case Readers Directed to
David Fanshel and John Grundy

As the case reading schedule is filled out, indicate any
noteworthy definitional problem about an item or indicate
idiosyncratic features of a case which make an item not
particularly relevant or problematic. This information will be
reviewed with you and will lead to definitions and coding
decisions to guide this and other cases (or the problem will be
resolved arbitrarily for this case without implications for other
cases.)

_____   _____
Case number   Case reader

Item number and page:_____

Item number and page:_____

Item number and page:_____

FOLLOWUP   Case No._____   -64-   TCFP 9/ 7/84

FUTURE EFFORTS TO LOCATE FORMER CASEY PROGRAM WARDS

List potential leads to the location of the child so that he/she
    can be approached about participating in a follow-up study in
    1985-86.

A. What is the date of the last contact with the child, the
    nature of the contact, and future plans indicated in the case
    record and residential status at the time?

B. Persons with whom child might be in contact (foster parents,
    natural parents, siblings, employer, etc.)
    Record names, addresses and telephone numbers.

	Name	Address	Telephone
1.	_____	_____	_____
2.	_____	_____	_____
3.	_____	_____	_____
4.	_____	_____	_____
5.	_____	_____	_____
6.	_____	_____	_____

C. Agencies who might know where the child is.

	Name	Address	Telephone
1.	_____	_____	_____
2.	_____	_____	_____
3.	_____	_____	_____

D. Other potentially useful location information.

SUMMARY   Case No._____   -65-   TCFP 7/31/84

Brief Summary of the Case

_____

_____

_____

_____

_____

_____

_____

_____

_____

_____

_____

_____

_____

_____

_____

_____

Case Reader: _____   Date read: _____

☐ Primary reader

☐ Secondary reader

☐ Other: _____

THE CASEY FAMILY PROGRAM

```
┌─────────────────────────────────┐
│                                 │
│         FOLLOW-UP STUDY         │
│                                 │
│           1985 - 1986           │
│                                 │
└─────────────────────────────────┘
```

INTERVIEWING SCHEDULE

David Fanshel, Project Director
Professor
Columbia University School
         of Social Work

Jaime Alvelo, Research Associate
622 West 113th Street
New York, New York 10025
(212) 280-3250

The Casey Family Program
Management Office
Suite 906 Joseph Vance Bldg.
1402 Third Avenue
Seattle, Washington 98101
(206) 624-6412

Arthur R. Dodson, ACSW
Executive Director

STATEMENT TO INTERVIEWEE

We wish to talk to you about your experience in life now and while in care with 'The Casey Family Program'. We represent Columbia University which has been given a contract by The Casey Program to study the quality of life of people like yourself. The Casey Family Program wants to do everything it can to better serve the children that come to its care.You are in a position to be of assistance in this study because you have experienced the services offered by The Casey Family Program directly and only you know what was helpful and not helpful, what you may have liked and what you may not have liked about the way your situation was handled. The Casey Family Program will of course be glad to hear reports that its efforts have been found helpful.However, it is also important to know when service was not helpful and if you were displeased with any aspect of the way you were treated.

What you say will be held strictly confidential. Responses from individuals will not be reported back to the agency. We will be interviewing 100 persons who at some point in their life came in to foster family care at The Casey Program, and we will summarize what everyone tells us so that the agency will receive an overall report. Any suggestions will be reported back to Casey staff but not in a way that individuals can be identified.

We will be paying you twenty-five dollars for your time and effort in participating in this interview. We are also offering payment because your cooperation is important to our study and, in this instance, you are being asked to give a service to the agency which can be very valuable.

You should feel free to ask questions before making up your mind about whether you wish to be interviewed. You should feel free to refuse to be interviewed if you experience discomfort about participation or object to such an interview for other reasons.

2   TCFP 9/12/85

CLIENT CONSENT

DATE _____

I have explained the purposes of the research to the interviewee, emphasized the voluntary nature of participation, and elicited the following response to the question, "Do you consent to being interviewed?"

_____ Subject agrees to being interviewed

_____ Subject refuses to be interviewed*

*Reason stated

_____

_____

_____
Interviewer

3
RESEARCH NO. _____ DIVISION_____ TCFP 9/12/85

NAME OF SUBJECT _____

ADDRESS _____
      NUMBER   STREET   CITY   STATE   ZIP

TELEPHONE# WHERE RESPONDENT CAN BE REACHED

NAME OF RELATIVE/ACQUAINTANCE: _____

ADDRESS _____
      NUMBER   STREET   CITY   STATE   ZIP

TELEPHONE# WHERE RELATIVE CAN BE REACHED

***********RECORDS OF ATTEMPTS TO CONTACT FORMER WARD***************

SOURCES OF CLUES:

__ CASERECORD(1)   __ SOCIAL AGENCY(8)
__ CASEREADER(2)   __ UTILITY COMPANY(9)
__ TELEPHONE BOOK(3)   __ MOTOR VEHICLE DEPT(10)
__ SOCIAL WORKER(4)   __ CREDIT BUREAU(11)
__ FOSTER PARENT(5)   __ POSTAL SERVICE(12)
__ RELATIVES(6)   __ LOCAL MERCHANT(13)
__ NEIGHBORS(7)   __ MILITARY LOCATOR SERVICE(14)

NOTE:Identify clue and write a running record of efforts at contact

Calls or Letters	Date and Time of Each Call (or date of letter)	What Happened?
1		
2		
3		
4		

DATE OF RESEARCH INTERVIEW _____ TIME BEGAN _____

A. CONDITIONS OF LIFE FOR FAMILY

As a way of getting started, let's talk about housing. We would like to have some sense of the conditions of your living arrangements and your feelings about them. For example, concerning your housing...

A01   What is your current housing situation? (e.g., Do you own a house, rent an apartment, have a room or live with relatives?)

    006   1 |_| Rented room

           2 |_| Rented aparment

           3 |_| Rented house

           4 |_| Own apartment

           5 |_| Own house

           6 |_| Live with relatives

           9 |_| Other (specify _____)

A02   How satisfied are you with your housing arrangements?
             In general, would you say...

    007   1 |_| Very satisfied?

           2 |_| Fairly satisfied?

           3 |_| Neither?

           4 |_| Fairly dissatisfied? [Ask a) & b)]

           5 |_| Very dissatisfied?   [Ask a) & b)]

           9 |_| Other (specify _____)

           a) Why are you dissatisfied?
              (PROBE: What conditions do you object to?)
              CHECK ALL THAT APPLY

A03   1 |_| Overcrowding of living quarters
    008
A04   1 |_| Seriously deteriorated housing
    009
A05   1 |_| Threat of loss of housing
    010
A06   1 |_| Lack of own housing (living with
    011   relatives or friends)

A07   1 |_| Other (specify _____)
    012

HOUSING

IF DISSATISFIED

A08   b) Have you made any effort to improve the situation?

013   1 |‾| Yes

2 |‾| No

Please tell me what you did?

A09
014-015 _____
A10
016-017 _____
A11
018-019 _____

A12   Going back to your experience after you left foster care, have you
encountered any particularly difficult times with housing since you
left foster care?

020 1 |‾| Yes

2 |‾| No---------------> GO TO Q.

A13   IF YES: What was your experience? _____
021-022
A14   _____
023-024
A15   _____
025-026

Concerning this neighborhood....

A16   How do you feel about this neighborhood (area) as a place in which to raise your family? Would you say it is...

    027   1 |‾| A very good place?---------->
                                              > GO TO A23
          2 |‾| A fairly good place?-------->

          3 |‾| Average/a mixture of good and bad?

          4 |‾| A pretty bad place?

          5 |‾| A very bad place?

          9 |‾| Other (specify _____)

A17   a) Why do you feel this way?
028-029

A18
030-031 _____

A19   b) How has living in this neighborhhod (area) influenced how you
032-033   live?

A20
034-035 _____

        IF R HAS CHILDREN
A21   c) How do you see the conditions of this neighborhood (area)
036-037   influencing your children?

A22
038-039 _____

A23   How long have you been living here?

040-041   NUMBER OF YEARS_____
A24
042-043   MONTHS_____

A25   How many times have you moved in the past five years?

044-045   NUMBER OF TIMES_____

B. INCOME AND FINANCIAL MATTERS

We are interested in knowing something about the role of
income and financial matters in your living situation.

What are the sources of income in your home?
(CHECK ALL THAT APPLY)

B01
    041 1 |__| Wages
B02
    042 1 |__| Public assistance (full support)
B03
    043 1 |__| Public Assistance (partial support)
B04
    044 1 |__| Social Security
B05
    045 1 |__| Student loan(s) or grants
B06
    046 1 |__| Unemployment insurance
B07
    047 1 |__| Supplemental Security Income (SSI)
B08
    048 1 |__| Business or profession (Own)
B09
    049 1 |__| The Casey Family Program
B10
    050 1 |__| No income at all at this time
B11
    051 1 |__| Other (specify _____)

IF RECEIVING WELFARE (AFDC, SSI, GENERAL ASSISTANCE)

B12   How long have you been receiving financial aid?
052-053 NUMBER OF YEARS_____
B13
054-055 NUMBER OF MONTHS_____

B14   Do you regard your income as providing you with an adequate
         amount of money to live decently or to raise your family properly?

    056 1 |__| Income is adequate

        2 |__| Income is somewhat adequate

        3 |__| Income is inadequate

        4 |__| Other (specify) _____

_____

B15   During the last few years, has your financial situation been getting
         better, stayed the same, or has it been getting worse?

    057 1 |__| Getting better

        2 |__| Stayed the same

        3 |__| Getting worse

B16   Compared with most people about your age you know, would you say
       your income is higher, about the same or less than theirs?

058   3 |‾| Higher

       2 |‾| Same

       1 |‾| Less

       9 |‾| Other

B17   Have you or your family needed financial help to get along during
       the last few years?

059   1 |‾| Yes

       2 |‾| No

       IF YES

B18   Who has given you help?_____
060-061
       _____

B19   Do you ever run short of funds so that you do not have the ability to
       buy food or pay your rent? Would you say this happens...

062   3 |‾| Often

       2 |‾| Sometimes

       1 |‾| Never

       9 |‾| Other (specify) _____

       _____

B20   Do you find yourself having more debts than you can handle?

063   1 |‾| Very much

       2 |‾| Somewhat

       3 |‾| Not at all

       4 |‾| Other (specify_____)

B21   How satisfied are you with your financial situation?

064   3 |‾| Very satisfied

       2 |‾| satisfied

       1 |‾| Not satisfied

       9 |‾| Other (specify) _____

       _____

INCOME AND FINANCES

B22   What is more or less your annual income before taxes?
        (SHOW INCOME CARD)

065-066 01. None   13. $12,000 - $12,999

        02. $1 - $1,999   14. $13,000 - $13,999

        03. $2,000 - $2,999   15. $14,000 - $14,999

        04. $3,000 - $3,999   16. $15,000 - $15,999

        05. $4,000 - $4,999   17. $16,000 - $16,999

        06. $5,000 - $5,999   18. $17,000 - $17,999

        07. $6,000 - $6,999   19. $18,000 - $18,999

        08. $7,000 - $7,999   20. $19,000 - $19,999

        09. $8,000 - $8,999   21. $20,000 - $24,999

        10. $9,000 - $9,999   22. $25,000 - $34,999

        11. $10,000 - $10,999   23. $35,000 AND OVER

        12. $11,000 - $11,999

B23   How many adults depend on this income? How many children?

067-068   NUMBER OF ADULTS _____

069-070   NUMBER OF CHILDREN _____

B24   During the past few months have you had to worry about money
        matters? Would you say...

    071   5 |‾| Very often

          4 |‾| Often

          3 |‾| Sometimes

          2 |‾| Hardly ever

          1 |‾| Never

          9 |‾| Other (specify)_____

C. PREVIOUS JOB NUMBER_____   REPEAT FOR UP TO FOUR JOBS
What type of work did you do, and what was your job title?

TYPE OF WORK:_____

JOB TITLE:_____

How long did you work at this job?

_____Months   _____Years

What was your annual take home pay? ---->ENTER ANNUAL SALARY_____

Were you ever promoted?

1 |‾| Yes

2 |‾| No

a) Why not?_____

_____

Were you happy with the type of work that you did?

3 |‾| Very happy

2 |‾| Pretty happy

1 |‾| Not too happy

What about your salary? How satisfied were you with what you earned?

4 |‾| Very satisfied

3 |‾| Somewhat satisfied

2 |‾| Not too satisfied

1 |‾| Not at all satisfied

Why did you stop working at this job? (CHECK ALL THAT APPLY)

1 |‾| Higher paying/better job	10 |‾| Other family responsibilities
2 |‾| Fired	11 |‾| Didn't like the job
3 |‾| Laid off/plant shut-down	12 |‾| Didn't want to work
4 |‾| Got married	13 |‾| Strike
5 |‾| Personal health reasons	14 |‾| Transportation problems
6 |‾| Got pregnant	15 |‾| Keep social service eligibity
7 |‾| Returned to school	98 |‾| DK
8 |‾| Moved away	99 |‾| Other (specify_____)
9	‾	Child care responsibilities	GO TO C25 PAGE 12

D. MARRIAGE AND COURTSHIP

D01   Are you married? Living with someone? Divorced? Separated?
        Widowed? or Single?

    148 1 |‾| Married ------------------->
                                                  > GO TO   PAGE 17 Q. D11
          2 |‾| Living with someone --------->

          3 |‾| Divorced

          4 |‾| Separated

          5 |‾| Widowed

          6 |‾| Single

        IF NOT MARRIED/LIVING

D02   a)Do you have any objections to questions about your current
          relationships with the opposite sex?

    149 1 |‾| Yes----------------> SKIP TO PAGE 17 Q. D12

          2 |‾| No

D03   b)Do you have a steady boyfriend/girlfriend?

    150 1 |‾| Yes ---------------> GO TO PAGE 17 Q. D11

          2 |‾| No

          9 |‾| Other (Specify_____)

D04   c)Have you been dating or participating in activities
          where you meet men/women?

    151 1 |‾| Yes

          2 |‾| No

          9 |‾| Other (Specify_____)

IF NOT MARRIED OR LIVING WITH SOMEONE

D05   d)Are you involved in a relationship which may lead to marriage or
             to your living with someone in the near future?

      152   1 |‾| Yes ---------------------> GO TO PAGE 17 Q. D11

             2 |‾| No

             IF NO

D06   Why not?
 153-154

D07
 155-156

D08   e)How have your relationships with the opposite sex turned out
             so far?

      157   5 |‾| Very satisfactory

             4 |‾| Satisfactory

             3 |‾| Neither satisfatory nor unsatisfactory

             2 |‾| Unsatisfactory

             1 |‾| Very unsatisfactory

             IF LESS THAN SATISFACTORY

D09
 158-159   Why is that? _____
D10
 160-161   _____

MARRIAGE AND COURTSHIP

(FOR THOSE INVOLVED IN AN ONGOING RELATIONSHIP)

D11   Overall, how would you rate the relationship you are involved in?
         Would you say it is...

         162 3 |‾| A happy one?

              2 |‾| Pretty happy?

              1 |‾| Not too happy?

D12   Have you ever permanently broken up with someone you lived with
         or were married to?

         163 1 |‾|Yes

              2 |‾|No--------------> SKIP TO PAGE 18

         IF YES
D13
 164-165 How many times?_____

              (FOR EACH RELATIONSHIP ASK THE FOLLOWING. RECORD RESPONSES
               IN CHART BELOW)

         In what year did your (first/second/etc) marriage begin?

         In what year did the marriage/relationship end?

         Was the marriage ended by death, divorce, separation, or annulment?

         (REPEAT FOR EACH BROKEN RELATIONSHIP)

		Year began	Year ended	Death	Divorce	Separation	Anulment	Other#
D14/D16 166-170	1st			1	2	3	4	9
D17/D19 171-175	2nd			1	2	3	4	9
D20/D22 176-180	3rd			1	2	3	4	9
D23/D25 181-185	4th			1	2	3	4	9

D26   #Other(describe)_____
 186-187
D27   _____
 188-189
          _____

D28   What do you think was the main reason for this(ese) separation(s)?
 190-191
D29   _____
 192-193
          _____

E. EDUCATION AND TRAINING

Now some questions about your education and aspirations...

E01   What was the highest grade you completed in school?

194-195   _____GRADE COMPLETED

While you were going to school how did you perform in the following areas? (FOR EACH ASK) Would you say very good,good,average,below average or poor?

PERFORMANCE

		Very Good	Good	Average	Below Average	Poor	DNA
		5	4	3	2	1	8
E02	196 a)Getting along with classmates	|_|	|_|	|_|	|_|	|_|	|_|
E03	197 b)Getting along with teachers	|_|	|_|	|_|	|_|	|_|	|_|
E04	198 c)Grades	|_|	|_|	|_|	|_|	|_|	|_|
E05	199 d)Sports	|_|	|_|	|_|	|_|	|_|	|_|
E06	200 e)Music,drama or art	|_|	|_|	|_|	|_|	|_|	|_|
E07	201 f)Attendance at school	|_|	|_|	|_|	|_|	|_|	|_|

E08   Did you have any special problems in doing your best in school?

202   1 |_| Yes

        2 |_| No

E09   IF YES What were these?_____
203-204
E10   _____

205-206 _____

E11 Do you have any regrets about how far you went or what you accomplished in school?

  207 1 |＿| Yes

     2 |＿| No

E12
208-209 IF YES What would you have preferred?_____
E13
210-211 _____

E14 Based on your training or education how well prepared were you for employment or a work career? (PROBE: Were you prepared to earn a living?)

  212 1 |＿| Very well prepared

     2 |＿| Sowewhat prepared

     3 |＿| Not that well prepared

     4 |＿| Altogether unprepared

E15 Have you considered obtaining further education?

  213 1 |＿| Yes

     2 |＿| No

    IF YES
E16
214-215 a) In what way?
E17
216-217

E18 b) What are the chances that you will actually get this education?

  218 1 |＿| Good

     2 |＿| Fair

     3 |＿| Poor

     9 |＿| Other (specify)_____

E19   Have you ever participated in a job training program?

　　219　　1 |‾| Yes

　　　　　2 |‾| No

　　　　　IF YES

E20   a)In what field? (i.e. banking, computers...)
220-221

E21   b)Did you complete it?

　　222　　1 |‾| Yes

　　　　　2 |‾| No
E22
223-224   IF NO Why not?_____
E23
225-226   _____

E24   Overall, how satisfied are you with the education and training you
          have acquired so far?

　　227　　5 |‾| Very satisfied

　　　　　4 |‾| Somewhat satisfied

　　　　　3 |‾| Neither satisfied nor dissatisfied

　　　　　2 |‾| Somewhat dissatisfied

　　　　　1 |‾| Very dissatisfied

E25   Did you ever apply to The Casey Family Program for scholarship
          assistance to obtain more education or training?

　　228　　1 |‾| Yes

　　　　　2 |‾| No

　　　　　IF YES
E26
229-230   a) In what?_____
E27
231-232   _____
E28
233-234   b) How did it turn out? Why?_____
E29
235-236   _____

F. HEALTH

F01   In general would you say that your health is: excellent, good, fair, poor, or very poor?

237   5 |__| Excellent

        4 |__| Good

        3 |__| Fair

        2 |__| Poor

        1 |__| Very poor

F02   Is there any particular physical or health problem that bothers you at present?

238   1 |__| Yes

        2 |__| No

        a)What are (is) these (this) condition(s)?

F03
239-240   1-First condition _____
F04
241-242   2-Second condition _____
F05
243-244   3-Third condition _____
F06
245-246   4-Fourth condition _____
F07
247-248   5-Others(INTERVIEWER LIST OTHER CONDITIONS)_____

            _____

F08   Considering your physical health condition, Do you feel it affects your ability to work? (negatively as a barrier)

249   1 |__| Yes

        2 |__| No

F09   IF YES In what way?_____
250-251
F10   _____
252-253

G.   WORRIES AND HAPPINESS

Everybody has some things he worries about more or less. What kind of things do you worry about most?

G01
254-255 _____

G02
256-257 _____

G03
258-259 _____

_____

G04   Do you worry about such things a lot, or not very much?

260   1 |‾| A lot

        2 |‾| Not very much

        9 |‾| Other

Everyone has things about their life they're not completely happy about. What are some of the things you're not too happy about these days? (PROBE FOR FULL RESPONSES)

G05
261-262 _____

G06
263-264 _____

G07
265-266 _____

_____

Thinking now of the way things were in the past, what do you think of as the most unhappy time of your life? (probe for whole period of R's life)

G08
267-268 _____

G09
269-270 _____

Why do you think of that as an unhappy time? (Can you tell me more about that time?)

G10
271-272 _____

G11
273-274 _____

G12
275-276 _____

_____

Thinking now of the way things were in the past, what do you think
of as the most happy time of your life? (probe for whole period
of R's life)

G13
277-278 _____

G14
279-280 _____

Why do you think of that as a happy time? (Can you tell me more
about that time?)

G15
281-282 _____

G16
283-284 _____

G17
285-286 _____

_____

G18   Do you find yourself feeling bitter about the way things
       have turned out for you? Would you say...

287   1 |‾| Yes, very often?

                2 |‾| Yes, sometimes?

                3 |‾| No, hardly ever or never?

                9 |‾| Other (specify) _____

                _____

G19   a)   What generally causes you to feel this way?
288-289
G20
290-291

H.   WELL BEING
Now I some questions about how you've been feeling during the past month.

H01   How have you been feeling in   1 |⎯| In excellent spirits
        general?
  292   2 |⎯| In very good spirits

                                          3 |⎯| In good spirits mostly

                                          4 |⎯| I 've been up and down in spirits

                                          5 |⎯| In low spirits mostly

                                          6 |⎯| In very low spirits

H02   Have you been bothered by   1 |⎯| Extremely so--to the point
        nervousness or your nerves?   where I could not work
  293
                                          2 |⎯| Very much so

                                          3 |⎯| Quite a bit

                                          4 |⎯| Some--enough to bother me

                                          5 |⎯| A little

                                          6 |⎯| Not at all

H03   Have you been in firm control 1 |⎯| Yes, definitely so
        of your behavior,thoughts,
        emotions or feelings?
  294   2 |⎯| Yes,for the most part

                                          3 |⎯| Generally so

                                          4 |⎯| Not too well

                                          5 |⎯| No, and I am somewhat disturbed

                                          6 |⎯| No, and I am very disturbed

H04   Have you felt so sad,   1 |⎯| Extremely so--to the point
        discouraged,hopeless, or had   that I have about given up
        so many problems that you
        wondered if anything was   2 |⎯| Very much so
        worthwhile?
  295   3 |⎯| Quite a bit

                                          4 |⎯| Some--enough to bother me

                                          5 |⎯| A little bit

                                          6 |⎯| Not at all

H05   Have you been under or felt   1 |_| Yes--almost more than
       you were under any strain   I could bear or stand
       stress,or pressure?
  296   2 |_| Yes--quite a bit

                                         3 |_| Yes--more than usual

                                         4 |_| Yes--some--about usual

                                         5 |_| Yes-a little

                                         6 |_| Not at all

H06   How happy, satisfied, or   1 |_| Extremely happy--could not have
       pleased have you been with   been more satisfied or pleased
       your personal life?
  297   2 |_| Very happy

                                         3 |_| Fairly happy

                                         4 |_| Satisfied--pleased

                                         5 |_| Somewhat dissatisfied

                                         6 |_| Very dissatisfied

H07   Have you had any reason to   1 |_| Not at all
       wonder if you were losing
       your mind, or losing control
       over the way you act,talk,   2 |_| Only a little
       feel,or of your memory?
                                         3 |_| Some--but not enough to be
  298   concerned or worried about

                                         4 |_| Some & I 've been concerned a bit

                                         5 |_| Some and I am quite concerned

                                         6 |_| Yes,very much so and I am
                                               very concerned

H08   Have you been anxious,   1 |_| Extremely so--to the point
       worried, or upset?   of being sick or almost sick
  299
                                         2 |_| Very much so

                                         3 |_| Quite a bit

                                         4 |_| Some-enough to bother me

                                         5 |_| A little bit

                                         6 |_| Not at all

H09   Have you been waking up fresh   1 |__| Every day
300   and rested?   2 |__| Most every day

                                             3 |__| Fairly often

                                             4 |__| Less than half the time

                                             5 |__| Rarely

                                             6 |__| None of the time

H10   Have you been bothered by any   1 |__| All the time
        illness,   bodily   disorder,
        pains, or fears about health?   2 |__| Most of the time
301
                                             3 |__| A good bit of the time

                                             4 |__| Some of the time

                                             5 |__| A little of the time

                                             6 |__| None of the time

H11   Has your daily life been full   1 |__| All the time
        of   things   that   were
        interesting to you?   2 |__| Most of the time
302
                                             3 |__| A good bit of the time

                                             4 |__| Some of the time

                                             5 |__| A little of the time

                                             6 |__| None of the time

H12   Have   you   felt   down-hearted   1 |__| All the time
        and blue?   2 |__| Most of the time
303
                                             3 |__| A good bit of the time

                                             4 |__| Some of the time

                                             5 |__| A little of the time

                                             6 |__| None of the time

H13   Have   you   been   feeling   1 |__| All the time
        emotionally   stable   and sure
        of yourself?   2 |__| Most of the time
304
                                             3 |__| A good bit of the time

                                             4 |__| Some of the time

                                             5 |__| A little of the time

                                             6 |__| None of the time

H14   Have you you felt tired, worn   1 |_| All the time
        out, used up, or exhausted?
    305   2 |_| Most of the time

                                          3 |_| A good bit of the time

                                          4 |_| Some of the time

                                          5 |_| A little of the time

                                          6 |_| None of the time

H15   Do you discuss your problems   1 |_| Yes--and it helps a lot
        with any members of your
        family or friends?   2 |_| Yes--and it helps some
    306
                                          3 |_| Yes--but it does not help at all

                                          4 |_| No-I do not have anyone I can
                                                talk with about my problems

                                          5 |_| No-no one cares to hear about
                                                my problems

                                          6 |_| No-I do not care to talk about
                                                my problems with anyone

                                          7 |_| No-I do not have any problems

H16   Have you had severe enough   1 |_| Yes, and I did seek professional
        personal,emotional,behavior,   help
        or mental problems that you
        felt you needed help during   2 |_| Yes,but I did not seek
        the past year?   professional help
    307
                                          3 |_| I have had (or have now)
                                                severe personal problems, but
                                                have not felt I needed
                                                professional help

                                          4 |_| I have had very few personal
                                                problems of any serious
                                                concern

                                          5 |_| I have not been bothered
                                                at all by personal problems
                                                during the past year

H17   Have you ever felt that you 1 |⎽| Yes--during the past year
       were going to have,or were
       close to having, a nervous 2 |⎽| Yes--more than a year ago
       breakdown?
   308   3 |⎽| No

H18   Have you ever had a nervous 1 |⎽| Yes--during the past year
       breakdown?
   309   2 |⎽| Yes--more than a year ago

                                   3 |⎽| No

H19   Have you ever been a patient 1 |⎽| Yes--during the past year
       at a mental health facility
       for any personal,emotional, 2 |⎽| Yes--more than a year ago
       behavior,or mental problem
   310   3 |⎽| No

H20   Have you ever seen a
       psychiatrist, psychologist,or 1 |⎽| Yes--during the past year
       psychoanalyst about any
       personal,emotional,behavior, 2 |⎽| Yes--more than a year ago
       or mental problem concerning
       yourself?   3 |⎽| No
   311

       Have you talked with or had any connection with any of the following
       about some personal,emotional,behavior,or mental problem concerning
       yourself during the past year?

H21
       312 a)Regular medical doctor(not routine)   1 |⎽| Yes   2 |⎽| No
H22
       313 b)Brain or nerve specialist   1 |⎽| Yes   2 |⎽| No
H23
       314 c)Nurse (not routine)   1 |⎽| Yes   2 |⎽| No
H24
       315 d)Lawyer(not routine)   1 |⎽| Yes   2 |⎽| No
H25
       316 e)Police(not minor violations)   1 |⎽| Yes   2 |⎽| No
H26
       317 f)Clergyman,minister,priest,rabbi...   1 |⎽| Yes   2 |⎽| No
H27
       318 g)Marriage counselor   1 |⎽| Yes   2 |⎽| No
H28
       319 h)Social worker   1 |⎽| Yes   2 |⎽| No
H29
       320 i)Other formal assistance   1 |⎽| Yes   2 |⎽| No

                                       What kind?_____

For each of the four scales below, note that the words of each end of the 0 to 10 scale describe opposite feelings. Circle any number along the bar which seems closest to how you have generally felt during the past month.

H30

321

How concerned or worried about your health have you been?

```
0  1  2  3  4  5  6  7  8  9  10
|  |  |  |  |  |  |  |  |  |   |
|__|__|__|__|__|__|__|__|__|__|
Not                         Very
concerned               concerned
```

H31

322

How relaxed or tense have you been?

```
0  1  2  3  4  5  6  7  8  9  10
|  |  |  |  |  |  |  |  |  |   |
|__|__|__|__|__|__|__|__|__|__|
Very                        Very
relaxed                     tense
```

H32

323

How much energy, pep, vitality, have you felt?

```
0  1  2  3  4  5  6  7  8  9  10
|  |  |  |  |  |  |  |  |  |   |
|__|__|__|__|__|__|__|__|__|__|
No energy                   Very
at all                  energetic
```

H33

324

How depressed or cheerful have you been?

```
0  1  2  3  4  5  6  7  8  9  10
|  |  |  |  |  |  |  |  |  |   |
|__|__|__|__|__|__|__|__|__|__|
Very                        Very
depressed              cheerlful
```

SYMPTOMS DURING PAST WEEK

Please tell how often you have experienced the following during the past week....
(INTERVIEWER PROBE FOR FREQUENCY OF SYMPTOM)

		Rarely or None of the Time	Some or a little of the Time	Occasion-ally or a Mode-rate Amount of Time	Most or All of the Time
	DURING THE PAST WEEK:	(1 day)	(1-2) Days	(3-4) Days	(5-7) Days
H34	325 I was bothered by things that usually don't bother me......................	0	1	2	3
H35	326 I did not feel like eating;my appetite was poor............................	0	1	2	3
H36	327 I felt that I could not shake off the blues even with help from my family or friends.............................	0	1	2	3
H37	328 I felt that I was just as good as other people...............................	0	1	2	3
H38	329 I had trouble keeping my mind on what I was doing...........................	0	1	2	3
H39	330 I felt depressed......................	0	1	2	3
H40	331 I felt everything I did was an effort..	0	1	2	3
H41	332 I felt hopeful about the future.......	0	1	2	3
H42	333 I thought my life had been a failure..	0	1	2	3
H43	334 I felt fearful.......................	0	1	2	3
H44	335 My sleep was restless.................	0	1	2	3
H45	336 I was happy...........................	0	1	2	3
H46	337 I talked less than usual..............	0	1	2	3
H47	338 I felt lonely.........................	0	1	2	3
H48	339 People were unfriendly................	0	1	2	3
H49	340 I enjoyed life........................	0	1	2	3
H50	341 I had crying spells...................	0	1	2	3
H51	342 I felt sad............................	0	1	2	3
H52	343 I felt that people disliked me.........	0	1	2	3
H53	344 I could not get going.................	0	1	2	3

I.   ALCOHOL AND DRUGS

Now I'd like to ask you some questions about drinking.

I01   During the past month, about how often did you drink beer, wine or some other liquor? Would you say...

345   5 |＿| Every day

4 |＿| 3-5 times a week

3 |＿| 1-2 times a week

2 |＿| Less than 1-2 times a week

1 |＿| Never------------------------------> GO TO Q. I03

I02   About how often, during the past month, did you drink to the point where you felt high or "tight" or had "a buzz on"?

346   5 |＿| Every day

4 |＿| 3-5 times a week

3 |＿| 1-2 times a week

2 |＿| Less than 1-2 times a week

1 |＿| Never

I03   During earlier years, was there any time that you were drinking more, about the same, or less than now?

347   4 |＿| More than now

3 |＿| About the same as now

2 |＿| Less than now

1 |＿| Never drank------------------------> GO TO PAGE 33 Q. I08

I04   About how old were you when you started to drink alcohol?

348-349   AGE_____

I05   Has drinking ever been a source of problems in your life?

    350 1 |__| A lot

         2 |__| Somewhat

         3 |__| Not at all

         8 |__| DNA

         9 |__| Other (specify_____)

         IF YES
I06   In what way?_____
351-352
I07   _____
353-354
             _____

ALCOHOL AND DRUGS
I08   Have you ever used any non-prescribed drug in your life? (LIKE POT, COCAINE, ETC...)

355   1 |__| Yes

      2 |__| No--------------->GO TO PAGE 35 Q. I22

On this sheet please check aproximately how often you have used each of the drugs during the the the past year.

	NEVER (1)	ONCE OR TWICE A YEAR (2)	3-10 TIMES A YEAR (3)	ONCE OR TWICE A MONTH (4)	ONCE OR TWICE A WEEK (5)	NEARLY EVERY DAY (6)
I09 356 Marijuana (pot, grass) or hashish						
I10 357 Amphetamines (speed, pep pills, bennies, uppers), other than prescribed by an MD						
I11 358 Cocaine						
I12 359 Barbiturates or other downs						
I13 360 Heroin (H, smak) or morphine						
I14 361 LSD, Angel Dust						
I15 362 Quads, qualudes						
I16 363 Valium, librium, etc.						

I17   During earlier years were you using drugs more, about the same amount, or less than now?

364   1 |‾| More

2 |‾| The same

3 |‾| Less

4 |‾| Never used drugs

I18   a)About how old were you when you started using drugs?

365-366   AGE_____

I19   b)Has the use of drugs been a source of problems in your life?

367   1 |‾| A lot

2 |‾| Somewhat

3 |‾| Not at all------------> GO TO   PAGE 35

I20   c)In what way has it been a problem? _____
368-369   _____

I21
370-371   _____

CONFLICTS WITH THE LAW

I22   Have you ever received a ticket, or been charged by the police, for
        a traffic violation--other than illegal parking?

        372 1 |__| Yes

             2 |__| No

I23   Were you ever picked up, or charged, by the police, for any other
        reason whether or not you were found guilty?

        373 1 |__| Yes

             2 |__| No----------------> GO TO PAGE 36

        IF EVER CHARGED

        a)For what? (INTERVIEWER CHECK OFF ALL THAT APPLY)
I24/I25
374-375 |__| Shoplifting/vandalism |__| Assault

I26/I27
376-377 |__| Parole/probation violations |__| Arson

I28/I29
378-379 |__| Drug charges |__| Rape

I30/I31
380-381 |__| Forgery |__| Homicide/manslaughter

I32/I33
382-383 |__| Weapons offense |__| Disorderly conduct/
                                                        vagrancy
I34/I35
384-385 |__| Burglary/larceny/B & E |__| Driving while drunk
I36/I37

386-387 |__| Robbery |__| Major driving violation

I38
    388 |__| Other (specify_____)

I39   b) About how many times has this happen since you left foster care?

389-390   NUMBER_____

I40   c) About how many times were you convicted?

391-392   NUMBER_____

I41   d)IF CONVICTED--->Were you sentenced to jail or prison?

    393 1 |__| Yes------------> For how long?_____
I42
 394-395 2 |__| No

J.   SOCIAL HEALTH BATTERY

We are interested in the social activities you and members of
of your family are able to participate in.

J01   About how many families in your neighborhood (or area) do you know
        well enough that you visit each other in your homes?

396-397   0 |‾| None

            _ |‾| One or more (number:_____)

            9 |‾| Other (specify _____

            _____)

J02   About how many close friends do you have - people you feel at
        ease with and can talk with about what is on your mind? (You
        may include relatives.)

398-399   0 |‾| None

            _ |‾| One or more (number:_____)

            9 |‾| Other (specify _____

            _____)

J03   Over a year's time, about how often do you get together with
        friends or relatives, like going out together or visiting in
        each other's homes? Would you say....

400   7 |‾| Every day?

        6 |‾| Several days a week?

        5 |‾| 2 or 3 times a month?

        4 |‾| About once a month?

        3 |‾| 5 to 10 times a year?

        2 |‾| 1 to 5 times a year?

        1 |‾| Never or almost never?

        9 |‾| Other (specify:_____)

J04   During the past month, about how often have you had friends
           over to your home? (Do not count relatives.) Would you say....

    401   6 |⁻| Every day?

               5 |⁻| Several days a week?

               4 |⁻| About once a week?

               3 |⁻| 2 to 3 times in past month?

               2 |⁻| Once in past month?

               1 |⁻| Not at all in past month?

               9 |⁻| Other (specify: _____

               _____)

J05   About how often have you visited with friends at their homes
           during the past month? (Do not count relatives.) Would you
           say....

    402   6 |⁻| Every day?

               5 |⁻| Several days a week?

               4 |⁻| About once a week?

               3 |⁻| 2 to 3 times in past month?

               2 |⁻| Once in past month?

               1 |⁻| Not at all in past month?

               9 |⁻| Other (specify: _____

               _____)

J06   About how often were you on the telephone with close friends
           or relatives during the past month? Would you say....

    403   6 |⁻| Every day?

               5 |⁻| Several times a week?

               4 |⁻| About once a week?

               3 |⁻| 2 or 3 times?

               2 |⁻| Once?

               1 |⁻| Not at all?

               9 |⁻| Other (specify: _____)

J07   About how often did you write a letter to a friend or relative during the past month? Would you say....

404   6 |_| Every day?

         5 |_| Several times a week?

         4 |_| About once a week?

         3 |_| 2 or 3 times in past month?

         2 |_| Once in past month?

         1 |_| Not at all in past month?

         9 |_| Other (specify: _____

                                 _____)

J08   In general, how well are you getting along with other people these days - would you say better than usual, about the same, or not as well as usual?

405   3 |_| Better than usual?

         2 |_| About the same?

         1 |_| Not as well as usual?

         9 |_| Other (specify: _____

                                 _____)

J09   How often have you attended a religious service during the past month?

406   6 |_| Every day?

         5 |_| Several times a week?

         4 |_| About once a week?

         3 |_| 2 or 3 times in past month?

         2 |_| Once in past month?

         1 |_| Not at all in past month?

         9 |_| Other (specify: _____

                                 _____)

J10   About how many voluntary groups or organizations do you belong to - like church groups, clubs, parent groups, etc. ("Voluntary" means because you want to)

    407   0 |‾| None

            _ |‾| One or more (specific number:_____)

            9 |‾| Other (specify _____

                     _____)

J11   How active are you in the affairs of these groups or clubs you belong to? Would you say....

    408   3 |‾| Very active, attend most meetings?

            2 |‾| Fairly active, attend fairly often?

            1 |‾| Not active, but hardly ever go?

            0 |‾| Do not belong to any groups or clubs?

K. PARENTING

K01   How many living children do you have who were born to you?

409-410   NUMBER OF CHILDREN_____   IF NONE------> GO TO PAGE 44

What are their names? (PLEASE START WITH THE OLDEST)

How old are they? Male or female? With whom do they live with?

CHILD NUM	NAME	AGE	SEX	LIVING ARRANGEMENT
1				
2				
3				
4				
5				
6				
7				
8				

K02/K04 411-415
K05/K07 416-420
K08/K10 421-425
K11/K13 426-430
K14/K16 431-435
K17/K19 436-440
K20/K22 441-445
K23/K25 446-450

K26   Have you ever been separated from your children for an extended period of time?

451   1 |__| Yes

        2 |__| No

        IF YES

K27   Were they staying with relatives, in foster care, child's parent, or in some other living arrangement?

452   1 |__| Living with relatives

        2 |__| In foster care

        3 |__| With spouse (CHILD'S PARENT)

        4 |__| Other child care arrangement? (specify_____)

K28   What were the circumstances?_____
453-454
K29   _____
455-456

        _____

IF NOT WITH RESPONDENT

a)How long have you been separated from _____ (MENTION CHILD)?

K30/K31 457-460	CHILD1 __	MONTHS __	YEARS __
K32/K33 461-464	CHILD2 __	MONTHS __	YEARS __
K34/K35 465-468	CHILD3 __	MONTHS __	YEARS __
K36/K37 469-472	CHILD4 __	MONTHS __	YEARS __
K38/K39 473-476	CHILD5 __	MONTHS __	YEARS __
K40/K41 477-480	CHILD6 __	MONTHS __	YEARS __
K42/K43 481-484	CHILD7 __	MONTHS __	YEARS __
K44/K45 485-488	CHILD8 __	MONTHS __	YEARS __

K46   b)How satisfied are you with this arrangement?

489   1 |__| Very satisfied

2 |__| Somewhat satisfied

3 |__| Neither satisfied nor unsatisfied

4 |__| Somewhat unsatisfied

5 |__| Very unsatisfied

K47
490-491
K48

What would you say is the nicest thing about having children?

_____

492-493   _____

K49
494-495
K50
496-497
K51
498-499

Most parents have had some problems in raising their children. What are the main problems you've had in raising your child(ren)?

_____

_____

K52   Many persons feel that they are not as good a parent as they would like to be. Have you ever felt this way?

500   1 |__| Yes

2 |__| No

K53
501-502
K54
503-504

IF YES: Why do you say that?_____

_____

THE PARENTING EXPERIENCE

K55   How much satisfaction do you experience these days in being
           a parent to your children? Would you say...

    505   4 |‾| A great deal of satisfaction?

            3 |‾| Some satisfaction?

            2 |‾| Just a little satisfaction?

            1 |‾| None or almost none?

            9 |‾| Other (specify) _____

                   _____

K56   a)   What accounts for this?
 506-507
K57
 508-509
K58
 510-511

K59   When you consider the experience you have had raising your
           children, and compare them with the experiences of friends
           and relatives, would you says yours have been easier,
           about the same, or harder?

    512   1 |‾| Easier

            2 |‾| About the same

            3 |‾| Harder

            9 |‾| Other (specify) _____

                   _____

K60   Why is that?
 513-514
K61
 515-516

K62   When being a parent to your child(ren) has been hard or
           discouraging in the past, what kinds of things have you found
           most helpful in order to get over this feeling? (OPEN-ENDED)

 517-518   _____
K63
 519-520   _____
K64
 521-522   _____

K65   What do you find the hardest thing about being a parent these
523-524 days?

K66
525-526

K67   a)   Why is that?
527-528
K68
529-530

K69   Do you have any feelings, positive or negative, about
        the age at which you first became a parent. For instance,
        do you think that you became a parent at too young an
        age, or too old, or just right?

    531   1 |_| Too young

                 2 |_| Too old

                 3 |_| Just right

                 9 |_| Other (specify) _____

        _____

K70   a)   What has made you feel this way?
532-533
K71
534-535

K72   Do you have any feelings, positive or negative, about
        the number of children you have had?

    536   1 |_| Yes, positive

                 2 |_| Yes, negative

                 3 |_| No

                 9 |_| Other (specify) _____

        _____

K73   a)   How has the number of children you had affected you?
537-538

K74
539-540

L. BIOLOGICAL FAMILY

We are interested in knowing about your relation with your biological family after you left foster care. Primarily we want to know if you have kept in touch with them and how close you feel towards them.

L01   After you left foster care, did you establish any contact with your biological family?

541   1 |⎯| Yes

      2 |⎯| No------------------GO TO PAGE 46

IF YES: INTERVIEWER ASK FOR THE NAMES OF THE FAMILY MEMBERS AND FOR EACH ASK THE FOLLOWING QUESTIONS

          a) How often have you had contact with her/him?
          b) When was the last time you saw _____ (NAME)?
          c) How close do you feel towards her/him?
          d) How far does he/she live from you?
          e) How satisfied are you with your relation to her/him?

Contact Code: Closeness Code:

  1 |⎯| None at all   1 |⎯| Very close

  2 |⎯| Once a year   2 |⎯| Somewhat

  3 |⎯| Several times a year   3 |⎯| Hardly

  4 |⎯| Monthly   4 |⎯| Not at all

  5 |⎯| More than once a month

  6 |⎯| Daily or in same home

Satisfaction Code: Proximity Code:

  1 |⎯| Very satisfied   1 |⎯| Out of State

  2 |⎯| Somewhat satisfied   2 |⎯| Within state

  3 |⎯| Neither satisfied   3 |⎯| Within one hour ride
         nor dissatisfied

  4 |⎯| Somewhat dissatisfied   4 |⎯| Within 30 minutes by car

  5 |⎯| Very dissatisfied   5 |⎯| Same town, block,
                                               walking distance

                                        6 |⎯| Same house or building

```
| FAMILY SYSTEM
|
|
|                                            Date   Close- Proxi-Satis-
|Family Members       Identity  Contact  Seen   ness   mity  faction
|(Last name, First)
|Parents:
|
```

	Family Members (Last name, First)	Identity	Contact	Date Seen	Close-ness	Proxi-mity	Satis-faction
L02/L06 542-549	1. _____	Mother		___	___	___	___
L07/L11 550-557	2. _____	Father#1		___	___	___	___
L12/L16 558-565	3. _____	Father#2		___	___	___	___
L17/L21 566-573	4. _____	Father#3		___	___	___	___
L22/L26 574-581	5. _____	Other (Specify_____)		___	___	___	___

Siblings (in birth order)

(Circle respondent)

	Family Members	Identity	Contact	Date Seen	Close-ness	Proxi-mity	Satis-faction
L27/L31 582-589	1. _____	Sibling1		___	___	___	___
L32/L36 590-597	2. _____	Sibling2		___	___	___	___
L37/L41 598-605	3. _____	Sibling3		___	___	___	___
L42/L46 606-613	4. _____	Sibling4		___	___	___	___
L47/L51 614-621	5. _____	Sibling5		___	___	___	___
L52/L56 622-629	6. _____	Sibling6		___	___	___	___
L57/L61 630-637	7. _____	Sibling7		___	___	___	___
L62/L66 638-645	8. _____	Sibling8		___	___	___	___

M. CONDITIONS THAT MADE FOSTER CARE EXPERIENCE NECESSARY

Considering all the time you spent in foster care, in The Casey Family Program, we are interested in obtaining your impressions of why foster care became necessary, why you had to be in foster care.

In your own words, please tell me what factors made it necessary for you to be cared for by foster care arrangements.

M01
646-647 _____
M02
648-649 _____
M03
650-651 _____
M04
652-653 _____
M05
654-655 _____

_____

What do you think was the MAIN reason that you came into foster care?

M06
656-657 _____
M07
658-659 _____
M08
660-661 _____
M09
662-663 _____
M10
664-665 _____

_____

What was your experience in the foster homes prior to coming to the Casey Family Program?

M11
666-667 _____
M12
668-669 _____
M13
670-671 _____
M14
672-673 _____
M15
674-675 _____

_____

EXPERIENCE IN CASEY FOSTER HOMES

(Foster Home Number 1)

Please think back to the last foster family you were placed with while you were under the care of The Casey Family Program. Let's see - - this was the _____ home?

What was the foster father's name? _____

What was the foster mother's name? _____

M16
676-677 At what age did you enter this foster home? _____ (years)
M17
678-679 At what age did you leave this foster home? _____ (years)

Please tell me in your own words what it was like to be in this foster home. (IF NEEDED, PROBE: How did it feel to be in this foster home?)

M18
680-681
M19
682-683
M20
684-685

M21   Did you feel secure in this home - that you belonged and you were part of the family?

686   1 |‾| Secure?

        2 |‾| Somewhat secure?

        3 |‾| Somewhat insecure?

        4 |‾| Insecure?

        IF SOMEWHAT INSECURE OR INSECURE
M22   Why was that?
687-688
M23
689-690

M24   To what extent do you feel the _____'s understood you? Would you say.......

691   1 |‾| Very much?

        2 |‾| Quite a bit?

        3 |‾| Somewhat?

        4 |‾| Hardly?

        5 |‾| Not at all?

M25   Trying to think of yourself objectively, what kind of a child
         were you to care for while in this home? Would you say..

    692   1 |⎯| Easy to care for - presented few problems?

             2 |⎯| Somewhat easy to care for - had problems but they were not
                   severe?

             3 |⎯| Somewhat hard to care for - had some pretty serious
                   problems?

             4 |⎯| Hard to care for - had serious problems?

         IF SOMEWHAT HARD OR HARD TO CARE FOR
M26   Please describe what you mean.
 693-694
M27
 695-696

M28   How close did you and the _____'s become? Would you say..

    697   1 |⎯| Very close?

             2 |⎯| Somewhat close?

             3 |⎯| Not too close?

             4 |⎯| Not at all close?

M29   Why did you leave the _____ home?
 698-699
M30
 700-701

M31   Do you keep in touch with the _____'s?

    702   1 |⎯| Yes

          2 |⎯| No
M32
 703-704 IF YES: How often do you see them? _____

M33   Did you live in another foster home while you were in the care of
         The Casey Family Program prior to the home of the _____ family?

    705   1 |⎯| Yes

                2 |⎯| No

                If YES, how many other Casey foster homes did you
                reside in?
M34   Foster Home Number (circle each)

    706   2   3   4   5   6   7   8

         (INTERVIEWER: INQUIRE ABOUT EACH OF THE CASEY FOSTER FAMILIES
         USE SUPPLEMENTARY SHEETS FOR EACH ADDITIONAL HOME)

N.   EXPERIENCE WITH TCFP FOSTER PARENTS
     Let's talk about the foster home you were at the longest.
     Please tell if any of the following took place:

		Yes (1)	No (2)	DK (8)	DNA (9)
NO1	707	a)Were you treated kindly and accepted as part of the family by your foster family?	I_I	I_I	I_I	I_I
NO2	708	b)Did anyone in the foster home ever try to take advantage of you sexually?	I_I	I_I	I_I	I_I
NO3	709	c)Did you have the right clothes to wear?	I_I	I_I	I_I	I_I
NO4	710	d)Did your foster parents have reasonable rules for you to follow, like when to go to bed, what time to be in the evening, chores to do?	I_I	I_I	I_I	I_I
NO5	711	e)Did your foster parents show interest in your school work?	I_I	I_I	I_I	I_I
NO6	712	f)Did your foster parents do things with you like teach you things, play games, take you places for fun?	I_I	I_I	I_I	I_I
NO7	713	g)Were you allowed to have your friends come to your home to play or visit?	I_I	I_I	I_I	I_I
NO8	714	h)Did you have enough to eat?	I_I	I_I	I_I	I_I
NO9	715	i)Was the home kept clean?	I_I	I_I	I_I	I_I
N10	716	j)Did your foster parents always remember your birthday?	I_I	I_I	I_I	I_I
N11	717	k)Were you allowed to go to the homes of your friends to play or visit?	I_I	I_I	I_I	I_I
N12	718	l)Were you ever whipped or punished in any severe way by your foster parents?	I_I	I_I	I_I	I_I
N13	719	m)Were you given a regular allowance or spending money?	I_I	I_I	I_I	I_I
N14	720	n)Could you talk to your foster parents about things that were bothering you?	I_I	I_I	I_I	I_I
N15	721	o)Did your foster parents talk with you about the facts of life, or changes in your body as you became a teen-ager?	I_I	I_I	I_I	I_I

EXPERIENCE WITH TCFP SOCIAL WORK SERVICE

Now I would like to know about your experience with the social workers while you were in care at the Casey Family Program. Please tell me if the worker did any of the following:

		Yes (1)	No (2)	DK (8)	DNA (9)
N16 722	a)Discussed with you in private how you liked your foster placement and the treatment you were receiving there.	|_|	|_|	|_|	|_|
N17 723	b)Explained to you why you were in foster care.	|_|	|_|	|_|	|_|
N18 724	c)Arranged for you to visit your natural parents	|_|	|_|	|_|	|_|
N19 725	d)Asked your opinion about choosing a different place to live, like a new foster home or going to live with a relative	|_|	|_|	|_|	|_|
N20 726	e)Went to your school to see how you were doing	|_|	|_|	|_|	|_|
N21 727	f)Told you how long you would be in foster care and whether or not you would be returning home	|_|	|_|	|_|	|_|
N22 728	g)Gave you information about your real family	|_|	|_|	|_|	|_|
N23 729	h)Took you to see your brothers or sisters	|_|	|_|	|_|	|_|
N24 730	i)Talked to you about the facts of life	|_|	|_|	|_|	|_|

I would now like to ask you some general questions:

		Yes (1)	No (2)	DK (8)	DNA (9)
N25 731	j)Did you feel your worker cared about what happened to you?	|_|	|_|	|_|	|_|
N26 732	k)Did your worker visit you regularly and keep in touch with you?	|_|	|_|	|_|	|_|
N27 733	l)Did you feel that your worker was easy to talk to?	|_|	|_|	|_|	|_|
N28 734	m)Did you find that you could depend on your worker to help you with problems?	|_|	|_|	|_|	|_|

N29   Overall, what was the most gratifying experience while in foster
735-736   care in The Casey Family Program? Why?

N30   _____
737-738
            _____

N31   Looking back, what was the most unpleasant experience while in
739-740   The Casey Family Program? Why?

N32   _____
741-742
            _____

N33   What suggestions do you have to improve foster care services in
743-744   The Casey Family Program?
N34
745-746   _____
N35
747-748   _____

N36   Do you want to make any additional comments?

    749   1 |‾| Yes

            2 |‾| No

N37   IF YES
750-751   What?_____
N38
752-753   _____

O.   INTERVIEWER REPORT

RESPONDENT'S RACE OR ETHNICITY

001
    754

| |_| White |_| Central American
| |_| Black |_| Cuban
| |_| American Indian |_| Puerto Rican
| |_| Chinese |_| Mexican
| |_| Japanese |_| South American
| |_| Filipino |_| Other Spanish
| |_| Korean |_| Other (specify_____)

HOW GOOD WERE THE CONDITIONS FOR THE INTERVIEW?

002
    755   CHECK ALL
         THAT APPLY |_| Noise interfering with audibility
003
    756 |_| Distractions (Source: _____)
004
    757 |_| Interruptions (Source: _____)
005
    758 |_| Lack of privacy
006
    759 |_| Other (specify) _____

WERE ANY OF THE FOLLOWING BEHAVIORS MANIFESTED BY THE

RESPONDENT DURING THE INTERVIEW?

			Very much 3	Some-what 2	Not at all 1	
007	760	a. Suspicious or guarded	|_|	|_|	|_|	
008	761	b. Anxious or uncertain	|_|	|_|	|_|	
009	762	c. Inappropriate in responses	|_|	|_|	|_|	
010	763	d. Interested	|_|	|_|	|_|	
011	764	e. Long-winded responses	|_|	|_|	|_|	
012	765	f. Friendly	|_|	|_|	|_|	
013	766	g. Found interview too long	|_|	|_|	|_|	
014	767	h. Difficulty in understanding about agency	|_|	|_|	|_|	

WHAT WAS THE RESPONDENT'S OVERALL ATTITUDE TOWARD THE
CASEY FAMILY PROGRAM?

			Very much 3	Some-what 2	Not at all 1	NA/Other 9
015	768	a. Had good recall of experience with agency	|_|	|_|	|_|	|_|
016	769	b. Had positive things to say about agency	|_|	|_|	|_|	|_|
017	770	c. Had negative things to say about agency	|_|	|_|	|_|	|_|
018	771	d. Seemed clear about agency's program	|_|	|_|	|_|	|_|
019	772	e. Appeared to have positive feeling for agency staff	|_|	|_|	|_|	|_|
020	773	f. Felt agency had serve him/her well?	|_|	|_|	|_|	|_|
021	774	g. Other (specify) _____				

022
775 Interviewer_____   Time Interview Ended:_____
023
776-777

NOTES

1 Doing good for children: a man named Jim Casey

1. A sense of the formative years of The Casey Family Program is available in Jaffee and Kline. Their description of the agency is: "The Casey Family Program is a foster care agency established by the Board of Trustees of The Casey Family Foundation in 1966, with the broad purpose of using foundation funds in the field of juvenile delinquency. This is interpreted by the trustees to include prevention of delinquency as well as the care and rehabilitation of delinquent children of any race or religion. . . . It was recognized that many children whose parents are 'unable or unwilling' to provide adequate care require carefully selected foster parents able to provide opportunities for self-development equal to those of any normal child of a family in moderate circumstances" (1970:14).

2. This approach to public funding was examined in recent years and consideration given by the Board of Trustees to a relaxation of the policy under certain quite restricted conditions.

3. For the period covered by the study reported here, the division located in Seattle was known as the Western Washington Division. In 1985 the name was changed to the Seattle Division.

4. In 1987 and 1988, the upper limit on the size of division caseloads was raised about ten children per division to 65 children.

5. Comment to Fanshel by Dr. Charles P. Gershenson whose research leadership in the United States Children's Bureau spanned some twenty-five years. In his view, funding for residential treatment institutions is being withdrawn nationally because of the steep climb in costs and be-

cause the gains to children in residential care have not been sufficiently documented.

2 Research methods: an overview

1. See, for example: Jessor and Jessor (1977)
2. Dr. Henry Ilian was the supervising reader. The three readers who completed the project were Jeanne Bertrand Finch, Mary Fitzpatrick, and Margaret Schmidt. Amelia Chu was the research assistant who helped edit and manage the database.
3. More precisely, the reexpression is

$$m + (M-m)(X-m)/(M-m).$$

4. Dr. Qimei He, Dr. Ten Shang Joh, and Finch simulated the use of factor analysis techniques for data such as appeared in this study. Their analyses supported the techniques used in this study. Dr. He's simulations suggested that oblique rotations may be somewhat more effective as a variable extraction technique. Unfortunately, it was prohibitively expensive in computer time, and we used varimax rotation here.
5. However, in an exploratory study we have to work with greater uncertainty; our simulation studies have suggested that coefficients as low as .25 in absolute value may have some merit. We have considered this choice of .35 carefully. On the basis of our previous research, an item with a loading less than .35 usually does not produce an item-criterion correlation of materially significant size. We do not know of other research to inform us here. In our view the choice produces satisfactory results, but it may not be the "best" choice.
6. This is called "listwise deletion" in SPSS-X.
7. Although the case-reading schedule provided three categories of information about a child's need for foster care (reason for placement, reason for referral to The Casey Family Program, and contributory conditions) these were collapsed into a single category (factor present/not). The case record material did not support the earlier elaboration of factors involved in the need for care. This modified approach was used for factors related to the child, factors related to the natural mother, and factors related to the natural father.
8. The ratings of foster families proved to be too unreliable to use. The records usually did not contain sufficient information to support an evaluation rating by the case reader.
9. Ratings of the presence of behavioral symptoms were supported by the presence in the case records of monthly reports about the children sent to the agency by the foster mothers.

3 Characteristics of the children and their experiences before entering care

1. Fanshel and Shinn (1978) did not find such a strong sense of parents being almost totally out of the picture in their longitudinal study of foster

children in New York City because that study was restricted to children who were experiencing their first placements in foster care. The children in this study, in contrast, had been in many placements.

2. The task of codification of the information so that it could be transformed into data and entered into the computer was challenging in its own right. A single case could generate many concrete items of information so that the amount of computer storage space required was very substantial. Grundy had to develop specialized software to summarize this information.

3. The Index of Child with Mental Illness in Background had an intraclass correlation coefficient of .34 and a Cronbach alpha coefficient of .36. The Index of Child Embedded in Abusive Family Situation had an intraclass correlation coefficient of .66 and a Cronbach alpha of .39. The Index of Child with Developmental Disability had an intraclass correlation of .15 and a Cronbach alpha of .49. The Index of Child in Conflicted Relationship with Parents had an intraclass correlation coefficient of .40 and a Cronbach alpha of .52. These indexes are very poor measures, but we use them here for exploratory purposes.

4. Two adoptions were disrupted while the child was in the care of The Casey Family Program.

4 How the children fared in Casey care

1. We refer to this type of property in a series of associations as a "Markov property." In the probabilistic modeling of time ordered events, when the conditional probability of an event at time t depends only on the event that occurred immediately before at time t-1 and the events that occurred prior to that time are not additionally associated with the probability of the event at time t, then the sequence of events is said to be "Markov." Our use of the term conforms to this definition.

2. The intraclass correlation for moodiness and depression was about .60, and so this measure is somewhat problematic.

3. The interrater reliability for the challenge rating during the first year of a child's experience in care using the contingency coefficient was .70.

4. Agreements between raters on these items with collapsed categories were also marginal with values of the intraclass correlation ranging between .50 and .60.

5. See Simon (1954), Lazarsfeld (1972).*The International Encyclopedia for the Social Sciences*, David Sills, ed. New York: Macmillan Company and the Free Press (1968) contains two discussions by these authors: Herbert A. Simon, Causation, 2:350–356; and Paul F. Lazarsfeld, Survey Analysis II: The Analysis of Attribute Data, 15: 419–429.

6. We feel that this model is the best description of moodiness while in Casey care, but the regression model with an additional association was also statistically significant (p<.05). The additional association was

difficult to interpret and was that a child with more living arrangements prior to entry into the Casey program was less moody while in care. This association increased the percentage of explained variation from .06 to .07. The result may reflect less depression because of a less final and complete loss of family in those who had families who provided turbulent living arrangements. We applied Occam's razor in deciding to report the simpler and smaller set of associations.

5 Modes of exit of the children from care and their adjustment at departure

1. The response categories were ordered as follows: (7) a normal "aging out" emancipatory process—generally devoid of any sense of conflict or crisis; (5) ending of care arrangement on a positive note but some elements of turbulence and associated problematic behavior shown by the child; (3) a less than serene ending with considerable evidence of emotional crisis and problematic behavior—some positive features to the ending phase give the exit from care a mixed quality; (1) an acute crisis in the child's foster care status (e.g., child is being thrust out of home)—a sense of failure accompanies the ending of care. This rating scale shows anchoring labels for odd-numbered steps; and the even-numbered steps are shown without labels, for the even numbers reflect the midpoints between two identified ordered states. This comment also applies to note 2 of this chapter as well.

2. The categories were ordered as follows: (7) child was making an excellent adjustment in all spheres of his life; (5) child was making an adequate adjustment—his/her strengths outweighed the weaknesses shown; (3) child was making a mixed adjustment—generally the problems faced were serious; (1) child was making an extremely poor adjustment. The two ratings were combined to form a single measure of the child's condition at the point of departure. The interrater reliability for the combined two-item measure using the intraclass correlation was calculated as .58.

3. The status term "emancipated" is taken from agency usage. It corresponds to the term "independent living" now widely used in the child welfare literature.

4. In a national study of children entering substitute care in 1983, the distribution of the children for age at admission was: less than 1 year - 8.4%; 1 to 5 years - 26.3%, 6 to 12 years - 25.8%, 13 to 20 years - 39.3%. From Technical Report, Administration for Children, Youth and Families, Office of Human Development Services, US Department of Health and Human Services. Prepared by Maximus (McLean, Virginia: 1985) p.22.

5. This somewhat counterintuitive finding suggests that the depressed child is viewed with less concern since aggression tends to be internalized rather than directed externally in the form of conduct problems.

6. The Casey program used interim group care placements at least once in 21.1% of the cases with the expectation that the children would

return to foster family homes after behavioral difficulties had modified. This is fully described in chapter 7.

6 How they fared after foster care

1. We are unable to account for the reason why one subject was not interviewed.

2. The three interviewers who were social workers were Sid Copeland, Patti Gorman, and Joan K. Heinmiller. Mary Kline was trained as a registered nurse and had postgraduate training and experience in psychotherapy. Their supervisor was Dr. Jaime Alvelo.

3. The interviewing schedule used in the follow-up study is shown in the appendix B.

4. Subject was asked: "Did anyone in the foster home ever try to take advantage of you sexually?" Question referred to the foster home of longest stay.

5. Subject was asked: "Were you ever whipped or punished in any severe way by your foster parents?" Question referred to the foster home of longest stay.

6. There were four associations that together explained .408 of the variance ($p<.0001$). A subject who had a greater extent of hostility and negativity at entry was in poorer condition at exit ($p<.01$). A subject who engaged in more extensive delinquent behavior while in Casey care was in poorer condition at exit ($p<.01$). A subject who spent more years out of his home was in better condition at exit ($p<.05$). A subject who had more extensive sexual acting out behavior was in worse condition at exit ($p<.05$). These associations paralleled those for the whole study population. There were no associations with the foster home or social worker variables.

7. The questions derived from a national health survey conducted by the federal government. See: U.S. Department of Health, Education and Welfare, Public Health Service, National Center for Health Statistics (June 1978) General Well-Being Questionnaire. pp. 46–50

8. There was a counterintuitive association that a subject who went through a disrupted adoption felt better about himself as an adult ($p<.05$).

9. The results of the regression analysis on this variable were troublesome to interpret. We report the results of a model with four significant associations as the clearest and most general of the models selected by the stepwise regression. There was a suggestion in other regression results that the eight girls who were both physically abused and exposed to a sexually disturbing event were not more disturbed as adults than children who were not sexually abused but that girls who were only exposed to a disturbing sexual event were more disturbed as adults. We discounted this result on the grounds that the relation was too complex compared with the amount of data available.

10. There was an association that a subject who had a higher regard

for the relatedness of the worker had an adult index reflecting greater disturbance (p<.05). This association appeared with another counterintuitive association that a subject who while in Casey care showed more extensive psychopathic behavior was less disturbed as an adult. We have discounted both of these associations.

11. When we included associations significant at the .05 level, there were three significant associations with adult reports on the state of finances that together explained .194 of the variance (p<.0001). A child who was in better condition at exit from Casey care was in better shape financially on average (p<.0001). A subject who had experienced a greater number of living arrangements away from the natural parents before entry into the Casey program was in a more adequate financial situation (p<.05), a somewhat counterintuitive finding. Subjects who had come into care with The Casey Family Program with identified developmental disabilities, including in some cases problems of mental retardation, tended to report less adequate financial situations as adults (p<.05). Our application of Occam's razor led us to report the simpler model.

12. The regression with six associations explained .453 of the variance In addition to the three associations reported, a subject who had more extensive psychiatric evaluation while in Casey care reported a poorer measure of adult education (p<.001). A subject who had a greater extent of mental illness reported a better measure of adult education (p<.05), a counterintuitive finding. A subject who had a better school performance while in Casey care reported a better measure of adult education (p<.05).

13. An alternative model has three associations that together explained .183 of the variance. In addition to the association with number of pre-Casey returns to parents, a subject who spent more years out of the natural family's home had a better measure of current job (p<.01), and a subject whose father had a greater role in his life while the subject was in Casey care had a better measure of current job (p<.05).

14. The model using associations significant at the .05 level explained .299 of the variance of the measure. The three additional associations did not deal with foster care issues. Those who had been out longer tended to have larger families meeting a common sense expectation that age is an important factor in family building (p<.01). Male subjects had larger families (p<.05). White subjects had smaller families (p<.05).

15. When we ran the same regression using just male subjects, we found the associations with physical abuse, destructive delinquency while in Casey care, and an adverse sexual experience in the Casey foster home.

16. The same regression analysis using just males found a strong association that a man who had a strong attachment to his last Casey foster home had a less extensive involvement in serious adult crime (p<.01).

17. There was a counterintuitive association that a child who had an adverse sexual experience in the Casey foster home of longest stay was less extensively involved in adult drinking (p<.05).

7 Group care and replacement as a tactic in maintaining foster care

An earlier version of the findings reported in this chapter has previously appeared in publication. See: David Fanshel, Stephen J. Finch, and John F. Grundy, Group Care in the Lives of Children in Long-Term Foster Care: The Casey Family Program Experience, in Edwin A. Balcerzac, ed. 1989. *Group Care of Children: Transitions Towards the Year 2000.* (Washington, D.C. Child Welfare League of America, 1989), pp. 37–66.

1. It is no doubt coincidental that the care of children by their own families usually requires little if any governmental expenditure; foster boarding home care, moderate governmental expenditure; and institutional placement, the greatest expenditure!

2. There was an additional association that a boy who was physically abused was in poorer condition at exit (p<.05).

*8 From birth to exit: seeking life course patterns
in the experiences of foster children*

1. Of the 585 case records subjected to the content analysis procedures, 9 cases were deleted from the factor analyses reported here because they contained problems of missing information.

2. The summary measure of delinquent/acting out behavior while in Casey care is a strong index composed of eleven items. Its interrater reliability coefficient was .75, and the Cronbach alpha coefficient was .79.

9 Into the adult years; further exploratory factor analyses

1. We are in the process of developing more objective procedures for deciding how to interpret the results of factor analyses with multiple solutions such as these. The guidelines we have followed here are primarily those of good sense.

10 Former foster children speak for themselves

1. We have replaced all case identifiers with an alphabetical letter beginning with A and ending with AW. FA would designate the foster father, MA would designate the foster mother, and WA the Casey social worker for Child A.

11 Conclusions and commentary

1. A report prepared by Maximus for the Administration for Children, Youth and Families, Office of Human Development Services, U.S. Department of Health and Human Services, Comparative Statistical Analysis of 1984 State Child Welfare Data (dated June 6, 1986) showed that for 22

reporting states 21.4 percent of the children in substitute care had experienced 3 to 5 placements and 7.2 percent had experienced 6 or more placements. Maximus, Inc., 6723 Whittier Avenue, McLean, Virginia 22101. Also: A recent study of 10,000 children in care in California showed that for the social service system 23.8 percent of the children had 3 to 5 prior placements and 8.6 percent had 6 or more prior placements (Fitzharris 1985:65).

2. Geiser points out that in 1910, of the 176,000 children in foster care, 65 percent were in institutions for the neglected and dependent and the emotionally disturbed child. By 1965, with 287,000 children in care, only 28 percent were in child welfare institutions. Robert L. Geiser, *The Illusion of Caring: Children in Foster Care*. (Boston: Beacon Press, 1973) p.167. In a national study relative to the year 1977, it was estimated that 21% of some 500,000 children in foster care in the United States were in residential institutions. Ann W. Shyne and Anita G. Schroeder, *A National Study of Social Services To Children and Their Families*. (Rockville, Md.: Westat, 1978).

REFERENCES

Akins, Faren R., Dianna L. Akins, and Gillian S. Mace. 1981 *Parent-Child Separation: Psychosocial Effects on Development*. New York: IFI/Plenum.

Allen, MaryLee and Jane Knitzer. 1983. Child Welfare: Examining the Policy Framework. In Brenda G. McGowan and William Meezan, ed., *Child Welfare: Current Dilemmas, Future Directions*, pp. 93–141. Itasca, Ill.: F. E. Peacock.

Allen-Mearas, Paula. 1981. Content Analysis: It Does Have a Place in Social Work Research. *Journal of Social Services Research* 7:51–68.

American Psychological Association. 1966. *Standards for Educational and Psychological Tests and Manuals*. Washington, D.C.: APA.

Anderson, Andy B., Alexander Basilevsky, and Derek P. J. Hum. 1983. Measurement, Theory and Techniques. In Peter H. Rossi, James D. Wright, and Andy B. Anderson, ed., *Handbook of Survey Research*. New York: Academic Press.

Billingsley, Andrew and Jeanne M. Giovannoni. 1972. *Children of the Storm: Black Children and American Child Welfare*, pp. 231–287. New York Harcourt Brace Jovanovich.

Bostwick, Gerald J., Jr. and Nancy S. Kyte. 1988. Validity and Reliability. In Richard M. Grinnell, Jr., ed.,*Social Work Research and Evaluation*, pp. 111–136. Itaska, Ill.: F. E. Peacock.

Cantley, Patricia W. 1980. *New Foster Parents*. New York: Human Sciences Press.

The Casey Family Program, Western Washington Division. 1977. Report of Advisory Committee on Evaluation of Program (Unpublished Report).

Child Welfare League of America. 1964. *Standards for Services of Child Welfare Institutions.* New York: Child Welfare League of America.

Children's Defense Fund. 1978. *Children Without Homes.* Washington, D.C.: Children's Defense Fund.

Cronbach, Lee J. 1951. Coefficient Alpha and the Internal Structure of Tests. *Psychometrica* 16:297–334.

Fanshel, David and Eugene B. Shinn. 1978. *Children in Foster Care: A Longitudinal Investigation.* New York: Columbia University Press.

Fanshel, David, Stephen J. Finch, and John F. Grundy. 1987. Collection of Data Relating to Adoption and Foster Care. Washington, D.C.: Administration for Children, Youth and Families, Office of Human Development Services, U.S. Department of Health and Human Services. Technical Appendix to the Report of the Advisory Committee on Adoption and Foster Care Information.

Fanshel, David, Stephen J. Finch, and John F. Grundy. 1989. Modes of Exit from Foster Family Care and Adjustment at Time of Departure of Children with Unstable Life Histories. *Child Welfare* 68:391–402.

Fanshel, David and Henry Maas. 1962. Factorial Dimensions of the Characteristics of Children in Placement and Their Families. *Child Development* 33:123–144.

Festinger, Trudy. 1983. *No One Ever Asked Us. . . A Postscript to Foster Care.* New York: Columbia University Press.

Festinger, Trudy. 1986. *Necessary Risk: A Study of Adoptions and Disrupted Adoptive Placements.* Washington, D.C.: Child Welfare League of America.

Fisher, Ronald A. 1970. Statistical Methods for Research Workers, ed. 14. New York: Hafner.

Fitzharris, Timothy L. 1985. *The Foster Children of California.* Sacramento, Calif.: California Association of Services for Children.

Galdston, Richard. 1979. Disorders of Early Parenthood: Neglect, Deprivation, Exploitation, and Abuse of Little Children. In Joseph D Noshpitz, ed., *Basic Handbook of Child Psychiatry*, vol. 2. *Disturbances in Development.* New York: Basic Books.

Jaffee, Benson and Draza Kline. 1970. *New Payment Patterns and the Foster Parent Role.* New York: Child Welfare League of America.

Janchill, Sister Mary Paul. 1983. Services for Special Populations of Children. In Brenda G. McGowan and William Meezan, ed., *Child Welfare: Current Dilemmas—Future Directions*, pp. 345–375. Itaska, Ill.: E. F. Peacock.

Jessor, Richard and Shirley L. Jessor. 1977. *Problem Behavior and Psychosocial Development: A Longitudinal Study of Youth.* New York: Academic Press.

Joh, Tenshang. 1989. The Performance of Factor Analysis on Linear Recursive Path Models. Doctoral Dissertation. State University of New York at Stony Brook.

Kagan, Jerome. 1973. Cross-Cultural Perspectives on Early Development. *American Psychologist* 28:947–961.

Kadushin, Alfred. 1967. *Child Welfare Services.* New York: Macmillan.

Kadushin, Alfred. 1978. Children in Foster Families and Institutions. In Henry S. Maas, ed., *Social Service Research: Review of Studies.* New York: National Association of Social Workers.

Kadushin, Alfred and Judith A. Martin. 1988. *Child Welfare Services,* ed. 4. New York: Macmillan.

Krippendorff, Klaus. 1980. *Content Analysis: An Introduction to Its Methodology.* Beverly Hills, Calif.: Sage Publications.

Langner, Thomas S. and Stanley T. Michael. 1963. *Life Stress and Mental Health.* New York: Free Press.

Lazarsfeld, Paul F. 1972. The Algebra of Dichotomous Systems. In Paul F. Lazarsfeld, Ann K. Pasanella, and Morris Rosenberg eds. *Continuities in the Language of Social Research,* pp.193–207. New York: Free Press.

Lipset, Seymour M., Martin Trow, and James Coleman. 1956. *Union Democracy* Chicago, Ill.: Free Press.

Maas, Henry S. and Richard E. Engler, Jr. 1959. *Children in Need of Parents.* New York: Columbia University Press.

Martin, Harold P. and Patricia Beezley. 1976. Foster Placement: Therapy or Trauma. In Harold P. Martin, ed. *The Abused Child: A Multidisciplinary Approach to Developmental Issues and Treatment.* Cambridge, Mass.: Ballinger.

Maximus, Inc. 1988. *Child Welfare Statistical Fact Book, 1985: Substitute Care.* Washington, D.C.: U.S. Department of Health and Human Services.

Mosteller, Frederick and John W. Tukey. 1977. *Data Analysis and Regression.* Reading, Mass.: Addison-Wesley.

National Commission for Children in Need of Parents. 1979. *Who Knows? Who Cares? Forgotten Children in Foster Care.* New York: National Commission for Children.

Nelson, Thorana, David Rosenthal, Robert G. Harrington, and Danny Mitchelson. 1986. Assessment of Adolescent Substance Abuse. In Robert G Harrington, ed. *Testing Adolescents: A Reference Guide for Comprehensive Psychological Assessments.* Kansas City: Test Corporation of America.

Quevillon, Randal P., Steven Landau, W. B. Apple, and Patricia Petretic-Jackson. 1986. Assessing Adolescent Conduct Disorders and Oppositional Behaviors. In Robert G. Harrington, ed. *Testing Adolescents: A Reference Guide for Comprehensive Psychological Assessments.* Kansas City: Test Corporation of America.

Reid, Joseph H. 1959. Actions Called For—Recommendations. In Henry S. Maas and Richard E. Engler, Jr. eds. *Children in Need of Parents,* pp. 378–397. New York: Columbia University Press.

Rogeness, Graham A., Suchakorn A. Amrung, Carlos A. Macedo, William

R. Harris, and Charles Fisher. 1986. Psychopathology in Abused and Neglected Children. *Journal of the American Academy of Child Psychiatry* 25:659–665.

Rosenblum, Barbara. 1977. *Foster Homes for Adolescents.* Hamilton, Ont.: Children's Aid Society.

Sandberg, David N. 1989. *The Child Abuse-Delinquency Connection.* Lexington, Mass.: Lexington Books.

Selltiz, Claire, Lawrence S. Wrightsman, and Stuart W. Cook. 1976. *Research Methods in Social Relations,* ed. 3. New York: Holt, Rinehart and Winston.

Simon, Herbert A. 1954. Spurious Correlations: A Causal Interpretation. *Journal of the American Statistical Association* 49:467–479.

Stein, Theodore J. 1981. *Social Work Practice in Child Welfare.* Englewood Cliffs, N.J.: Prentice-Hall.

Stein, Theodore J. 1987. Foster Care for Children. In *Encyclopedia of Social Work,* ed. 18, vol. 1. Silver Spring, Md.: National Association of Social Workers.

Sullivan, P. L., Christine Miller, and W. Smelser. 1958. Factors in Length of Stay and Progress in Psychotherapy. *Journal of Consulting Psychology* 22:1–9.

U.S. Department of Commerce, Bureau of Census. 1985. *Statistical Abstract of the United States 1985.* Washington, D.C.: U.S. Government Printing Office.

U.S. Department of Health, Education, and Welfare, Public Health Service, National Center for Health Statistics. 1978. General Well-Being Questionnaire. In *Plan and Operation of the HANES I Augmentation Survey of Adults 25–74 Years, United States, 1974–1975.* Hyattsville, Md.: DHEW Publication No. (PHS) 78–1314, series 1, no. 14, pp. 46–50.

Weber, R. P. 1985. *Basic Content Analysis.* Beverly Hills, Calif.: Sage Publications.

Whittaker, James K. 1985. Group and Institutional Care: An Overview. In Joan Laird and Ann Hartman, eds. *A Handbook of Child Welfare.* New York: The Free Press.

Wiltse, Kermit T. 1985. Foster Care: An Overview. In Joan Laird and Ann Hartman, eds. *A Handbook of Child Welfare,* pp. 565–584. New York: The Free Press.

Zeitz, Dorothy. 1969. *Child Welfare: Services and Perspectives,* ed. 2. New York: John Wiley & Sons.

INDEX